MW00604627

Dedicated to all the people who, over time, have made Las Cruces what it is today,
and to the award-winning team of writers, editors, graphic designers, marketers and staff of the Las Cruces Bulletin,
who have put their hearts into this special Centennial book –
a project that will be cherished by future generations of Las Crucens.

NEW MEXICO CENTENNIAL 1912-2012

Las Cruces

A PHOTOGRAPHIC JOURNEY

Las Cruces: A Photographic Journey is a copyrighted book of the Las Cruces Bulletin,
designed and published by FIG Publications, LLC, 840 N. Telshor Blvd., Suite E,
Las Cruces, NM 88011. Inquiries regarding content may be directed to 575-524-8061.

© Copyright 2011 FIG Publications, LLC. All rights reserved.

Library of Congress Control Number: 2011941545

ISBN 978-0-615-54517-2

Unless stated otherwise, all text and images in this book are property of or have been licensed by
FIG Publications, LLC and may not be reproduced without explicit permission. FIG Publications, LLC has made
every effort to properly credit ownership and/or determine ownership of each image.

Cover photos/images: Aerial photos of Las Cruces contributed by Mike Groves and New Mexico State University
Library Archives & Special Collections; 1887 map of Las Cruces and Mesilla contributed by Moy Surveying Inc.

Back cover: Olin Calk's Recycled Roadrunner overlooking Las Cruces, photo by Jessica Grady-Mauldin

End flaps: Las Cruces postcard, New Mexico State University Library Archives & Special Collections;
David and Jaki McCollum; Las Cruces Bulletin staff photo by Nicolas Bañalas

End sheet photos: Organ Mountains photo by Theresa Montoya Basaldua

Foreword: Snowcapped Organ Mountains photo by Jim Hilley

FOREWORD

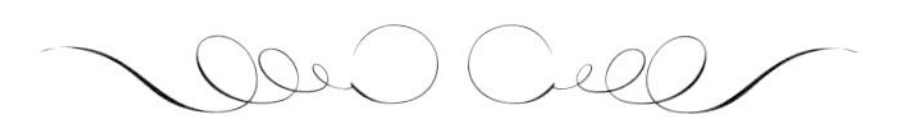

New Mexico is our state.

Las Cruces, located in the verdant Mesilla Valley along the historic Rio Grande in southern New Mexico, is our home.

One hundred years ago, on January 6, 1912, President William H. Taft signed the declaration that proclaimed New Mexico as the forty-seventh state in the United States of America. For a brief 40-day period, before Arizona was added as the forty-eighth state on February 14, 1912, a unique 47-star American flag was displayed across our great nation.

One hundred years later, in 2012, New Mexico celebrates its Centennial year of statehood. Our company, FIG Publications, LLC founded in 2003, is a family-owned and operated publishing company, based in Las Cruces. The Las Cruces Bulletin newspaper is our primary publication.

We are not book publishers.

We are newspaper people.

However, because of our love for the wonderful place we have chosen to make our home, we felt a driving need to contribute something that would not only commemorate our state's Centennial, but would also share our region's unique character and history.

This special book, "Las Cruces: A Photographic Journey," is our company's contribution to New Mexico's 100th birthday.

As our award-winning team of journalists, graphic designers and support staff embarked on this ambitious project, we learned very quickly that compiling a pictorial history book is not an easy task.

Fortunately, we were wise enough to engage the assistance of our friends at the New Mexico State University library. Their advice and hands-on support throughout this process proved invaluable as we developed our book's concept.

In order to complete the book and have it available prior to the start of the Centennial year, we split the workload among our staff. We chose to divide the book's content among thirteen chapters including nine full decades (1920 through 2010), plus two partial decades (1912-1919 and 2011-2012) and chapters for the pre- and post-statehood time periods.

Each decade was assigned a different "champion" from among our news, design and marketing teams. The champions were responsible for researching photos, news items, features and interviews that would comprise the content of each chapter.

Team members quickly became engrossed in their research, despite the fact that most of their work was having to be accomplished outside of their normal work schedule, as we had to continue to publish our weekly newspaper and other projects on our regular seasonal schedule.

Writing, editing, proofing and production of this book truly became a labor of love. This was especially true over the last several weeks of production when many team members were working 15-hour-per-day shifts in order to meet the printing schedule for the book in addition to the regular workload.

An unanticipated benefit of the time investment we have made into the research for this project is that our staff, many of whom are younger, just a few years out of college, has gained a deeper understanding of the history and culture of our area. These insights will prove to be a great benefit over time as we publish our local newspaper.

The result of our work is this wonderful pictorial book that provides readers a historical glimpse back in time and gives an insight as to how the Las Cruces region has contributed to the state of New Mexico over the past 100 years.

While the book offers a broad perspective on the history of Las Cruces, it is by no means a complete history of Las Cruces. To accomplish that objective, the book would require many more than the 288 pages found in "Las Cruces: A Photographic Journey." We will leave the in-depth history narratives to the fulltime professional historians.

We hope that readers will be entertained and informed by this book. We also expect that "Las Cruces: A Photographic Journey" will become an heirloom for others who live in Las Cruces and love our city as much as we do.

CONTENTS

FIRST NATIONAL BANK
LAS CRUCES DOWNTOWN MALL
SUSANA MARTINEZ GOVERNOR

State of New Mexico

Susana Martinez
Governor

Dear Fellow New Mexican:

On January 6, 2012, our state will celebrate a historic occasion – its Centennial anniversary. New Mexico's 100th birthday is not only a reminder of our rich past, but is also a gateway to what we are sure will be a bright future.

The last hundred years have shaped an identity in our state that exists nowhere else. A unique convergence of many cultures has made New Mexico a land as diverse as anywhere in the world. Our communities are recognized as much for their hard-working ranchers, farmers, and family business owners as they are for accomplishments in the fields of art, science, and technological development - and the city of Las Cruces and Doña Ana County play a major role in the success of our ever-growing economy.

The Mesilla Valley is home to dramatic landscapes, wonderful neighborhoods and a cultural identity like no other place in the world – Southern New Mexico has a storied past that has played a central role in the growth and success of New Mexico in the past century. As Las Cruces and the surrounding communities in Doña Ana County continue to grow and prosper, New Mexico will benefit from the many valuable contributions of the border region. I am proud to call Las Cruces home and I look forward to the bright and promising days that lie ahead.

As we celebrate the 100th anniversary of statehood, we should not just reflect on a century of history, but we should also look toward the opportunities that await us down the road. Our next hundred years will be just as important as the last, giving us a chance to create a legacy that generations of New Mexicans can reflect upon as we approach future landmarks. We have begun to build upon the qualities that make New Mexico great, advancing efforts to make sure that every child receives a quality education and every business has a chance to succeed. We are committed to the well-being of every New Mexican, through a healthier economy and safer communities.

New Mexico's Centennial celebration is an appropriate time for each of us to pause and appreciate the distinct characteristics of our people and our communities; express gratitude for past generations of New Mexicans who shaped our state into the Land of Enchantment; and make a commitment that we will use our proud heritage to build an even stronger future.

Sincerely,

SMartinez

Susana Martinez
Governor

State Capitol • Room 400 • Santa Fe, New Mexico 87501 • 505-476-2200 • fax: 505-476-2226

NEW MEXICO STATE UNIVERSITY LIBRARY ARCHIVES & SPECIAL COLLECTIONS

INTRODUCTION

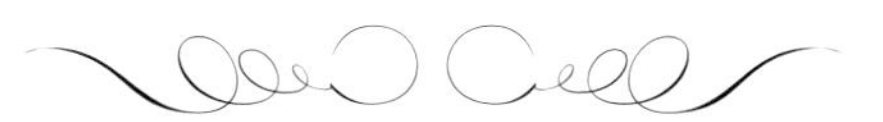

The story of Las Cruces is a reflection of America.

Las Cruces is a unique blend of the fiercely independent Wild West and a growing economic enterprise center. Strategically located at the convergence of two highways, Interstate 10 and Interstate 25, Las Cruces is poised to be among the fastest-growing cities in America over the next 20 years.

The history of Las Cruces and the Mesilla Valley is a truly American story, as cultures have blended into what has become the city we know today as "The Crossroads."

Starting in prehistoric times with nomadic Native American tribes moving in and out of the area, our rich heritage has evolved as the land was explored and settled, first by Spanish conquistadores, then by northern Mexican families and other hardy adventurers who were searching for a new life out West.

By the 1900s, Las Cruces was "home" to a diverse group of former easterners.

The rugged lifestyle of the dusty desert town was not for everyone.

Life was difficult. Often, people struggled just to survive.

Farming was done, but not for commercial purpose. People farmed to provide just enough to feed themselves.

Floods were a common problem among the low-lying areas that flanked the Rio Grande.

Ranching evolved as a livelihood, although the grazing land was sparse and required vast acres of land to support enough cattle to make a living. General supplies were limited and often expensive for the average resident.

Somehow, the little Western town not only survived, but also began to thrive.

Forward-thinking leaders recognized the need for education and founded a college in Las Cruces that evolved into New Mexico State University.

Retail businesses, hotels and bars began to sprout in and around Downtown.

Agriculture had always been an essential part of life in Las Cruces, and over the next 100 years, the Las Cruces area would become one of the most important areas in the nation for agriculture research and development.

Primary crops raised among the fertile farmlands along the Rio Grande include chile, cotton, pecans and onions.

World War II had a profound impact on the development of Las Cruces. The nearby White Sands Proving Ground served as the base for strategic military research and brought in an entirely new group of people – rocket scientists and researchers. Las Cruces also received hundreds of prisoners of war who were placed in camps within the city limits.

After the war, more and more people were attracted to Las Cruces by the temperate climate, the beautiful blue skies, fiery sunsets and the small town quality of life.

More people meant the need for more businesses and services. More schools and churches were also needed.

By the end of the first 100 years of New Mexico statehood, Las Cruces had grown to become the second largest city in the state with nearly 100,000 residents.

This book, "Las Cruces: A Photographic Journey," attempts to take readers back in time through a pictorial review of the past 100 years. It is our hope this book will serve as a reminder of the origins of Las Cruces, and of the people and businesses that have made the city what it is today.

1846–1911

SHAPING THE MESILLA VALLEY

BENEATH GRANITE SPIRES

The Cox Ranch – also known as the San Augustine Ranch – on the east side of the Organ Mountains around 1900 is bustling with activity as cowhands and members of the Cox family are saddled up and ready for an excursion.

JIM HILLEY

THE WINDS OF CHANGE

When Col. Alexander W. Doniphan and his column of troops descended from the Jornada Basin into the dusty adobe settlement of Doña Ana in December 1846, there was a remarkable change in the weather.

During the company's passage down the Jornada del Muerto from the north, the invading Americans had battled through a bitter New Mexico winter storm. However, as they entered the tiny village along the Rio Grande, the bright sun chased the clouds away and the heralds of a new era of American government enjoyed one of those perfect winter days inhabitants of this area know so well.

To the members of Doniphan's campaign, it was like discovering a new climate.

But it was Doniphan who brought the first gust of climatic change to the fertile valley, a long-neglected gem in the heart of a vast desert wilderness.

No longer would the tedious stretch along the Rio Grande be only a tiresome segment in the long journey north or south along the dreaded Camino Real de Tierra Adentro. The first breeze of a different civilization had arrived, though it would take decades for fruits of that civilization to take root and blossom. The wind was blowing from a new direction.

The tempest of the American Civil War first brought the Confederates under Gen. Henry H. Sibley to the valley in 1862. They declared Mesilla the capital of the Arizona Territory, but after being defeated at Glorieta Pass in northern New Mexico, their campaign to make New Mexico a part of the Confederate States of America quickly came to an end.

LAS CRUCES' FIRST COURTHOUSE

This Doña Ana County Courthouse was in use around 1900. The building was located on the site where Court Junior High was built, later known as Court Youth Center.

NEW MEXICO STATE UNIVERSITY LIBRARY ARCHIVES & SPECIAL COLLECTIONS

Soon, troops from California hurried east across vast stretches of desert to take control of New Mexico. After a nearly 1,000-mile march and battles with the great Apache warrior Cochise,

280 million years ago
Dimetrodons and other creatures sun themselves on the shores of a warm sea and leave markings and footprints in the sand. In the late 1980s, the resulting fossils are uncovered in the Robledo Mountains by amateur paleontologist Jerry MacDonald. The discoveries are later called the "Rosetta Stone" of the Paleozoic era and lead to the creation of the Prehistoric Trackways National Monument.

1846
On Dec. 25, 500 cavalry under Col. Alexander W. Doniphan meet an army of 1,300 Mexican troops at Brazito, southeast of Mesilla. The battle results in more than 70 dead and about 150 wounded on the Mexican side, and eight Americans wounded. The hastily assembled Mexican force flees the battlefield, and the American troops continue their march to Chihuahua, Mexico.

1853
The Gadsden Purchase is ratified. The entire Mesilla Valley becomes part of U.S. territory, including villages in the southern portion of the valley, such as La Mesa and its San Jose Catholic Church, below, which were settled to escape American sovereignty.

1878
The Atchison, Topeka and Santa Fe Railroad builds its line just west of Las Cruces, bypassing Mesilla, the most important settlement in the area at that time. With the arrival of the railroad, Las Cruces becomes the center of commerce in the Mesilla Valley and the second largest city in New Mexico.

LAS CRUCES BULLETIN/U.S. LIBRARY OF CONGRESS/NMSU LASC

1900s

Who's Who

Las Cruces Mayor

1908-12 .... R.L. Young

New Mexico A&M Presidents

1888-94 .... Hiram Hadley
1894-96 .... Samuel P. McCrae
1896-99 .... Cornelius Jordan
1899-1901 .... Frederick W. Sanders
1901-08 .... Luther Foster
1908-13 .... Winfred Garrison

Doña Ana County Sheriffs

1854-60 .... Samuel G. Bean
1860 .... Lupindo Borunda
1861 .... L. Armijo
1861-63 .... J.C. Roberts
1863 .... Fred Barker
1863-65 .... Apolonio Barela
1865 .... Reyes Escontria
1865-69, '71-79, '92 .... Mariano Barela
1870-71 .... Fabian Gonzales
1879-80 .... Henry J. Cuniffe
1880-81 .... James W. Southwick
1881-82 .... Thomas J. Bull
1883-84 .... Guadalupe Escarate
1884-87 .... Eugene Van Patten
1893-94 .... Martin Lohman
1895-96 .... Nuna Raymond
1897-1900 .... Pat Garrett
1901-05, '09-12, ... Jose R. Lucero
1906-08 .... Felipe Lucero

By the Numbers

14 .... Settlers in Doña Ana Bend Colony when reinforced (April 1843)

Casualties at Battle of Brazito (Dec. 25, 1846)

71 .... Mexicans died
0 .... Americans died
150 .... Mexicans wounded
8 .... Americans wounded

New Mexico College of Agriculture & Mechanic Arts enrollment (Jan. 21, 1890)

2 .... Sophomores
15 .... Freshmen
10 .... Preparatory Students

66 .... Years New Mexico was a U.S. Territory
9 .... Casualties in the Mesilla Riot (Aug. 27, 1871)
24 .... Years Fort Selden was in commission

In the News

Dec. 29, 1890: The Battle of Wounded Knee, South Dakota, occurs in the last major battle between United States troops and Native Americans.

April 15, 1892: The General Electric Co. is formed, merging the Edison General Electric Co. with the Thomson-Houston Co.

April 6-15, 1896: The first modern Olympic Games are held in Athens, Greece.

Sept. 4, 1896: The Apache chief Geronimo surrenders on the Arizona-New Mexico border, bringing an end to centuries of warfare between Native Americans and European immigrants.

1898: The U.S. declares war on Spain, and gains control of Cuba, Puerto Rico and the Philippines.

March 14, 1900: The Gold Standard Act is ratified, placing the U.S. currency on the gold standard.

Sept. 6, 1901: President William H. McKinley is shot in Buffalo, N.Y.

Jan. 28, 1901: The American League, the so called "junior circuit," goes head to head with the established National League, resulting in the first World Series in 1903.

April 2, 1902: The first movie theater in the U.S. opens in Los Angeles..

Dec. 17, 1903: Inventors Wilbur and Orville Wright succeed in the first sustained and manned airplane flight.

Jan. 1, 1908: The tradition of dropping a ball in New York's Times Square to signal the beginning of the New Year is inaugurated.

Sept. 27, 1908: The first production Model T was built at the Ford plant in Detroit.

May 30, 1909: The National Conference of the Negro is conducted, leading to the formation of the National Association for the Advancement of Colored People (NAACP).

1888
Hiram Hadley founds Las Cruces College and begins offering instruction in a two-room abandoned adobe structure at the corner of Lohman Avenue and Alameda Boulevard in Las Cruces. A year later, the college moves to land donated east of Mesilla Park and becomes the New Mexico College of Agriculture & Mechanic Arts. In 1958, the name is changed to New Mexico State University.

1896
Col. Albert Jennings Fountain disappears in the Tularosa Basin on Feb. 1 while returning to Mesilla from Lincoln County. His 8-year-old son Henry is also the apparent victim of murder. Fountain's blood-stained buggy and horse are found at the scene, but the bodies of Fountain and his young son were never located.

1901
Toribion Huerta, left, and Sheriff Jose R. Lucero just prior to Huerta's hanging for murder in May 1901, the only legal hanging ever carried out in Las Cruces. Huerta admitted his guilt and gave a rambling, incoherent 35-minute speech before his execution. Lucero and his brother Felipe alternated as sheriff and undersheriff between 1901 and 1936.

1908
Famous lawman Pat Garrett is shot to death by Wayne Brazel on the trail between Las Cruces and the Organ Mountains on Feb. 28. The man who gunned down Billy the Kid has his own life ended at the end of the barrel of a gun. Brazel successfully claimed self-defense after the incident.

the California Column, as they became known, found themselves guarding the small Mexican pueblos and villages of southern New Mexico from Apache and Navajo Indians instead of fighting invading rebel armies.

The Confederate troops quickly came and went, but the California Column stayed long enough for many of the young soldiers to be ensnared by the strange, captivating spell of Nuevo México.

After being discharged from military duty, they were allowed to stay in the territory, if they so desired.

One who stayed was a soldier named Albert Jennings Fountain.

Fountain married Mariana Perez from Mesilla, learned to speak Spanish and quickly became a dominating political force, first in nearby El Paso, but later back in his wife's hometown.

The California Column was just a breeze off the Pacific compared to the strong wind that soon came blowing from the east. With the end of the Civil War, the lawless badlands of New Mexico were the perfect place to escape from the changes imposed on the south after the end of the war. Former troops, dispossessed civilians and just plain ruffians and outlaws blew into southern New Mexico. Over the next half a century, much of the turmoil in the Land of Enchantment was stirred up by struggles between remnants of the California Column and the new settlers from Texas and the old South.

The El Paso Salt War, the Lincoln County War, the Mesilla Riot and the eventual murder of Fountain and his young son Henry in the Tularosa Basin are just a few of the many incidents of violence and lawlessness that plagued the area. Men such as Billy the Kid, Pat Garrett, Victorio and Elfego Baca would shed and spill blood in the hot desert sands.

The lawless character of southern New Mexico was used as an excuse to deny New Mexico statehood time and time again.

But slowly, what was a hinterland of Spanish colonial rule, a backwater of the Mexican Republic and the badlands of the American West, would find itself a fertile ground for the roots of civilization.

The modern world could not be kept out forever. First the telegraph, then the railroad, would find their way into the area.

Like cottonwood seeds blowing in the wind, men like Hiram Hadley, Albert Fall, Thomas Branigan and Hunter "Preacher" Lewis would make the valley their home. They, and many others, would put their stamp upon southern New Mexican history.

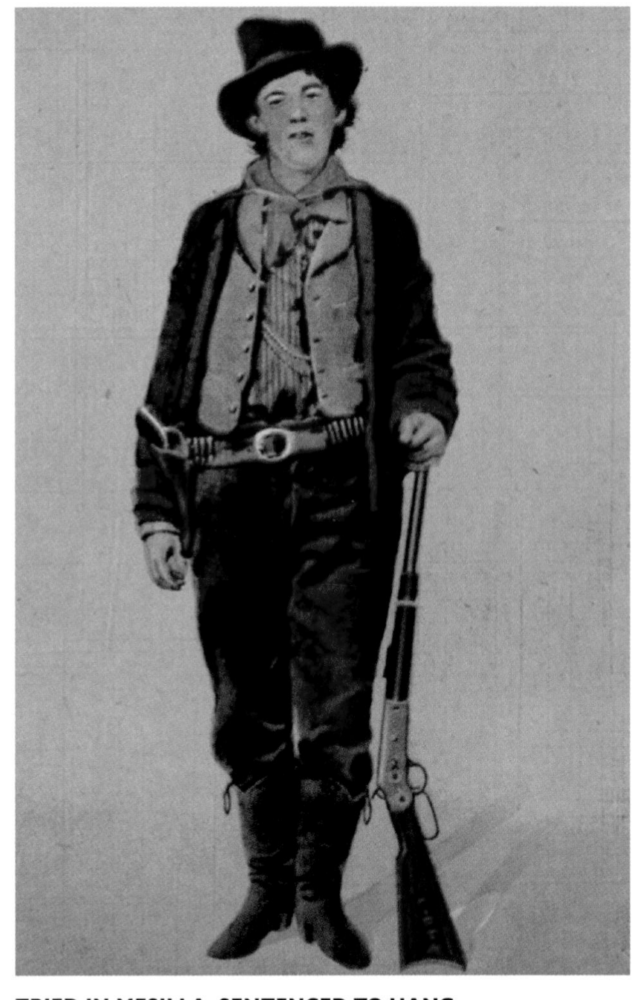

TRIED IN MESILLA, SENTENCED TO HANG

The famous outlaw Billy the Kid was tried in a Mesilla courtroom and sentenced to hang. He was later killed by Pat Garrett.

NMSU LASC

Mesquite thickets would be cleared to become farms, adobe villages would become growing towns. Churches, businesses and schools sprang up. A university would be built and a great river would be tamed.

From a wilderness there came an oasis – the Mesilla Valley.

Albert Jennings Fountain

Albert Jennings Fountain came to New Mexico with the California Column in 1862, and spent the next several years fighting Navajo and Apache Indians along the Rio Grande.

He married Mariana Perez of Mesilla. The young couple moved to El Paso, where Fountain began a law practice and became a major organizer for the Republican Party in Texas. In 1869, he was elected state senator and became Senate Majority Leader. When his political prospects in Texas dimmed, he returned to Mesilla and set up his law practice there.

His reputation as a lawyer and prosecutor grew and he was elected to the territorial legislature in 1888, and was then elected Speaker of the House.

An effort he led to attain statehood for New Mexico was defeated in 1889, but he was instrumental in getting a land grant college for New Mexico located in the Mesilla Valley. At a time when it was not popular, he was committed to public education for both sexes.

As a prosecutor, he battled to rid southern New Mexico of gangs of cattle rustlers and thieves, and after obtaining indictments of several prominent local ranchers, he disappeared along with his young son, Henry, near what later became White Sands National Monument. His death deprived southern New Mexico of perhaps its ablest advocate, and it will never be known what he could have accomplished had he been granted a longer life.

THE MATRIARCH

Fountain's wife, Mariana Perez Fountain, was a native of Mesilla and stayed in the Mesilla Valley until her death in 1915.

STEPHANIE JOHNSON-BURICK

LIVING IN LAS CRUCES

Homes in early Las Cruces were mostly constructed of mud, but many could see the potential of the small New Mexico town and the valley surrounding it.

NMSU LASC

THE PEOPLE

Above left is Rafaela Lucero in the early 1900s. Above right is a wedding photo from around the same era. At right is Albino Montes Sr., born in 1856, and Albino Montes Jr., born in 1889, with the family dog in this portrait, circa 1895.

CHARLES AND MARY ANN LUCERO/BARRIO FAMILY/ OLIVIA MCDONALD

ANYONE FOR TENNIS?

Left, the Las Cruces Tennis Club in 1896; standing are Dr. Elmer Otis Wooton, Dr. Jordan, Miss Freeman, H.B. Holt, Sue Meade, Mr. Freeman and F.C. Barker. Seated in the middle row are Edith Dawson, Fannie Blakesley, Miss Granger and Millicent Barker. Seated on floor is C.W. Ward and additional members whose identities are unknown.

NMSU LASC

THE ARCADIAN CLUB

The Arcadian Club on Feb. 20, 1895, in Las Cruces. In the back row are Mrs. F.W. Smith, Mrs. F.C. Barker, Mrs. S.B. Newcomb, Mrs. J.W. Dawson, Mrs. A.L. Christy, Mrs. H.L. Miles and Mrs. H.B. Holt. In the center row are Mrs. Corrie Lyon, Mrs. A.E. Davidson, Mrs. E.E. Day, Mrs. A.B. Fall, Mrs. U.R. Baker and Susie Young. In the front row are Mrs. P.H. Curran, Mrs. J. Branigan, Miss R. Meeker and Mrs. S. A. Steele.

NMSU LASC

MUSIC AND DANCE

Above, Antonio Loya and his cousin Emeterio Loya are dressed in their finest, possibly to attend a dance. At right, a band entertains onlookers in Mesilla around 1910.

NMSU LASC

THE RITTER FAMILY

Not many people can say they office in a 163-year-old building. Fewer still can say their great-great grandfather once used the same office. Buddy Ritter can say those things, demonstrating the deep connection this fifth-generation New Mexican has to the Mesilla Valley.

A prominent Las Cruces businessman, John Barnes Ritter, and Billie Ruth Carter Ritter were Buddy's parents. John Ritter's grandfather was New Mexico Supreme Court Judge Richmond Barnes, and John Ritter's great grandfather was Dr. Edwin Burt of Mesilla. When Buddy married Margaret Bonnell, she seemed a relative newcomer, only being a fourth-generation New Mexican. They raised three children – John, Elizabeth and Winfield – and have three grandsons.

Born Charles Winfield Ritter in 1936, Buddy assembled a prolific career, centered primarily on hotels, restaurants and investments.

In the 1980s, Ritter had the opportunity to purchase the Double Eagle restaurant on the Mesilla Plaza, the very building in which his great-great grandfather, one of the first surgeons in Mesilla, once practiced. Ritter continued restoration of the building that had begun in 1973, and filled it with unique antiques from throughout Europe and the Americas. The Double Eagle restaurant remains nearly 44 years later as a vibrant destination for dining and celebration.

He studied at New Mexico Military Institute, Tulane University, and graduated from New Mexico State University with a B.A. in banking. A graduate degree at Michigan State University enabled him to be the first Certified Hotel Administrator in New Mexico.

During his career in New Mexico and Arizona, he would own four hotels, 11 restaurants and two breweries. His skills would be recognized statewide and nationally.

NMSU has recognized Ritter's decades of service to the university, naming him the Distinguished Alumnus of the College of Business in 1981 and an Outstanding Centennial Alumnus of the College of Business in 1988. Ritter supported the establishment of the School of Hotel, Restaurant and Tourism Management, funds an annual scholarship and offers internships to NMSU students.

For six years, he served as president of the Board of Regents of the Museums, State Monuments and State Parks of New Mexico.

In 1984, he was named Citizen of the Year by the Las Cruces Association of Realtors. Twenty-five years later, he was named Citizen of the Year by the Greater Las Cruces Chamber of Commerce.

His involvement left an imprint on numerous groups and organizations, such as the New Mexico Cancer Society, the New Mexico Bicentennial Commission, Mesilla Valley Hospice, the Doña Ana County Historical Society, the New Mexico Heritage Preservation Alliance and the Save the Amador Hotel Committee.

Ritter served on boards and commissions for six consecutive governors and, in 2003, was inducted into the New Mexico Tourism Hall of Fame. Ritter even had his own day, when Dec. 7, 2010, was proclaimed "Buddy Ritter Day" throughout the state.

Through it all, Ritter has never stopped working and innovating. In the 2000s, Ritter added to Double Eagle a casual dining restaurant, Peppers Café. He also never stopped being a New Mexican. The featured item on the Peppers menu? The World's Largest Green Chile Cheeseburger.

FAMILY TRADITION

Buddy Ritter, a fifth-generation New Mexican, has built a long and decorated career in the hotel and restaurant business.

DOUBLE EAGLE/CHRIS MORTENSON

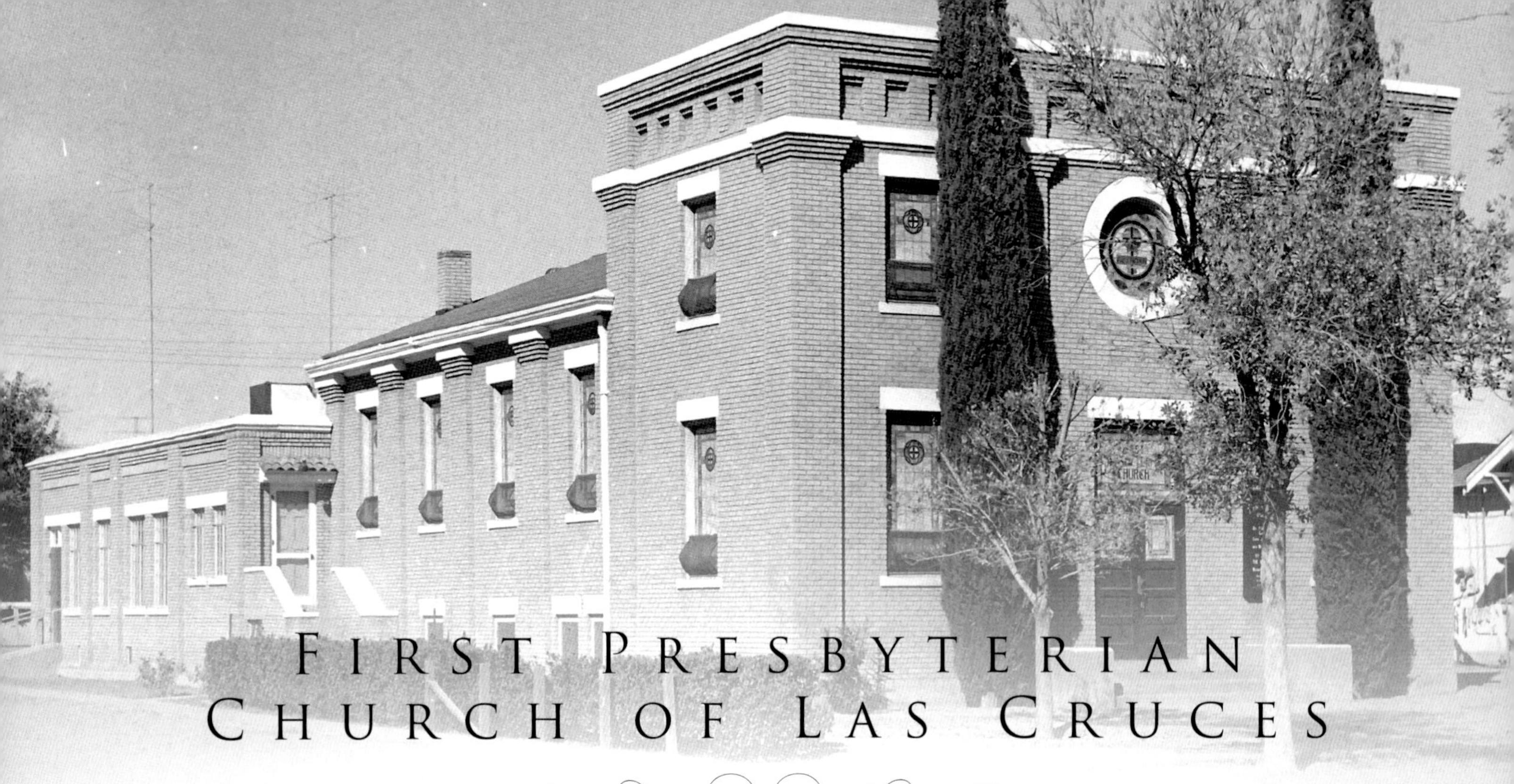

First Presbyterian Church of Las Cruces

The First Presbyterian Church of Las Cruces has a rich history dating back to 1883. Prior to 1883, a Presbyterian church existed in Mesilla Park. It was a mission church established by the Home Mission Board in New York City. The mission eventually closed and the Presbytery of Santa Fe commissioned Rev. Mathieson to sell the mission's property. There was not much to sell; vandals had succeeded in removing most of the furniture and fixtures.

With no Protestant church in Las Cruces, Rev. Mathieson felt called to begin one. On March 25, 1883, the church was officially organized, with seven charter members.

The first meeting place was at Las Cruces Avenue and Alameda Boulevard. The original building was purchased by the Women's Presbyterian Board of Missions for $200. It wasn't long before that building had served its purpose and a larger facility was needed. A new building was completed in November 1883.

At first, the Congregation was composed of Anglo- and Spanish-Americans. Because of the language difference, two separate services were held each Sunday. By 1886, the demands made by the two groups were more than could be handled by one minister. By action of the Santa Fe Presbytery, the congregations were separated. Spanish-speaking congregants continued to use the existing structure while the Anglos moved across the street where a larger adobe building was constructed at a cost of $1,657.

Until 1909, the church received financial support from the Presbyterian Board of Missions. As membership continued to grow, so did the ability to become self-supporting. By 1916, the church had grown to the size where it was deemed necessary to construct larger facilities. World War I made it necessary to postpone construction until 1924, when a new edifice was completed for the sum of $20,000.

The church continued to grow and to expand its ministries. In 1960, the members decided the old building would either have to be enlarged or the congregation would need to relocate. The decision was made to move and construct new facilities. On Sept. 19, 1965, the present sanctuary and educational buildings at 200 E. Boutz Road were dedicated.

Heading into New Mexico's second century, First Presbyterian Church of Las Cruces, with its blend of all ages and family backgrounds, is serving more than 350 members with its services and a variety of programs and activities.

GROWING IN THE FAITH

The First Presbyterian Church of Las Cruces was the city's first Protestant church. During its first 128 years, the church has held services in three primary locations: 1883-1924 at Las Cruces Avenue and Alameda Boulevard, 1924-65 at Las Cruces Avenue and Armijo Street and, since 1965, at 200 E. Boutz Road.

FIRST PRESBYTERIAN CHURCH OF LAS CRUCES/NMSU LASC

METHODIST MEMORIES

The Methodist Episcopal Church, above left, was built in 1899 where the modern St. Paul's United Methodist Church stands in 2011. The little church was dismantled and replaced in 1912. Above right, members of the Methodist Episcopal Church enjoy a Sunday School picnic.

NMSU LASC

UTOPIA ON THE RIO GRANDE

The residence building at the Shalam Colony as it appeared in 1889. The colony was established in 1884 by John Newbrough – writer of the book "Oahspe" – and wealthy Boston merchant Andrew Howland as an orphanage and commune. Newbrough died in 1891 and the colony was abandoned in 1901.

NMSU LASC

IN THE CATHOLIC TRADITION

Left, St. Genevieve's Catholic Church in Las Cruces in the early 1900s. Above, the San Albino Catholic Church in Mesilla as it appeared after the bells were installed in 1887. The first San Albino Catholic Church on the site was built of mud and logs and was replaced in the mid-1850s. The church above was built in 1885 and replaced by a new church consecrated in 1908. The Vatican elevated the status of San Albino to a minor basilica in 2008.

NMSU LASC/COURTESY PALACE OF THE GOVERNORS PHOTO ARCHIVES (NMHM/DCA), 122144

NEW MEXICO A&M

The New Mexico College of Agriculture & Mechanic Arts was founded in 1888 as an institution chartered under the Morrill Act of 1862 and the Hatch Act of 1887.

Albert Fountain, who, as speaker of the House in the New Mexico Territorial Legislature, was instrumental in getting the college placed in Doña Ana County and spoke at a gathering at the Amador Hotel about the new school:

"Las Cruces is to be congratulated on this prize it has secured from the last Legislature … not an ordinary common school, but a greatly endowed institution … our children will be able to obtain the highest education at minimal cost," Fountain said.

Local residents were required to donate at least 100 acres of land on which to locate the new school, and soon 220 acres were acquired partly on the Mesilla Valley flood plain and partly on the nearby desert foothills.

Hiram Hadley, who founded Las Cruces College in 1887, turned his attention to the new land-grant college and became its first president.

The new college officially opened on Jan. 21, 1890. The cornerstone for McFie Hall, below, was laid in 1890 and the building was completed in 1891. The Science Hall, the Agricultural Hall (Wilson Hall) and the Women's Dormitory (renamed McFie Hall after the original McFie Hall burned) were soon added to the new campus.

Sam Steel was set to be the institution's first graduate in May 1893, but was robbed and murdered, so the ceremony was canceled.

The following year, five students graduated, including the first woman graduate, Agnes Williams, and a promising young agricultural student named Fabian Garcia.

THE DUSTY BEGINNINGS OF HIGHER EDUCATION

Hiram Hadley came to Las Cruces in 1887 from Indiana. Below, the educator stands next to the two-room adobe on the corner of Amador Avenue and Alameda Boulevard in which he founded Las Cruces College in 1888. A year later, the school and its small faculty formed the nucleus of New Mexico A&M, with Hadley as its first president.

NMSU LASC

KNOWLEDGE BLOSSOMS IN LAS CRUCES

The photo below shows a stenography class, circa 1904. Fourth from left is Alice Ford, who was a freshmen in 1904-05.

NMSU LASC

THE AG COLLEGE TAKES ROOT

In the1890s, New Mexico A&M was rising from the desert east of Mesilla Park. At left is the Science Hall, and the building on the right is Old Main, which burned to the ground in 1911. After its destruction, leaders at the college entertained the idea of turning its basement level foundation into a pool, but the idea never came to fruition.

NMSU LASC

WORK AND PLAY

Above, students, faculty and family members posed on the steps of Old Main in 1893. Left, female students are shown enjoying a taste of dormitory life in 1903.

NMSU LASC

CAMPUS ROYALTY

"Queen Elizabeth the First," the 1901 May Day Queen at New Mexico A&M, donned a regal gown and held court at the home of Professor Goss.

NMSU LASC

PATRIOTIC THESPIANS

A dramatic production on the stage at McFie Hall in 1907 included a patriotic theme – and romance.

NMSU LASC

AGGIES, GO AGGIES!

The ladies above were New Mexico basketball champions in 1904. In the back row is Dorris Foster, Vivian Redding and Nethie Durling; the front row includes Merle Blinns, Ruth Miller and Margie Ingram. At right, is the first Aggie football squad in 1894, which must have included a majority of the male students enrolled.

NMSU LASC

SISTERS OF SOUTHWESTERN DESTINY

Left, Annie and Sam Steel Sr. at their wedding in 1886. Center, Judge John and Mary McFie. Right, John and Eliza DeMier in 1872.

STEEL FAMILY

THE STEEL FAMILY

Eliza, Annie, Mary and Maggie Steel.

Sisterhood was strong in these four college-educated siblings. Mary's husband, John McFie, was appointed territorial land commissioner in southern New Mexico in the early 1880s. Mary and all of her sisters and all of their husbands packed up, left Illinois and headed for Las Cruces.

Maggie Steel Cooper and her husband would leave to settle in Colorado.

But the others – Eliza and John DeMier, Annie and Samuel Steel, Mary and John McFie – left a lasting impact on Las Cruces.

John DeMier rented a building to a fledgling campus that would become New Mexico A&M College, later New Mexico State University.

Judge John McFie would become the last territorial supreme court justice for New Mexico. The first building constructed specifically for the college was McFie Hall, which opened in 1891 and commonly called Old Main. Mary McFie helped found, in 1894, the Women's Improvement Association. Their son Ralph McFie rode with Teddy Roosevelt and the Rough Riders. At his home, at what later became McFie Street, John McFie started a vineyard, an enduring passion and vocation in the family.

NEW FAMILY, NEW MEXICO, 1890s

The first four children of Annie and Sam Steel Sr. were Sam Steel Jr., Ella, Matthew and the smallest, Richard. Matthew, Richard and a later son, James, all became doctors. Sam Jr. was not as fortunate.

Annie and Samuel Steel Sr. had several children, two of them long tied to history in Doña Ana County.

James Steel graduated from New Mexico A&M in 1908, then earned a medical degree from Columbia University in New York. He returned to southern New Mexico and for nearly 50 years was the doctor in Hatch. Dr. Steel delivered as many as 3,000 babies.

The short life of James' older brother, Sam Steel Jr., ended in tragedy. In 1893, the promising 17-year-old was studying at New Mexico A&M College, and was set to be the lone member of the college's first graduating class.

While delivering milk one day in a horse-drawn wagon, young Sam was murdered. The accused was a cowboy named John Roper. With Col. Albert Fountain as prosecutor, Roper was convicted and sentenced to hang, but a higher court overturned the decision.

At Sam Jr.'s funeral, Hiram Hadley, the college president, gave the eulogy. More than a century later, in 1995, a frontage road near the university was named Sam Steel Way.

Sam Steel Sr. began his vineyard in 1891. It grew along what was later to be known as South Main Street in Las Cruces, from University Avenue north for about two miles on both sides of the railroad tracks.

James Steel, the country doctor, kept the thought of wine alive, always dabbling with a grape arbor. When James was 67, he had another child named Gordon, who eagerly learned the art of wine from his father.

Gordon went to NMSU and, in 1975, joined the Air Force. Grapes were always in the back of his mind. During his military career, which included stays in Europe, he regularly made wine.

When it came time to retire, he and his wife, Sandi, knew exactly what to do. He felt the tug of the homeland, returned to the Mesilla Valley and established the Rio Grande Winery. The vineyard was planted in 2004, and the first harvest came in 2007.

Today, New Mexicans can taste the wine that carries the legacy of those four pioneering Steel sisters from long ago.

A HEAD TURNING DISPLAY

The REO Motor Car Co. showed off its new vehicles in front of First National Bank and the Bank Saloon on Main Street in Downtown Las Cruces in June 1909.

NMSU LASC

HOTELS AND HARDWARE

Above left, the Hotel Don Bernardo looking north of Main Street in the early 1900s. The above center photo shows a general store circa 1880. Blacksmith's shops, such as Rynerson's Blacksmith Shop in 1897, at right, were the hardware stores of their day.

NMSU LASC

CENTERS OF COMMERCE

The Frank Oliver store, above left, was a major retailer in its day. Above center, some fashionable ladies hang out at the millinery in Mesilla. The corral in back of Martin Lohman's Trading Post, above right, was often used as a location for trading with Indians from the Mescalero Apache Reservation.

NMSU LASC

A FAMOUS VISITOR

Former President Theodore Roosevelt spoke to an enthusiastic crowd of about 300 who gathered at the Las Cruces Depot on March 15, 1911. With Roosevelt on the platform was Las Cruces Mayor R. L. Young. Roosevelt noted the presence of many New Mexico A&M students in the crowd and encouraged them to work hard and become productive citizens.

NMSU LASC

STRENGTH IN NUMBERS

Victoria Garcia. Isaac Garcia the soldier. From1932: Isaac and Leroy Garcia; Elodia, Reymundo, Mary Jane; Victoria, Emma and Angelina Garcia. Soldiers Leroy and Jerry in the 1950s. At bottom, the Garcia siblings, 1990s, seated: Angelina G. Lucero, Reymundo Garcia, standing: Mary Jane Garcia, Elodia Garcia, Emma G. Chavez, Yolanda G. Gonzales, Jerry Garcia, Leroy Garcia. Emma's daughter Christina Chavez Kelley. The family farm in the 1970s.

MARY JANE GARCIA/CHRISTINA CHAVEZ KELLEY

THE GARCIA FAMILY

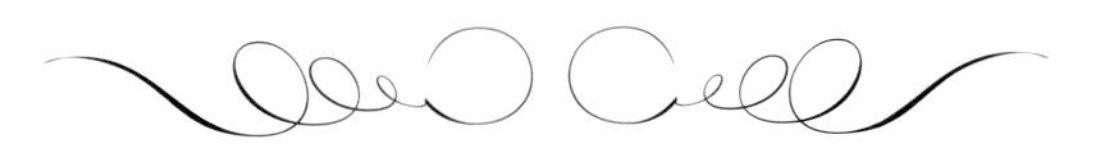

Driven by 1840 floods in Chihuahua, Mexico, 13 bold colonists headed north into the Mesilla Valley. Jose Inez Garcia was one of the 13. In 1842, they founded the Village of Doña Ana.

To see Doña Ana through the eyes of the present Garcia family is to look at New Mexico itself.

The family arrived in hardship, and worked with the land to carve out a life. Success with crops led to success in business and mercantile. Aspirations led to education. A nation at war called, and the Garcia men answered. More service took the form of law enforcement and politics.

Jose Inez Garcia married Francisca Perea (Mary Jane's great-grandparents), and they began farming, mostly cotton and corn.

It was clear the Garcia children would not be content with farming alone. Jose and Francisca's son Ruperto broadened their farm by adding watermelon, cucumber, squash and, of course, chile. He also took on the duty of Doña Ana's first justice of the peace.

Among Ruperto's children were Sylvestre Garcia, who would become the first Methodist pastor in Doña Ana, and Isaac Garcia, who threw himself into farming and business.

Isaac married Victoria, and they had 10 children.

The girls were Angelina, Emma, Elodia, Mary Jane and Yolanda. The boys were Leroy, Reymundo and Jerry. Two other boys, Max and Roy, did not live to see age two.

The children worked on the farm and in the family store. Issac and Victoria started the store, Doña Ana Mercantile, in the late 1930s. Before long, they added a second store, a dance hall, a pool hall and a saloon known as the Half Moon Bar.

"We were brought up in the store," Mary Jane said. "We learned our lessons in business and all of us had chores. I used to sweep the store before walking to elementary school. On the farm, we were there picking cotton. My sister Elodia was expert at picking chile."

Brother Reymundo and his wife, Emma, always had ideas. One was the barrel-style chile roaster. He envisioned it, and now you see them every harvest season at stores where crews roast chile.

Leroy served in the Army during the Korean conflict. Jerry served in the National Guard, as did their father Isaac, who served in the guard during the Pancho Villa era.

Education was a priority for the Garcias. Mary Jane earned a master's in anthropology from New Mexico State University in 1985, and wrote and published the first documented history of the Village of Doña Ana in 1986.

The family's emphasis on education is also illustrated by Yolanda, who got her degree from New Mexico State University and all four of her children earned degrees at NMSU.

Emma's daughter, Christina Chavez Kelley, has worked at NMSU for more than 20 years, serving as an assistant to five university presidents. Mike Gonzales, Yolanda's husband, worked as a Las Cruces police officer and in the district attorney's office.

For Mary Jane, public service was an unexpected calling. She never dreamed of becoming a state senator, but when her mother, Victoria, passed away in 1988, Mary Jane was inspired to run. She won, and kept winning. In 1996, she began a long tenure as Senate Majority Whip.

"Three things I'm most proud of," she said of her work in Santa Fe's Roundhouse. "The child abuse law (which gave teeth to keep convicted abusers in prison without parole), the cockfighting ban (the law passed in 2007, culminating an 18-year effort for Garcia, who brought it up in her very first session, 1989), and the human trafficking law (passed in 2010)."

THE RAILROAD

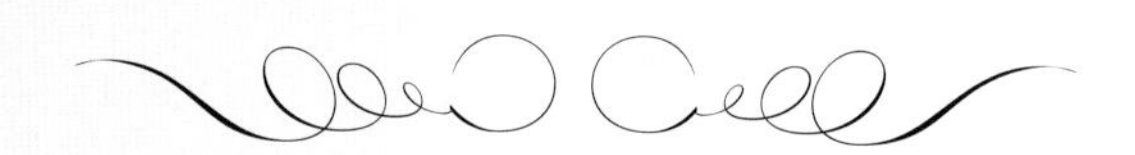

The Railroad Museum sits upon one of the most significant sites in Las Cruces history. The decision to entice the Atchison, Topeka and Santa Fe Railroad (AT&SF) to Las Cruces enriched the lives of the Mesilla Valley and brought the town to the forefront of Doña Ana County.

The railroad allowed local merchants and farmers to reach suppliers and buyers quicker and more efficiently. It also allowed people to travel to and from Las Cruces faster and safer.

When the railroad entered the Mesilla Valley in 1878, the area had long been part of major travel routes. For centuries, Native Americans took part in trade networks that stretched throughout the Southwest and Mexico. An important trading center at Casas Grandes, in western Chihuahua, Mexico, connected to trails in New Mexico. One main trail, the Rio Grande Pueblo Indian Trail, stretched from El Paso to the upper Rio Grande. These ancient trade routes brought goods such as coral, shells, parrot feathers and copper bells into New Mexico from the south. Many of these trade routes were active until the Spanish settlement of New Mexico.

The first train entered New Mexico in 1878 through Raton Pass on the AT&SF line. The route had been previously used by the Santa Fe Trail, but Ritchens Lacey "Uncle Dick" Wooten built a toll road through the pass. The AT&SF purchased the toll road and by building through Raton Pass first, established itself as the major player in New Mexico. The race to have tracks cover New Mexico was more for exporting minerals and materials than moving freight and passengers in and out.

The AT&SF railroad company approached both Mesilla and Las Cruces about providing a right of way to bring the main line to their towns. Mesilla did not respond positively to the deal, but in Las Cruces, four forward-looking men decided that the AT&SF was right for Las Cruces. William Rynerson, Henry Cuniffe, Simon Newcomb and Jacinto Armijo formed the New Mexico Town Company. Together they bought land west of town and then gave right of way to the railroad. Rynerson actually retained the deeds to the land east of the tracks which he would later develop into the Alameda-Depot District.

LIVING ON THE RAILROAD

Above left, coaches from the local hotels were on hand to ferry railroad passengers from the Las Cruces depot. The sights, sounds and smells of locomotives such as this 2-6-2 steam engine, above right, were part of everyday life in the years after the Atchison, Topeka & Santa Fe Railroad came to the Mesilla Valley. For many years, the quickest and most reliable way to ship goods, visit and shop in neighboring towns or anywhere in the nation was by rail. The coming of the railroad helped put an end to the isolation of Las Cruces and the Mesilla Valley, made it possible for friends and relatives to stay in contact and for businesses to ship and receive goods more quickly and easily.

NMSU LASC

With their right of way in place, the AT&SF started laying track toward Las Cruces. There were delays due to weather and lack of supplies when a fire took out a bridge across the Rio Grande. The local newspaper reported that the depot grounds would be laid out in February 1881. Finally on April 26, 1881, the first train arrived at the new Las Cruces Depot to much fanfare. The first passenger train arrived in June 1881.

A VISIONARY

Henry Cuniffe was one of the investors who sold land to the Atchison, Topeka & Santa Fe Railroad west of Las Cruces, causing Las Cruces to flourish at the expense of neighboring Mesilla.

NMSU LASC

The coming of the railroad changed Las Cruces forever. The railroad brought new businesses, products and people to the City of the Crosses. It provided the foundation for the push by Rynerson, Cuniffe and others to move the county seat from Mesilla to Las Cruces. New products available with the railroad were name-brand items, such as soap and sewing machines, and larger items too bulky to be moved in wagons. Farmers had much wider markets in which to sell their products, too.

The railroad also changed the physical appearance of Las Cruces. The first paved street led passengers off the train into Downtown where the hotels, restaurants and saloons were located.

With the railroad came new architectural ideas and materials, which can still be seen in the varied houses in the adjacent neighborhood, divided into lots and sold by Rynerson. In these few blocks there are Italianate, Queen Anne, bungalow, mission revival, Tudor revival, gothic revival and international style buildings.

The railroad offered a reduced rate of 6 cents per mile for people wanting to attend the first New Mexico Agricultural, Mineral and Industrial Exposition (now the State Fair) held in October 1881 in Albuquerque.

Between the telegraph and the mail being delivered by train, business and personal correspondence was much easier.

The railroad supplied new employment opportunities for both men and women. Local men were hired to lay track, build the depot and then after the railroad arrived both local men and women worked on the line. Other workers moved to Las Cruces for their railroad related jobs.

For safety and effective scheduling, the railroad industry created standard time zones – Atlantic Railway Time Zone, Eastern Railway Time Zone, Central Railway Time Zone, Mountain Railway Time Zone and Pacific Railway Time Zone. These time zones became so prevalent that in 1918 the U.S. government adopted the system, eliminating the "Railway" from the title. Previous to this standardization, there had been 1,183 time zones in the U.S. in almost 80 separate regions.

Courtesy the Las Cruces Railroad Museum

NO MORE BOOKS

When Hal Cox wasn't studying under the tutelage of a governess, the boy got to work up a thirst and appetite with his father and the ranch hands. Shown in this photo from 1899 are W.W. Cox (1); Ed "Panky" Fierro (2): Ince Rhodes (3); Jim Hester (4); Hal Cox (5); A.P. Rhodes (6); Tom Rhodes (7); and a cowboy whose name was not recorded (8).

JOHN YARBROUGH

TOUGH JOBS

Above, miners pause for some fresh air near Dripping Springs in 1900. At right, the Stephenson-Bennett Mine was one of numerous mines in the Organ Mountains that were a mainstay of the local economy. The mine produced silver and lead among numerous other ores.

NMSU LASC

HOW 'BOUT THEM APPLES

El Manzinal Orchard, left, was owned by the Stuart family and was one of the largest orchards in the Mesilla Valley before a rising water table after the completion of Elephant Butte Dam killed the trees. At first, farmers speculated the water table was rising because the dam was holding back silt, but it soon became apparent that some farmers were being "ten-foot water hogs," and were flooding the valley with their irrigation. The federal government eventually brought in diesel-powered dredges to dig a system of drainage ditches, and the irrigation district began to monitor and restrict the amount of water farmers were using on their farms. Below left, workers prepare to spray the apple orchard with pesticide. Below right, the Stuart family and friends spend a pleasant afternoon in the shade of the apple trees.

STUART MEERSCHEIDT

A LAND OF PLENTY

For much of the year, farmers depended on wells to keep their crops irrigated before the Rio Grande was tamed and became a more reliable source of water.

STUART MEERSCHEIDT

THE LORETTO ACADEMY

The Sisters of Loretto Academy at Amador Avenue and Main Street was established in 1870 and operated until 1943. The pictures above show the front of the academy around 1909 after the wings were added and students and faculty enjoying the garden grounds, which were used to feed the poor.

NMSU LASC

HOME SCHOOLING, 1900 STYLE

A portrait of W. W. Cox keeps watch over a school room at the Cox ranch in January 1900. Despite the ranch's remote location near Aguirre Springs, Lena Orpa Cox, 14; Hal Riley Cox, 6; Annie Laura Cox, 10; and Blanche Cox, 8, had to attend to educational matters under the guidance of governess Maggie Hagan, at right.

JOHN YARBROUGH

PUBLIC SCHOOLS

Above left, Las Cruces students Sophie Christie and Katherine Lohman are shown in their basketball uniforms from around 1900. Above center, a Las Cruces public school shown in 1906 eventually became Central Elementary. Above right, a group of Las Cruces school children and educators are shown in front of the old South Ward school in 1900.

NMSU LASC

1912-1919

A NEW ERA BEGINS

WITH THE STROKE OF A PEN

President William Howard Taft signs the proclamation making New Mexico a state at a ceremony in the White House in Washington, D.C., on Jan. 6, 1912. A group of witnesses from the 47th state, including Congressmen George Curry and Harvey Fergusson, W. H. Andrews, Mr. and Mrs. A. B. McGaffey, Charles Curry and John W. Roberts, looked on as Taft ended 66 years of territorial rule in the Land of Enchantment.

HARRIS AND EWING, COURTESY PALACE OF THE GOVERNORS PHOTO ARCHIVES (NMHM/DCA), 089760

TAFT SIGNS PROCLAMATION; NEW MEXICO NOW FINALLY INSIDE THE UNITED STATES

FATEFUL SIGNATURE ATTACHED TO DOCUMENT SHORTLY AFTER NOON; EXECUTIVE WAIVES ALL DELAY

"It is All Over. I Am Glad to Give You Life and I Hope You Will Be Healthy," Says President Taft to Jubilant New Mexicans at Capital; Receipt of News Hailed With Rejoicing All Over State and Last Obstacle in Way of the New Star is Believed to Have Been Removed.

THE 47 STAR FLAG

On Jan. 6, 1912, New Mexico was the 47th state to join the Union, which required the new American flag have a unique, uneven star pattern. However, just 40 days later, Arizona became the 48th state, making the 47-star version one of the shortest-lived and rarest of American flags. At right, the Jan. 7, 1912, headlines in the newspapers let folks know it was time to celebrate.

NMSU LASC

1912
The people of New Mexico cast their ballots in November, 1911, and after waiting 66 years for statehood, New Mexicans were able to convene the state's first Legislature in 1912.

1912
On March 26, Las Cruces attorney Albert B. Fall is appointed by the New Mexico Legislature as one of the first two United States Senators from New Mexico. In a contentious joint session, Fall was in last place on the first ballot, but with a solid block of supporters, he and Thomas B. Catron were elected over Thomas Mills and former statehood delegate W. H. Andrews.

1915
A building boom takes place in Las Cruces with many fine homes being built, including the stately home of H.B. Holt designed by renowned architect Henry Trost. The home still stands at the corner of Picacho Avenue and Alameda Boulevard.

NMSU LASC

1912-19

Who's Who

Las Cruces Mayors

- 1908-12 .... R.L. Young
- 1912-13 .... J.P. Mitchel
- 1913-14 .... Edward C. Wade
- 1914-16 .... R.P. Porter
- 1916-18 .... John H. May
- 1918-20 .... A.I. Kelso

Postmasters

- 1907-12 .... Thomas Branigan
- 1912-14 .... Vincent B. May
- 1914-21 .... Bliss Freeman

New Mexico A&M Presidents

- 1908-13 .... Winfred Garrison
- 1913-17 .... George E. Ladd
- 1917-21 .... Austin D. Crile

Doña Ana County Sheriffs

- 1901-05, '09-12, '17-20, ... Jose R. Lucero
- 1905-09, 1912-17 .... Felipe Lucero

New Mexico Governors

- 1912-17 .... William C. McDonald
- 1917 .... Ezekiel C. de Baca
- 1917-19 .... Washington E. Lindsay

U.S. Senators

- 1912-17 .... Thomas B. Catron
- 1912-1921 .... Albert B. Fall
- 1917-27 .... Andrieus A. Jones

U.S. Representatives

- 1912-13 .... George Curry
- 1912-15 .... Harvey B. Fergusson
- 1915-17, '19-21 .... Benigno C. Hernández
- 1917-19 .... William Bell Walton

By the Numbers

New Mexico A&M students (1917-18)

- 1 .... Graduate student
- 8 .... Seniors
- 14 .... Juniors
- 15 .... Sophomores
- 26 .... Freshmen

- 17 .... Number of Americans killed in Pancho Villa's Raid
- 9 .... Albert Fall's years in the U.S. Senate
- 141 .... Miles of canal in the Rio Grande Project
- $7.2 million .... Cost of Elephant Butte Dam
- 306 feet .... Height of Elephant Butte Dam
- $125 .... Cost of an irrigated acre of farmland in the Mesilla Valley (1915)
- 3 cents .... First-class stamp (1917)
- 2 cents .... First-class stamp (1919)

In the News

March 12, 1912: The Girl Scouts of America is formed by Judith Gordon Low in Georgia.

April 15, 1912: The Titanic sinks after colliding with an iceberg in the North Atlantic Ocean – 1,517 lives are lost.

Feb. 1, 1913: Grand Central Station, the world's largest rail terminal, opens in New York City.

Dec. 1, 1913: The first moving assembly line is introduced and adopted for mass production by the Ford Motor Company, allowing automobile construction time to decrease by almost 10 hours per vehicle.

June 28, 1914: Archduke Francis Ferdinand is assassinated in Austria by a Bosnian fanatic, an event that led to World War 1.

Aug. 3, 1914: Germany declares war on France.

Nov. 3, 1914: New York socialite Mary Phelps Jacob patents the brassiere, which she had invented one year earlier.

Jan. 25, 1915: Alexander Graham Bell and Thomas A. Watson conduct the first telephone conversation between New York and San Francisco.

Jan. 28, 1915: The United States Coast Guard is established, replacing the responsibilities formerly entailed within the services and stations of the U.S. Life-Saving Services.

April 20, 1916: Chicago Cubs play their first game at Wrigley Field.

April 2, 1917: President Woodrow Wilson asks Congress for a declaration of war against Germany.

May 29, 1917: Future U.S. President John F. Kennedy is born in Brookline, Mass.

1918: A flu epidemic kills more than 20 million people around the world and thousands in the United States

Jan. 6, 1919: Former President Theodore Roosevelt dies of a heart attack in his sleep in Oyster Bay, N.Y.

Jan. 16, 1919: Prohibition begins.

1915
H. H. Brook was the first county agent in Doña Ana County. A few years after his appointment, when the Mesilla Valley became waterlogged due to over irrigation, he was a leader in the effort to convince Mesilla Valley farmers to support the construction of drainage canals.

1916
Major construction on Elephant Butte Dam is completed, boosting the already considerable output of agricultural goods from the fertile Mesilla Valley.

1916
More than 400 Mexican revolutionaries under the command of Gen. Francisco "Pancho" Villa attack the village of Columbus, N.M., on March 9, leading to the "Punitive Expedition," in which American troops chase the charismatic Mexican revolutionary into northern Mexico. It is the last major use of mounted American cavalry troops.

1918
"The Great War" comes to an end in Europe. On Nov. 11, Las Crucens celebrate the end of the conflict with a bonfire at St. Genevieve's Catholic Church.

TAMING THE RIO GRANDE

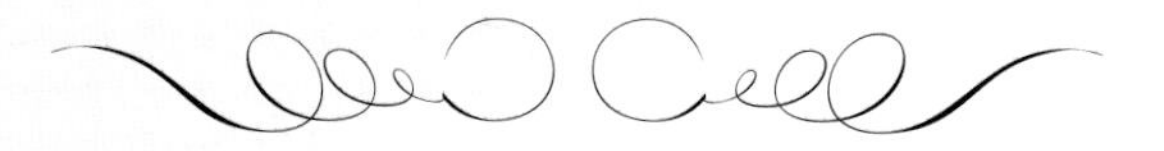

Early in the morning of Jan. 6, 1915 – the third anniversary of New Mexico statehood – a thunderous blast of dynamite echoed through the Rio Grande Valley at the construction site of Elephant Butte Dam.

The explosion sent a cascade of rubble into the channel constructed to carry water while the foundations and support structures at the huge dam were built. Some of the explosive charges failed, reported the Rio Grande Republican, but enough rubble was loosed to "greatly check the flow." An army of men descended into the trench to close the gap.

By noon, the flow had been checked well enough for work to begin on the flume.

During the night, the Republican reported, work was "nip and tuck" as workers labored to block any seepage. Two 4,000-gallon-per-minute pumps were brought in, and then a third, to keep the water from rising faster than masonry could be laid. By 7 p.m. Jan. 7, the water had risen to the point the pumps had to be moved. At 9 p.m., enough masonry had been laid to divert the water through the dam's lower gates and pipes.

Forty hours after the blast of earth and rock shook the countryside, the dam had been built to a height of 24 feet.

"The Rio Grande has been placed under absolute control," the Republican reported.

For southern New Mexicans a century later, it may be difficult to comprehend just what a momentous event it was.

No longer would spring runoff be a monster waiting to wash away anything in its path. What once was a bane, would now be a boon.

While the people along the lower Rio Grande in New Mexico were as excited about the prospects of statehood as the rest of New Mexico, it probably was not the leading topic of discussion when valley residents discussed the future. For this part of the world, the dam was much bigger.

Three hundred feet high, 1,674 feet long and constructed of 618,785 cubic yards of cement, the Elephant Butte Dam had evolved from a pipe dream to a concrete reality.

The idea for large irrigation projects in the West can be traced back to the reports of famed geologist and explorer John Wesley Powell, who noted a problem common in the western United States while surveying in Utah.

"The snows of winter are dissipated too early in the spring to be

NOT JUST A DAM

An incredible amount of work was done as part of the Rio Grande Project before construction on the actual dam could begin. Miles of railroad were built. A support "city," complete with machine shops, hospitals and housing, was constructed. Heavy equipment had to be moved into place, such as the locomotive shown above being moved across the river by a tram system.

NMSU LASC

A NEW LAKE

Elephant Butte Lake fills for the first time behind the still unfinished dam in 1915. The town built to support the massive construction project can be seen in the valley below. The derricks at right in the above photo were part of a tram system that hauled heavy materials across the Rio Grande.

NMSU LASC

of use for irrigation … the greater part of the future extension of the cultivated areas will be accomplished only by expensive engineering works, including the damming of the principal rivers and the construction of long canals."

In 1902, Rep. Francis Newlands of Nevada introduced legislation supporting involvement by the federal government in large irrigation projects and the Reclamation Act of 1902 approved funding for projects throughout the West.

Secretary of the Interior Ethan Hitchcock authorized construction of the Rio Grande Project on Dec. 2, 1905, under the provisions of the Reclamation Act. In 1906, construction began on the Leasburg Diversion Dam and six miles of canal, which were completed in 1908. Congress authorized the construction of the Engle Dam on Feb. 25, 1905.

On Oct. 8, 1910, the Republican described the scene at the construction site near Engle: "Clinging to the ledges overhanging the canyon, hundreds of men are working like ants. Dotting the hillside are groups of two, three or four, laboriously putting down drill holes. Over the hill comes an endless procession of men carrying ominous black cans – powder. One-thousand pounds to the hole. At noon and in the evening, great blasts are set off, in a single moment changing the face of the landscape."

In late 1910, local landowners were buoyed by news that work on the new dam would be hastened by a government takeover of private contracts. Advocates of the move believed it would eliminate problems with ordering materials and hiring labor that were slowing construction. Reports of the move contained some of the first official references to the project as "Elephant Butte Dam" instead of "Engle Dam."

THE FLEETING FLUME

Above, in preparation for construction of Elephant Butte Dam, a concrete flume, right, was built on the west side of the river to divert water away from the dam's foundation. In early 1915, the flume was removed and water was allowed to collect behind the dam as construction continued, above.

NMSU LASC

Interest in the construction was high in the region, and in April 1910, the Mesilla Valley and El Paso chambers of commerce arranged an excursion to the Elephant Butte Dam site on May 10. The train left El Paso in the morning and picked up passengers in Las Cruces in time to have lunch at the dam site. The fare was $6. It was the first of many such excursions that took place until the dam was completed in 1916.

Additional Rio Grande Project works included Mesilla Diversion Dam, East Side and West Side Canals, Percha Diversion Dam, the Rincon Valley Canal and an extension of Leasburg Canal that were constructed from 1914-19.

COWTOWN

Agricultural exhibitions were not relegated to rural fairgrounds in the years after statehood. Here, prized cattle are being displayed on Main Street in the heart of Downtown Las Cruces. The Rio Grande Theatre building is seen on the far left.

NMSU LASC

CHANGING LIFESTYLES

Above left, by the early 1900s, more modern buildings replaced many of the old adobe structures in Las Cruces, although a windmill still pokes above the roof lines. Above right, the Hotel Don Bernardo was a popular destination in Las Cruces, but the era of the automobile would change Downtown Las Cruces forever.

NMSU LASC

PUBLIC LIFE

Above left, this brick building served as a Wells Fargo & Company Express office as well as Las Cruces City Hall. Above right, interior of the Las Cruces post office in 1912 with Postmaster Thomas Branigan, Dave Chauvin, Alice Branigan, Wilson Wade, Johnny Lerma and Donald W. Young.

NMSU LASC

A GIANT AMONG GIANTS

Albert B. Fall, above center, was never more content than when at his Three Rivers, N.M., home, above left. Above right, Fall with his friend Eugene Manlove Rhodes, a rancher in the San Andres Mountains and a well-known author of Western novels.

NMSU LASC/JOSHUA SMITH

ALBERT B. FALL
POLITICS, LAW AND CORRUPTION

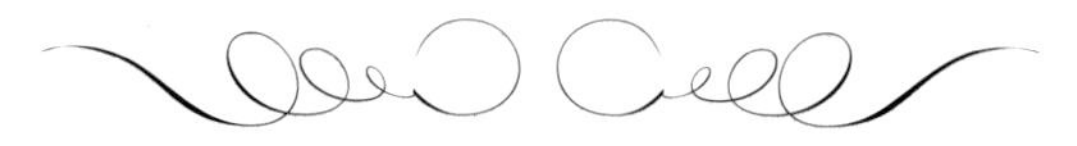

Though Albert Bacon Fall had an impressive political career, he will always be remembered for his involvement with the Teapot Dome Scandal.

Fall was born in 1861 to an educated family in Kentucky and received most of his education from his grandfather and his father, who was a teacher.

He worked in a cotton factory as a youth, but later developed respiratory problems and sought dry, warm weather to improve his health.

Moving to Las Cruces with his wife Emma and their children in 1887, Fall pursued a variety of careers before he enrolled in law school, taking night classes until he was admitted to the New Mexico Territory Bar.

Fall was charismatic and not afraid to make an enemy. A longtime feud between Fall and Albert Fountain began when the men ran against each other for the Territorial House of Representatives. The grudge between Fall and the Fountain family was heightened in 1886, when Fountain, an attorney, and his 8-year-old son went missing. Fall defended the three suspects in the case, Oliver Lee, Jim Gilliland and Billy McNew. Since bodies of the father and son were never found, charges against the suspects were dismissed.

Fall was known to take any case he was offered. One of Fall's most notorious cases was defending the accused killer of Pat Garrett.

After winning a series of offices, such as Irrigation Commissioner for Doña Ana County, Fall was one of the first two U.S. Senators from New Mexico to be elected by the Legislature.

Fall, a Republican, was disliked by fellow Republicans as well as the Democrats because of his involvement with Thomas B. Catron, who was selected to New Mexico's other U.S. Senate seat. Though many attempts were made to remove him from office, Fall was reelected through 1918, serving until he was appointed Secretary of the Interior by President Warren G. Harding in 1921.

Just one year later, Fall made history for being the first former cabinet officer sentenced to prison as a result of misconduct in the office.

An investigation sparked by allegations in the Wall Street Journal led to Fall's indictment on corruption charges after Fall allowed friends Harry F. Sinclair and Edward L. Doheny to drill for oil on Naval Reserve land without open bidding. Fall was found guilty of accepting bribes and kickbacks from the oil company executives. The Naval Reserves were located on land near Teapot Dome, Wyo., which gave the scandal its name.

Oyster Bay,
Long Island, N.Y.
June 17th 1916.

My dear Senator:
I wish to thank you most cordially for your support & for your nominating speech, & even more, my dear Senator, for your gallant fight on behalf of Americanism & humanity, & the performance of international duty; a fight you have valiantly waged for over four years in the Senate of the United States.

You have been the kind of a public servant of whom all Americans should feel proud. I congratulate the whole country that you are in the United States Senate.

With high regard & renewed thanks,

Faithfully yours

Theodore Roosevelt

Hon Albert Fall
United States Senate
Washington, D. C.

Every Vote for
ALBERT B. FALL
Is a vote for the winning of this War in the quickest possible time, and the earliest return of the boys from "over there."

Fall stands in the senate for the maximum of fighting strength, forced into the minimum of time.

SEND HIM BACK TO WASHINGTON
THE NATION NEEDS HIM

VOTE FOR
ALBERT B. FALL
A FIGHTING AMERICAN

REPUBLICAN CANDIDATE FOR THE UNITED STATES SENATE

A SAILOR FROM THE DESERT

Marcos L. Carbajal, pictured around 1917, was in the U.S. Navy from 1916 to 1921 and served in World War I. Carbajal was born in Las Cruces in 1890, and was a 1914 graduate of Carlisle Indian Industrial School, the school in Pennsylvania made famous by Jim Thorpe.

DOLORES ARCHULETA

ON DUTY

Members of the New Mexico National Guard pose for the camera while serving near Deming, N.M., in 1916.

JIM BRADLEY

IN UNIFORM

ROTC cadets are inspected by an officer at New Mexico A&M in 1914.

NMSU LASC

PANCHO VILLA

Early on the morning of March 9, 1916, Mexican revolutionary general Francisco "Pancho" Villa led a group of nearly 500 men in an unprovoked and unexpected military attack against Columbus, N.M., and the 13th U.S. Calvary that was stationed in the area.

Before the U.S. troops succeeded in driving the Mexican force back across the border, 18 Americans, including 10 cavalrymen, and more than 60 Villistas lay dead. Many businesses in Columbus had been looted and numerous buildings were burned. A new chapter had been written in the long history of southern New Mexico.

Immediately, President Woodrow Wilson ordered the military to pursue Villa into Mexico, capture the Mexican revolutionary and break up his band. Brig. Gen. John J. "Black Jack" Pershing was put in charge of the "Punitive Expedition." Over the next 11 months, American forces chased the elusive Villa into northern Mexico, but were never able to capture or kill him.

Villa was angered by the United States' recognition of Venustiano Carranza as the head of the Mexican government. A subsequent embargo of arms to the Villistas and assistance to Carranza's troops, leading to the defeat of Villa's army at Sonora and Hermosillo, would also contribute to his resentment of the neighbors to the north.

By late December 1915, with his army a shell of its former self, Villa made it known that he considered the United States to be an enemy, and threatened to attack the border town of Presidio, Texas.

After the attack on Columbus, National Guard troops were ordered to Columbus, including the 1st New Mexico Infantry. Units from New Mexico were not involved in the pursuit into Mexico, but spent their time in Columbus or on the Mexican border assisting the Border Patrol.

INTERVENTION IMMINENT
The dastardly Villa massacre at Columbus and the issuing of orders for the American army to go in pursuit of Villa and other bandits, cannot mean anything other than intervention in the very near future, as the Mexicans in general, barring no classes, are so thoroughly imbued with the idea that they can whip this country, that it means but a few days till all factions will turn against Americans, Carranza's utterances to the contrary notwithstanding; it will also eventually mean the annexation of the five northern Mexican states, Wilson's assertions to the contrary notwithstanding. On to Mexico City!

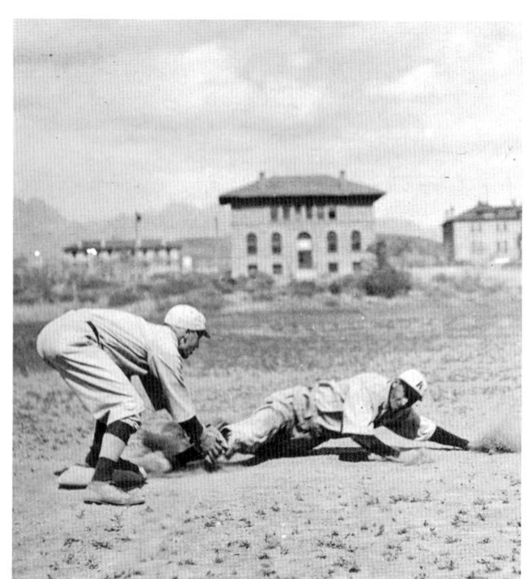

YOU'RE OUT!

Students, above, play baseball at New Mexico A&M in 1915 or 1916. Below, this view from the athletic fields shows the campus as it looked in the late teens.

NMSU LASC

MARCHING STUDENTS

Above, coeds from New Mexico A&M proudly display their class banners during a march. Below, a group of coeds show pride for their school on the steps of the original Hadley Hall.

NMSU LASC

LAS CRUCES SCHOOL CHILDREN

Children stand in front of Mesilla Park Elementary School around 1917. As of 2011, the school was still in use as the Mesilla Park Recreation Center.

BARRIO FAMILY

SCHOOL PIONEERS

Lee Woodson was superintendent of the county school system in 1899, and his wife Mary was later principal of Grandview Elementary.

JIM BRADLEY

A LAWN FOR THE OLD SOUTH WARD

Above left, Las Crucens turned out to help plant grass at the old South Ward School at the corner of Alameda Boulevard and Lohman Avenue in 1915. Left, Superintendent R.W. Twining addresses the crowd of volunteers. The school stood at the site of the two-room adobe that was Hiram Hadley's Las Cruces College, a building that became the first public school in Las Cruces in 1893.

NMSU LASC

NOT JUST BRANDING ANYMORE

At a corral on the Jornada Experimental Range, cowboys brand and vaccinate livestock in 1915.

NMSU LASC

STYLES OF THE TIMES

Above left, an unidentified lady poses for a portrait in a studio. Above right, Petra G. de Lucero, wife of Esteban Lucero, around 1919.

NMSU LASC/CHARLES AND MARY ANN LUCERO

TWO WHEELERS ARE THE RAGE

Left, two Las Crucens pose on a motorcycle in front of St. Genevieve's Catholic Church around 1915. Above, Corrine Woodson Bradley, daughter of Lee and Mary Woodson, sits atop a motorcycle in 1917, a few years before her long career in Las Cruces as a respected educator and matriarch of a line of successful high school football coaches. Below, the military experiments with motorcycles as a replacement for horses in this 1913 photo labeled "Motorcycle Machine Gun Corp."

NMSU LASC/JIM BRADLEY

Maxwell

"The "Wonder Car"

Electric Starting and Lighting

The new Maxwell is equipped with the Simms-Huff Electric Starting and Lighting System.

This system is a single unit type, combining in one instrument the generator and motor.

It is the simplest, "sure-fire" powerful self-starter made and has about one-half the wire of ordinary starters.

We are waiting to take you for a test ride in the car that has broken all low "First-Cost" records, and is breaking all low "After-Cost" records.

"One Man" Mohair Top
Demountable Rims
Rain Vision Windshield

$655
F.O.B. DETROIT

Electric Starter
Electric Lights
Magneto Ignition

"Every Road is a Maxwell Road"

H. F. BENNETT, Agent
Las Cruces, N. M.

GETTING AROUND IN THE TEENS

Above, an ad from the Las Cruces Citizen newspaper touted the latest in automobile technology, though Natalia and Martin Campbell, top right, have no intention of trading in their goat-powered Studebaker wagon just yet. Center right, Doña Ana County's first County Agent H.H. Brook uses his sturdy vehicle to advocate for much-needed drainage in the Mesilla Valley during Farmers' Prosperity Week. Right, at the end of the trail, weary travelers could relax with a stroll along the Acequia Madre and then spend a restful night at the Amador Hotel, near the center of Las Cruces.

NMSU LASC

ROOTED IN THE VALLEY: COMMITTED TO FAMILY AND COMMUNITY VALUES

Left, the Apodaca family – Mary Helen, Joe, Genevieve and Emma Jean Apodaca; Right, the Cervantes Family – Joseph, Emma Jean Apodaca Cervantes, Kristina, Orlando and Dino Cervantes.

EMMA JEAN CERVANTES

THE CERVANTES FAMILY

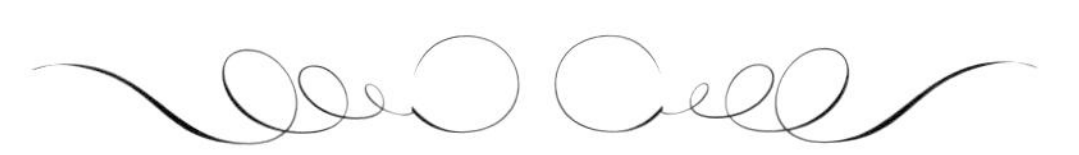

Emma Jean Cervantes started in agriculture picking cotton in the 1940s alongside her sister, longtime State Rep. Mary Helen Garcia, on the family farm established in the early 1900s by her grandfather, Andres Apodaca, and expanded by her parents, José "Joe" and Genevieve Apodaca. Today, Emma Jean is owner with her children – Joseph, Dino and Kristina – of Cervantes Enterprises, Inc., a cayenne and chile business that extends throughout the world.

Based in southern New Mexico's Mesilla Valley, Cervantes Enterprises produces, processes and distributes chile. The majority of the chile is processed in hot sauces. But if you have eaten at local Mexican restaurants, you've likely tasted the Cervantes family sun-dried chile. Joe Apodaca first sold his chile to local restaurants in the 1940s.

Emma Jean and her husband, Orlando, took over operation of the family business in the mid-1960s, with her father in a consulting role. Under her third-generation leadership, Cervantes Enterprises has grown six-fold in size and revenue since the 1990s. In 1998, the business moved to a new, expanded site in south Mesquite.

Based on a commitment to family and community values, Cervantes Enterprises has involved five generations – Emma Jean's grandchildren were learning the business in 2011 – since Andres Apodaca first acquired 40 acres in Mesilla. A hundred years later, the family farmed 1,200 acres of cotton, corn, chile, pecans and alfalfa.

Community service has been a long-established tradition in the Cervantes family. Joseph Cervantes, an architect and a lawyer, was elected to the New Mexico House of Representatives in 2002 and by 2011 was serving his fifth consecutive term. Emma Jean's mother, Genevieve Apodaca, was a major force in the state Democratic Party.

Emma Jean has been a founder or co-founder of many important Las Cruces institutions, including the Ikard cancer center at Memorial Medical Center, the First Step Center, the Mesilla Valley Hospice, the New Mexico Farm & Ranch Heritage Museum and New Mexico State University Chile Pepper Institute. Trained as a nurse, she served on the MMC board of directors for 20 years.

The Apodaca and Cervantes families have been community leaders for generations, and Emma Jean has mentored her six granddaughters to take up the call to service. In 2011, four of them were serving on their student councils, and Alexandra Cervantes was following in the footsteps of her father, Joseph Cervantes, as president of the Las Cruces High School student council.

As for the chile, it can be found every day on the Cervantes family kitchen table, in the adobe home Joe Apodaca built for his family 65 years ago.

GENERATIONS OF LEADERSHIP

Left, Emma Jean Cervantes surrounded by her granddaughters, from left: Jaclyn Vanderlught, Juliana Cervantes, Alexandra "Alex" Cervantes, Isabella Cervantes, Elizabeth Vanderlught, Alyssa Cervantes. Center, the Apodaca family home was built by Joe Apodaca in the 1940s. Right, Kristina, Dino and Joseph Cervantes grew up to be the fourth generation co-owners of Cervantes Enterprises, Inc.

EMMA JEAN CERVANTES

St. Andrew's Episcopal Church

The first Episcopal Church service ever to be held in Las Cruces, with 50 people attending, was June 23, 1889. That early congregation shared a facility with the Southern Methodists.

George Bowman, a layman, petitioned Bishop John Mills Kendrick of Albuquerque to develop a fully separate Episcopal mission in Las Cruces, but little activity ensued until the advent of the Rev. Hunter "Preacher" Lewis, who began fundraising with friends in Cambridge, Mass., for a church building in 1910. With his support, land was purchased on Alameda Boulevard the following year, and Lewis himself laid the cornerstone in 1913 for St. Andrew's Episcopal Church. Also known as Kendrick Chapel, the building, which has an all-wood interior in a country Gothic style, is an architectural and spiritual treasure in the city of Las Cruces.

The Rev. Edward S. Doan, from Roswell, followed Lewis from 1919-27. The Rev. George Wood arrived in 1939 to collaborate along the Rio Grande from La Union to Belen with Preacher Lewis, by then a traveling missioner.

Under the leadership of Rev. Bancroft Smith (1949-69), St. Andrew's enjoyed a period of remarkable growth and expansion: a classroom and parish hall in 1954 and the main church in 1962, designed by architect John Gaw Meem of Santa Fe, stained glass window by John Tatschl of the University of New Mexico, stone work by Eugenie Shonnard and palladium and gold leaf ornamentation by Dorothea Weiss.

In the 1970s, St. Andrew's helped establish a foundation that operated a Thrift Store and a Day Care Center with a hot-meal program for children of working mothers.

The Rev. James Galbraith's leadership, from 1985-2002, placed importance on the activities and welfare of parishioners along with construction. The congregation grew to more than 400 through new programs such as the Soup Kitchen (later "El Caldito") which served more than 17,000 meals during its time at St. Andrew's.

In 1991, members of St. Andrew's joined with local doctors and nurses to create St. Luke's Health Care Clinic in order to provide services to the homeless and poor. The ministry of the soup kitchen and St. Luke's became too much for the parish to handle, so a parishioner, Dr. Nancy McMillan, led the way for the Community of Hope, under the direction of the City of Las Cruces, which took over feeding those in need.

The Rev. Scott Ruthven, who was called to St. Andrew's in 2003, placed an emphasis on mentoring people in their faith to serving outside the walls of the church. St. Andrew's sent mission teams to Ciudad Juárez to build houses, and reconstruction mission teams to help the poorest of the poor rebuild after hurricanes Katrina and Ike. St. Andrew's has a long history as a welcoming community with a strong lay ministry program of hospital and home visitation.

A WELCOMING COMMUNITY

Left, in the early 1970s, Joan Lamb, holds a child believed to be Heather Colburn as Rikki Lamb holds Amy and Michael Gardner. Center, Rev. George Wood, Rev. Bancroft Smith, Bishop Kinsolving and Bishop Stoney. Right, the St. Andrew's Choir, circa 1945.

ST. ANDREW'S EPISCOPAL CHURCH

CITY PARK

City Park, later known as Pioneer Park, was a lush oasis in the center of Las Cruces and a favorite place for a relaxing stroll.

NMSU LASC

BY THE WATERFALL

Some Las Crucens enjoy a waterfall near the Modoc Mine in the Organ Mountains in 1912.

NMSU LASC

LUNCH TIME

Three gentlemen pause for a meal during their travels.

NMSU LASC

INFORMATION

The Doña Ana Fair Committee waits to answer fairgoers' questions inside the main fair barn in 1918. The committee included Edward B. Hoagland, Mr. Thorpe, an unidentified man, Mr. Alvarez and Dan Williams.

NMSU LASC

PEACE DAY

Las Crucens prepare to light a bonfire at St. Genevieve's Catholic Church in celebration of the end of the "Great War" on Nov. 11, 1918.

NMSU LASC

PLACES OF WORSHIP

San Albino Catholic Church in Mesilla was completed in 1908, and was elevated to the status of minor basilica in 2008 by Pope Benedict XVI. At right, the altar at St. Genevieve's Catholic Church was the center of Catholic worship in Las Cruces for many decades before the church was torn down in 1967. The statue of St. Genevieve visible on the altar was imported from France in 1881.

NMSU LASC

1920-1929

FROM PROSPERITY TO DESPAIR

KOLLEGE KACTUS KARNIVAL

In 1927, May Queen Johnnie Odom poses with her "court" during the Kollege Kactus Karnival, an annual celebration that was held at New Mexico A&M on May Day. The May Queen was the "most popular girl" at the karnival.

NEW MEXICO STATE UNIVERSITY LIBRARY ARCHIVES AND SPECIAL COLLECTIONS

NEVAREZ-APODACA WEDDING DAY

The above photo was taken in front of Jesus Nevarez and Mary Kelsey's home at 316 S. Campo St. The group was gathered to celebrate the marriage of Maria Nevarez and Ricardo F. Apodaca Sept. 22, 1924. In 2011, the building housed the Saenz & Torres law firm. In the photo, Reymundo Apodaca stands at the back far right. He later had a son, Jerry Apodaca, who became governor of New Mexico in 1975.

THE NEVAREZ FAMILY

1921
Albert B. Fall is appointed Secretary of the Interior.

1922
Oil is discovered on the Navajo Reservation. Coinciding with Henry Ford's assembly line, the discovery changed transportation forever.

1925
With the signature of Gov. Arthur T. Hannett, New Mexico adopts the current state flag – a red Zia symbol on a field of yellow – that replaced the original flag.

1925
Las Cruces Union High School district was created and school built.

1926
Schools became segregated, and black students are taught at Phillips Chapel CME Church until 1954.

1926
Deane Stahmann bought 29,000 acres of Santo Tomas farms, growing cotton and cantaloupe.

NMSU LASC/JIM HILLEY/JONATHAN LARSON

1920s

Who's Who

Las Cruces Mayors

- 1918-20, 1922-24, 1926-29 .... A.I. Kelso
- 1920-22 .... J.H. Paxton
- 1924-26 .... Gus Manasse

Postmaster

- 1921 .... Charles C. Lee

New Mexico A&M Presidents

- 1917-20 .... Austin D. Crile
- 1920-21 .... Robert W. Clothier
- 1921-35 .... Harry L. Kent

Doña Ana County Sheriffs

- 1917-20, 1925-28 .... Jose R. Lucero
- 1923-24 .... Donaciano E. Rodriguez
- 1920-23, 1929-30 .... Felipe Lucero

Las Cruces Fire Chief

- 1920s .... J.S. Ruiz

New Mexico Governors

- 1921-23 .... Merritt C. Mechem
- 1923-25 .... James F. Hinkle
- 1925-27 .... Arthur T. Hannett
- 1927-31 .... Richard C. Dillon

U.S. Senators

- 1917-27 .... Andrieus A. Jones
- 1925-33 .... Sam G. Bratton
- 1927-35 .... Bronson M. Cutting
- 1928-29 .... Octaviano Larrazolo

U.S. Representatives

- 1919-21 .... Benigno C. Hernández
- 1921-23 .... Néstor Montoya
- 1923-29 .... John Morrow
- 1929-31 .... Albert G. Simms

By the Numbers

- 16,548 ... Doña Ana County population (1920)
- 53.6 years .... Male life expectancy
- 54.6 years .... Female life expectancy
- $1,236 .... Average annual income
- 14 cents .... Gallon of gas
- 2 cents .... First-class stamp
- $985 .... Average new car (1925)
- 5.2 percent .... Unemployment rate
- $970 .... Average teacher's salary
- 35 percent .... Homes with electricity (1920)
- 68 percent .... Homes with electricity (1929)
- 52 cents .... One pound of bacon (1920)
- 12 cents .... One pound of bread (1920)
- 47 cents .... One dozen eggs (1920)
- 33 cents .... One-half gallon of milk (1920)
- 42 cents .... price of cotton per pound (1921)

In the News

Jan. 10, 1920: The League of Nations holds its first meeting and accomplishes the ratification of the Treaty of Versailles, ending the hostilities of World War I.

Aug. 18, 1920: Women are given the right to vote with the 19th Amendment.

Sept. 7-8, 1921: The first Miss America pageant is held in Atlantic City, N.J. It is won by Margaret Gorman for the title of the Golden Mermaid trophy, later dubbed Miss America.

1922: The American Professional Football League changed its name, forming the National Football League.

Feb. 5, 1922: Reader's Digest is founded and the first issue published by Dewitt and Lila Wallace.

April 7, 1922: The Teapot Dome scandal begins when the U.S. Secretary of the Interior leases the Teapot Oil Reserves in Wyoming.

May 30, 1922: The Lincoln Memorial, on the National Mall, is dedicated in Washington, D.C.

March 2, 1923: Time Magazine is published for the first time.

April 1923: The first sound on film motion picture "Phonofilm" is shown in the Rivoli Theatre in New York City by Lee de Forest.

Feb. 14, 1924: The IBM corporation is founded.

May 10, 1924: J. Edgar Hoover is appointed to lead the Federal Bureau of Investigation.

Jan. 5, 1925: Nellie Tayloe Ross is inaugurated as the first woman governor of the United States in Wyoming.

Nov. 15, 1926: The NBC Radio Network is formed by Westinghouse, General Electric, and RCA, opening with 24 stations.

Aug. 10, 1927: Work on Mount Rushmore began. Sculptor Gutzon Borglum would complete the task 14 years later.

May 15, 1928: The first appearance of Mickey and Minnie Mouse on film occurs with the release of the animated short film, "Plane Crazy."

June 17, 1928: Amelia Earhart becomes the first woman to fly across the Atlantic Ocean.

1926 Mesilla Valley farmers saw produce prices fall from 29 cents to 6.5 cents over 11 years.

1926 Rio Grande Theatre opens.

1927 The Women's Improvement Association opened the WIA Club House, which served as the first formal library in Las Cruces.

1927 Holy Cross School opens.

1928 Las Cruces Country Club opens.

1929 The stock market crashed, a major contributor to the Great Depression.

ANNOUNCING
THE OPENING OF THE
RIO GRANDE
THEATRE
(Operated by the Central Theatres Corp'n of Denver)
THURSDAY, JULY 29th, 7:30, 9:30
Presenting
"MARE NOSTRUM"
REX INGRAM'S MASTERPIECE
A Powerful Story of the Sea
With
ALICE TERRY and ANTONIO MORENO
ADDED ATTRACTIONS

GROCERY STORES

Stores such as H.H. Brook Local were thriving during the Roaring '20s because Americans bought on credit and spent lavishly. In 1920, cabbage cost 2 cents per pound, six lemons cost 15 cents, one dozen oranges cost 63 cents, peaches cost 17 cents per pound and watermelon cost 1 cent per pound.

NMSU LASC

FROM ADVANCEMENTS TO SURVIVAL

1920S SEE HIGHEST OF HIGHS AND LOWEST OF LOWS

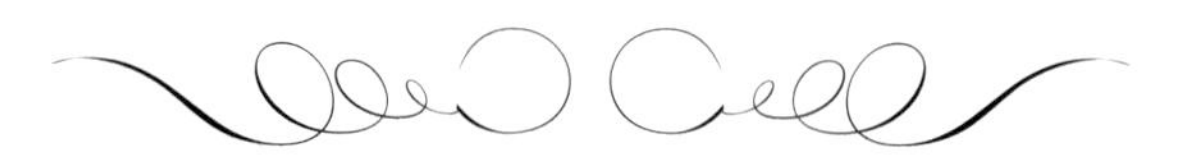

The 1920s, also known as the Roaring '20s, was a time of new culture, a heightened social scene and fine amenities. World War I had just ended, and homes were being "modernized."

Jumpstarted by the rapid growth of automobiles, the Roaring '20s was an era of great economic, political and construction growth. Henry Ford's assembly line produced and sold Fords for $290. The Miss America contest began in 1921, dance marathons began in 1923 and American baseball was made popular. The period was also called the Flapper Age because women's dress was transformed, and the short skirt became popular in 1925. The '20s also started the manufacturing of cosmetics, such as powder, lipstick, rouge, eye makeup and nail polish.

Another popular form of entertainment was traveling tent shows.

"My grandparents, mother and father and aunts and uncles called themselves the 'Musical Grays,' and they were a traveling tent show in the 1920s," said Bob Burns, a Las Cruces musician. "This was the No. 1 form of entertainment before talking movies killed it in 1929. They would travel to a town, set up tent and put on a parade when they first hit the town. Then they would perform a three-act play, with vaudeville in between acts and have a band concert before and play for a dance after this was over."

MESILLA VALLEY AGRICULTURE

Throughout the decades, the Mesilla Valley has been known for its fertile soil and ability to farm many types of crops, from cotton to corn.

NMSU LASC

Though the decade is characterized by expressionism, tolerance and fashion, it is also marred by the Great Depression.

In the fall of 1929, the New York Stock Exchange was more active than it had ever been, and economists predicted this to last. On Oct. 29, 1929 – Black Tuesday – the Roaring '20s were brought to a halt, and the Dow lost 30 points – 12 percent – adding to Monday's losses.

Lucrative lifestyles and structural weaknesses, such as bank failures and the stock market crash, led to the Great Depression, and the U.S. didn't recover until 1939, when World War II began.

On Black Tuesday, about $140 billion in assets disappeared almost overnight. Within six to eight months, more than 3 million Americans were unemployed.

Feature films including "Cinderella Man" and award-winning books such as "The Grapes of Wrath" depicted what life was like during the Great Depression, but only those who lived through it can truly know just how hard it was.

"(Barack Obama in 2011) calls this a depression, but he doesn't know what a depression is," said Bruce Cabot, a survivor of the Great Depression who moved to southern New Mexico in the 1930s. "We have it real good compared to back then."

DOÑA ANA COUNTY FARM BUREAU

The Doña Ana County Farm Bureau, which included Fabian Garcia, back center, was made up of Mesilla Valley farmers who banded together for better farming laws and assistance.

NMSU LASC

RACE TO THE FINISH

A popular pastime, automobile racing attracted men of all ages including Alec Hood, who would jump at the chance to race a car, such as the early, stripped-down Ford shown above. Left, judges and contestants pose after a race.

NMSU LASC

FATHER OF THE CHILE PEPPER

CHILES, PECANS, ONIONS AND MORE

Credited with being "the father of the chile pepper," it would be more accurate to describe Fabian Garcia as the father of the Mexican food industry in the United States as well as irrigated agriculture in New Mexico.

Born in 1871, Garcia fled Mexico with his grandmother and came to the United States as a young boy. He later attended New Mexico College of Agriculture & Mechanic Arts and was a member of its first graduating class in 1894.

"He was an excellent all-around horticulturist," said Paul Bosland, co-founder of the Chile Pepper Institute at New Mexico State University.

In 1913, Garcia became the director of New Mexico A&M's Agricultural Experiment Station and Extension Services, making him the first Hispanic to lead a land-grant agricultural research station.

"He was the head of the research side for everything – animals, plants, insects, food," Bosland said.

While Garcia researched and tested a variety of crops – including pears, grapes, plums, spinach, melons and cauliflower – possibly his greatest accomplishments were in green chile, onions and pecans.

FABIAN GARCIA

"The father of the chile pepper," Fabian Garcia pioneered agricultural engineering practices while he faced racism in southern New Mexico.

NMSU LASC

"He was a renaissance man," Bosland said. "He had an interest in everything."

Garcia was the first to plant pecan trees in the Mesilla Valley in the early 1900s. He planted the non-native trees on 4 acres after seeing its popularity on the East Coast, Bosland said.

"He decided to see how it would do here," Bosland said. "That was a common approach in that day and age."

Garcia also laid the groundwork for the onion industry in New Mexico. Obtaining a high-yielding variety named "babosa" from Spain, he planted the sweet onion, which also thrived in Texas.

At the heart of Garcia's legacy, however, is the chile pepper, which he began planting in the early 1900s.

"He created the first chile pod type taken from three different kinds of chile and combined them," said Bosland, adding that the pepper was known as New Mexico No. 9. "It had a more uniform, mild taste."

Crossing two dark chiles – chile negro and chile pasilla – with one red chile – chile colorado – Bosland said researchers were able to create the paprika industry in New Mexico in the 1970s because of Garcia's work.

While researching the chile pepper, Garcia also created the raised-bed planting concept, which helps drain water away from the plants to prevent fungus and molds from forming.

"The raised-bed concept is a big thing," Bosland said. "All row vegetables and crops are done this way."

Named as an American Society for Horticultural Science Hall of Fame member, Bosland said many around the country don't know about Garcia despite his incredible contributions to the food industry.

"He was very sensitive about being a Mexican," said Bosland, adding that even as an educator, Garcia faced racism and was treated as a second-class citizen. "It never seemed to get him down though. He kept moving forward."

After passing away in 1948, Garcia left his entire estate to the university, in part providing a dormitory and scholarships for Mexican-American youth. His legacy can still be seen around campus at the many buildings named in his honor, including his former farm, which is now the Fabian Garcia Research Center.

A PLETHORA OF PODS

Fabian Garcia, a former New Mexico A&M educator and director of the school's Agricultural Experiment Station and Extension Services, was best known for his contributions to the chile pepper industry. One of his most important innovations was a new planting technique known as raised-bed, a method still used today. Garcia left his estate to the college to build a new dormitory and provide scholarships to Mexican-American youth. The Colonia Latina Club, pictured below in 1906, represented the Hispanic students at New Mexico A&M.

NMSU LASC

MAY DAY COURT

The 1926 May Day Queen sits with her May Day court, a part of the Kollege Kactus Karnival held at New Mexico A&M.

NMSU LASC

LAS CRUCES HIGH SCHOOL FOOTBALL TEAM

Below, in 1921, the Las Cruces High School football team included, back, Tellos Lopez, Oscar Garrett, William Sutherland, Allen McCombs, J. Gloyd Miller, Mr. Uhl, Henry Summerford, coach F.M. Wilson, middle, Boyd Wayne, Enrique Miranda, Dewey Thomas, Alvin Limbaugh, Charles Shipe, Jack Turney, front, Gerald Hines, John Gregg, Frank Wayne, Daura Peacock and Harold Hines. The photo was taken in front of Las Cruces High School.

NMSU LASC

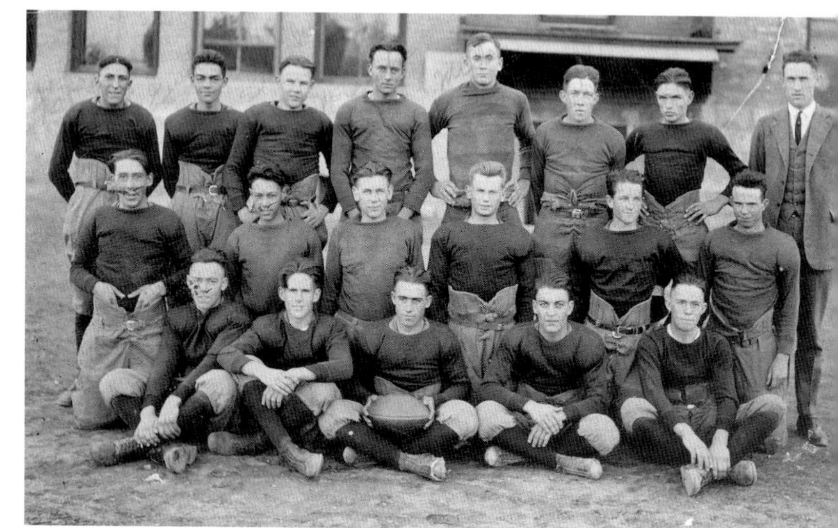

NEW MEXICO A&M FACULTY

New Mexico A&M faculty and staff posed in 1926 for a group photo. Pictured in the group is William A. Sutherland, who was known as "Mr. Aggie" because of his continuing support for the college. It was said Sutherland never missed an Aggie game.

NMSU LASC

NEW MEXICO A&M ORCHESTRA

The 17-member New Mexico A&M orchestra performed in 1926 on McFie stage.

NMSU LASC

SCHOOL CLASS

W. A. Sutherland's daughter Constance Sutherland is among dozens of school children in the photo taken in 1925. The photo also includes Miss Clymer's seventh-grade class.

NMSU LASC

CELEBRATING ACHIEVEMENTS

High school graduation was a time to honor graduates, who were showered with gifts and flowers. Local businesses showed their support with advertisements along the top of the stage.

NMSU LASC

DELTA SIGMA

Members of Delta Sigma sorority at New Mexico A&M, above, posed west of Hadley Avenue in 1928. Five consecutive May queens were from Delta Sigma. Some of the girls pictured include Mrs. Hannel, Lisa Courtney Howe, Era Rentfrow, Freddie Lee Bradford, Elizabeth Hoagland, Mandie Lowe, Peggy Evans, Maurine Dyne, Marry Will and Rhetla Brandon.

NMSU LASC

PRANKING AND BEING PRANKED

New Mexico A&M students earned the reputation for being the life of the party. Above, parades "initiated" freshmen who sometimes faced public embarrassment by older students. Right, professors were not safe from being pranked either, and the tradition of shoe-polishing cars seems to be as old as cars themselves.

NMSU LASC

Pioneering Radio

Goddard Makes Advancements in Engineering

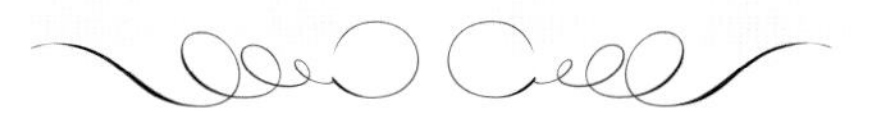

Ralph Willis Goddard was born in 1887, just 27 years before the pioneer of radio made advancements in engineering so significant that Americans still use some of his inventions today.

In 1913, Goddard received a telegram inviting him to join the faculty of New Mexico A&M as head of the electrical engineering division.

After moving to New Mexico, Goddard was approached about fixing a communications problem with New Mexico border agents. From 1915 to 1916, Mexican rebellions were prominent, and he helped set up temporary communication systems between border patrols. Goddard became the civilian director of instruction in electricity during World War I for the training detachment of the U.S. Army at New Mexico A&M. This, of course, had him wanting more and he began researching how to use permanent transmitting systems.

In 1919, Goddard started a radio club out of his home that moved to an old wooden building, which is now where Goddard Hall stands. The building became known as "Radio Shack" and was home to 5XD, a licensed radio station later developed into KOB, "The Voice of the Great Southwest."

Goddard was also excelling as a professor and was named dean of the School of Engineering in 1920.

In "Goddard's Magic Mast," a book by Ann Velia, an alumna of the college, "Several radio fans here are very much impressed with the Aggie broadcasting station, and when anyone asks me where I am from, I tell them State College, New Mexico, and they immediately connect it up with the radio broadcasting station. You may tell Dean Goddard for me …"

Though the dean had an inadequate budget, he developed the largest radio station at a college in the world.

He was also affiliated with several organizations, such as the Land Grant College Association, Institute of Radio Engineers and American Institute for Electrical Engineers, to name a few.

In 1921, Goddard was part of coordinating a rescue in Hatch and Santa Teresa after floods destroyed the areas. The following year, KOB accomplished another amazing feat – broadcasting the Aggies versus Albuquerque Indians football game.

Sadly, Goddard's passion also led to his demise. In 1929, Goddard prepared to broadcast a New Year's Eve special. While making adjustments to the 10,000-watt system, Goddard was killed when he was electrocuted through a wet yardstick, sending 12,000 volts of electricity through his arm.

"He was loved and admired by faculty and students alike. … He had built a strong engineering school both in physical equipment and reputation of graduates while in charge as dean," Linda Blazer wrote in her book "Building the Future," a tribute to the radio pioneer.

KOBE RADIO STATION

Though the call letters of the New Mexico State University station read KOBE in the 1950s, the name was KOB in the 1920s. In 1964, when KRWG-FM was created, the station changed its name to honor Goddard by using his initials – Ralph Willis Goddard.

NMSU LASC

ST. PAUL'S CONGREGATION

Members of St. Paul's United Methodist Church, above, gathered for a group photo outside of the church.

NMSU LASC

PHILLIPS CHAPEL

Another popular church at the time was Phillips Chapel CME Church, left. When schools segregated in the 1920s, black students went to Phillips Chapel until Booker T. Washington High School was built in 1954.

NMSU LASC

BAPTISM IN THE RIO GRANDE

In 1924, after a communitywide revival held at St. Paul's United Methodist Church, families and friends gathered along the Rio Grande to witness people from all denominations being baptized by the old bridge west of Las Cruces on the highway to Deming.

NMSU LASC

First Baptist Church

From the City of the Crosses, First Baptist Church has for more than 100 years held high the cross of Jesus Christ. Its members have sought in word, song and deed to "tell the next generation" (Psalm 48:13) God's message of love, redemption and guidance.

First Baptist Church of Las Cruces was organized in 1899. Initially, the body met in homes and then in rented buildings.

At first, pastors would come from El Paso or Albuquerque by train and walk from the nearby depot to the church site. However, in 1913 church members purchased and moved into an abandoned Methodist Episcopal Church at the corner of Organ Avenue and Miranda Street.

In addition, the group installed a baptistry and purchased a parsonage. The first baptistry was built in the center of the worship platform and was covered when not in use. The water had to be pumped by hand and delivered by a bucket brigade.

Historically, First Baptist Church has been a mission-minded congregation. Many churches in Las Cruces and Doña Ana County have First Baptist Church roots.

Since its inception, First Baptist has maintained strong ties to the Rio Grande Baptist Association, the Baptist Convention of New Mexico, and the Southern Baptist Convention. Over the years, different ministries found a place in the hearts of members. First Baptist Church has supported the Baptist Student Union (later termed the Christian Challenge) at New Mexico State University since 1932, when the organization formed. Students from the B.S.U. and First Baptist Church have served around the world as missionaries, pastors and Christian leaders.

In 1996 First Baptist Church launched the "Living Christmas Tree," a presentation that quickly became a community highlight of the Christmas Season. By 2011, more than 50 members made up the tree, featuring a computer-integrated lighting system with more than 60,000 lights programmed in sync with live music.

These are among the many ways church members have sought to reach the community and the world for Christ. First Baptist embraced an Acts 1:8 strategy to engage the city, state, nation and world for the glory of Christ.

First Baptist Church, a family of faith with a passion for worship, has sought to be a united family with sometimes differing tastes.

To meet the varied interests of its congregation, the church has offered contemporary and traditional worship, times of both powerful praise and celebration, and a traditional approach with hymns, a full choir and, periodically, an orchestra.

The First Baptist Church honors the dedication and courage of those who have gone before. Members strive to be faithful in meeting the challenges of a new century as they lead the way for future generations.

LET THERE BE LIGHT

First Baptist Church became a fixture on Miranda Street in 1913. The popular "Living Christmas Tree" event began in 1996. The building at top, and above second from left, was built in 1927.

NMSU LASC/FIRST BAPTIST CHURCH

1920S ABODES

Above, the S. M. Ashenfelter House represents a typical home in the 1920s, which included two bedrooms right next to each other with an adjacent bathroom. The kitchen and dining room were fairly small in comparison to the larger living room.

NMSU LASC

THE SUTHERLAND HOUSE

Above, this photo was taken from the front of the Sutherland house, looking east toward Las Cruces High School and the Organ Mountains.

NMSU LASC

SAN AUGUSTINE RANCH

Left, San Augustine Ranch, which was owned by Jim Cox.

NMSU LASC

LOHMAN AVENUE

A photo of Martin Lohman's house, front right of the photo, submitted by the Lemon family depicts a quiet Main Street – far from what took place 50 years earlier that led to the death of John Lemon. In 1871, Lemon participated in a Republican rally held in Mesilla the same day as a Democratic Party rally. As riots broke out, Lemon was clubbed in the head and killed by Democratic leader I.N. Kelley.

NMSU LASC

THE MITCHELL HOUSE

The Mitchell House, which was later a Safeway store, overshadowed other houses in the decade because of its size. Luciana Lemon and William Rynerson built the house after they married. The twin smokestacks are part of the Las Cruces Light and Ice Co.

NMSU LASC

DOWNTOWN MAIN STREET

Like many towns in the 1920s, Las Cruces' Main Street was full of entertainment, including derby races, parades and shops. Downtown Main Street served as a social scene as well as a place of business. For Alec C. Hood, below center, entertainment came from racing cars down the dirt roads and driving fast.

NMSU LASC/NEW MEXICO DEPARTMENT OF TRANSPORTATION

FIRST
NATIONAL
DRUGS
BOTICA
MOVIELAND
ENGLISH KITCHEN
RESTAURANT
CHOP SUEY AND NOODLES
DRY CLEANING WORKS

DEMOCRATIC AND REPUBLICAN CONVENTIONS OF 1924

Above, Democratic and, below, Republican conventions were held in Las Cruces in 1924, campaigning for Republican incumbent Calvin Coolidge and Democratic candidate John W. Davis. The United States presidential election of 1924 was won by Coolidge because of a split Democratic party. Since Davis was seen as "too conservative," liberal Democrats backed the third-party campaign of Sen. Robert M. La Follette of Wisconsin, who ran as the candidate of the Progressive Party.

NMSU LASC

LAS CRUCES COUNTRY CLUB 1928

Carved into the desert terrain on Main Street north of Downtown, the Las Cruces Country Club opened in 1928. For many years, the course was the only golf course within 50 miles. The country club closed Nov. 20, 2011.

NMSU LASC

EAST-TO-WEST CATTLE DRIVE

An unknown buyer and Jim Cox, riding Muskrat, drive cattle up San Augustine Pass from east to west in 1928. This was one of the last big drives from San Augustine to Leasburg where the cattle would be shipped to other parts of the country. In the 1920s, Mesilla Valley farmers produced cotton, below right, and ranchers herded sheep until cattle, below left, joined the industry, creating a third type of ranch – the sheep-cattle ranch. Just as useful for play as it was for farming, land in southern New Mexico also created popular hangouts, such as Dripping Springs, below center left, and Tortugas "A" Mountain, below center right. Both destinations are still popular in 2011.

JOHN YARBROUGH/NMSU LASC/BASON

BATTLING ECONOMIC WOES

In the 1930s, the Great Depression affected millions of Americans, kicking thousands out of their homes and forcing some to beg for basic necessities. Millions of Americans lost their jobs. When something was bad, it was referred to as "hard boiled." Ironically many things in this decade were hard-boiled as a result of the Great Depression. In this photo from the early 1930s, scores of Las Crucens crowd into a local Safeway grocery store, seeking to stretch their meager dollars to buy groceries for their families.

NEW MEXICO STATE UNIVERSITY LIBRARY ARCHIVES AND SPECIAL COLLECTIONS

1930-1939
HARD-BOILED TIMES

ENTERTAINMENT FOR ALL

In the late 1930s, the Queens of Mesilla entertain at a festival in front of the Griggs' home. Traveling troupes that performed at homes and public venues were a popular form of entertainment until talking movies became more popular in later decades. Located in Mesilla, the Griggs' home was built in the 1800s.

NMSU LASC

1932
Deane Stahmann gets a bargain on pecan trees after an El Paso farmer was unable to pay for the delivery. The saplings are the first pecan trees in what will become the expansive Stahmann Farms.

1933
Clyde W. Tombaugh discovered Pluto, a new planet. Tombaugh worked at White Sands Proving Ground in the early 1950s and taught astronomy at New Mexico State University from 1955-73.

1933
Because of an abundance of cotton, farmers were paid to not plant the crop.

1934
Las Cruces Board of Trustees prohibits stunt flying and regulates the flying of airplanes to no less than 1,000 feet.

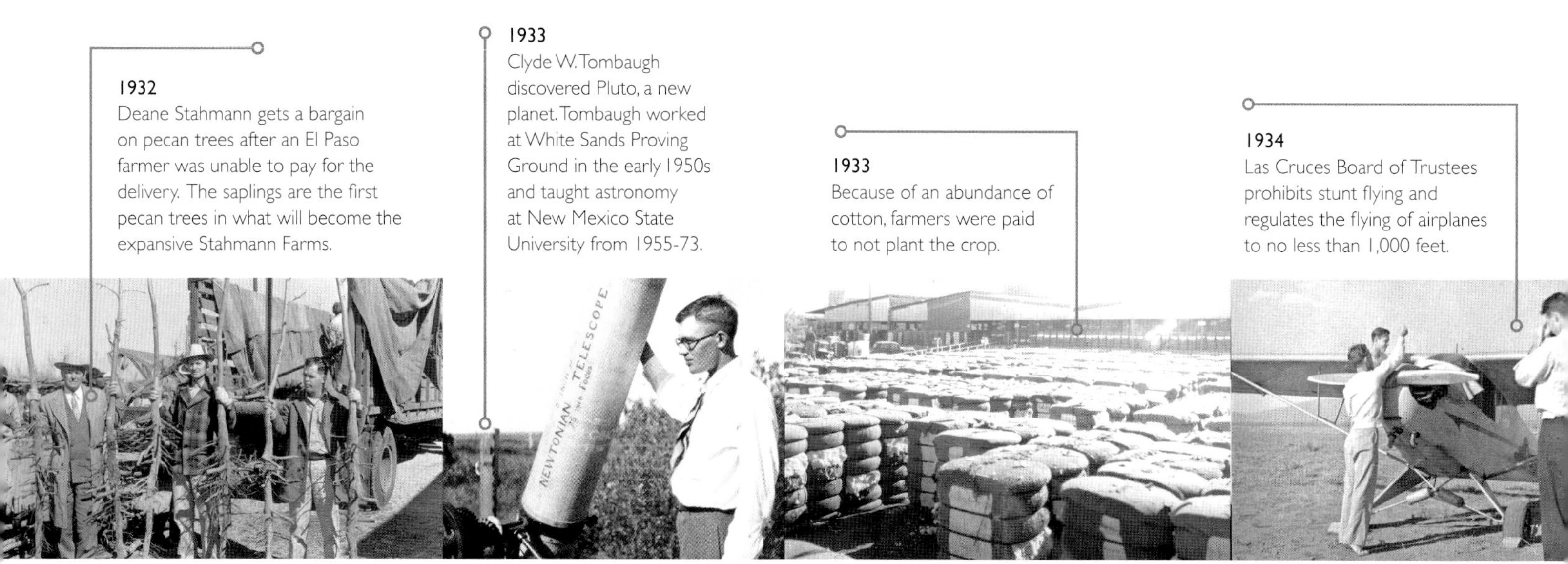

NMSU LASC/JESSICA GRADY-MAULDIN

1930s

Who's Who

Las Cruces Mayors

- 1929-30 ... Vil Lane
- 1930-32 ... T.C. Sexton
- 1932-34, 1938-44 ... Sam Klein
- 1934-36 ... J. Bensono Newell
- 1936-38 ... George Frenger
- 1938-1944 ... Sam Klein

Postmasters

- 1933 ... Alda M. O'Hara
- 1938 ... Lena B. Sexton

New Mexico A&M Presidents

- 1921-35 ... Harry L. Kent
- 1935-36 ... Hugh M. Gardner
- 1936-38 ... Ray Fife
- 1938 ... John W. Branson
- 1938-41 ... Hugh M. Milton

Doña Ana County Sheriffs

- 1929-30 ... Felipe Lucero
- 1931-34 ... Ricardo Triviz
- 1935-36 ... Jose R. Lucero
- 1937-40 ... Jose M. Viramontes

New Mexico Governors

- 1927-31 ... Richard C. Dillon
- 1931-33 ... Arthur Seligman
- 1933-35 ... Andrew W. Hockenhull
- 1935-39 ... Clyde Tingley
- 1939-43 ... John E. Miles

U.S. Senators

- 1925-33 ... Sam G. Bratton
- 1933-49 ... Carl Hatch
- 1929-35 ... Bronson M. Cutting
- 1935-61 ... Dennis Chavez

U.S. Representatives

- 1929-31 ... Albert G. Simms
- 1931-35 ... Dennis Chavez
- 1935-41 ... John J. Dempsey

By the Numbers

- 27,455 ... Doña Ana County population (1930)
- 58.1 years ... Male life expectancy
- 61.6 years ... Female life expectancy
- $1,970 ... Average annual income (1930)
- $1,730 ... Average annual income (1939)
- 10 cents ... Gallon of gas (1930)
- 3 cents ... First-class stamp
- $7,145 ... Home value (1930)
- $3,800 ... Home value (1939)
- $640 ... Cost of new car (1930)
- $3.85 ... Single Vision Glasses (1938)
- $79.85 ... 10-piece bedroom suite
- 25 percent ... Unemployment rate
- 2,787,400 ... Cars are sold
- 14 cents ... One-half gallon of milk
- 9 cents ... One loaf of bread
- 20 cents ... 1 pound of steak

In the News

March 3, 1931: The Star-Spangled Banner, by Francis Scott Key, is approved as the national anthem.

March 17, 1931: The state of Nevada legalizes gambling.

May 1, 1931: Construction is completed on the Empire State Building in New York City.

Jan. 23, 1932: Carlsbad Caverns National Park installs and inaugurates the use of high-speed elevators.

Dec. 5, 1933: The 21st Amendment to the U.S. Constitution is passed, ending prohibition.

1934: The first Master's golf tournament is held. The winner was Horton Smith at 4-under-par.

June 6, 1934: The U.S. Securities and Exchange Commission is established with the signing of the Securities Exchange Act into law.

June 1, 1935: Babe Ruth retires from Major League Baseball.

Sept. 30, 1935: Hoover Dam is dedicated.

June 28, 1938: The National Minimum Wage is enacted, establishing a minimum wage of 25 cents as well as time and one half for overtime and the prohibition of employment for minors.

October 30, 1938: Orson Welles created panic across America by broadcasting his War of the Worlds radio drama, including fake news bulletins stating a Martian invasion had begun on Earth.

1934
The Thomas Branigan Memorial Library, Las Cruces' first permanent public library, was formed with funds willed by Alice Branigan in memory of her husband, Capt. Thomas Branigan.

1937
Doc Noss, a prospector and adventurer, reportedly discovered gold and religious articles inside Victorio Peak, located in the San Andres Mountains.

1938
The second Rio Grande Compact is signed in Santa Fe by Colorado, Texas and New Mexico to distribute equal amounts of water from the Rio Grande Basin to each of the three entities.

Sept. 1, 1939
Nazi Germany's invasion of Poland engulfs the great powers of Europe in World War II. The U.S. remained neutral until 1941. Martin Amador Campbell and his friend were among the many to serve in the war.

A SERIES OF UNFORTUNATE EVENTS

GREAT DEPRESSION AND DROUGHT LEAD TO DUST BOWL

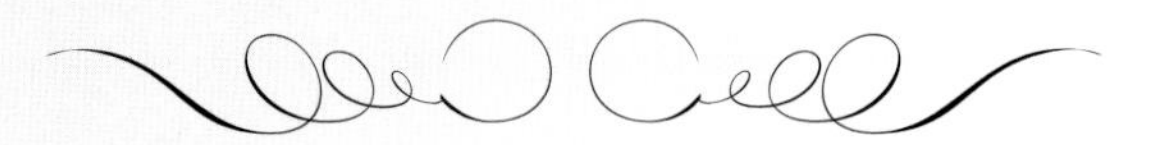

Though many people view the Dust Bowl of the 1930s as a series of natural disasters, man-made problems contributed to the storms that centralized in northeastern New Mexico, southeastern Colorado and the panhandles of Oklahoma and Texas, also known as the heart of the storms.

After World War I ended, America was left with an abundance of wheat crops grown on marginal land maintained with outdated technology and farming practices.

The oversupply led to decreased food prices. At the same time, America fell into the Great Depression.

In the fall of 1929, the New York Stock Exchange was more active than it had ever been, and economists predicted the increases to last. However, a series of events from Oct. 24-29, 1929, evoked fear and investors pulled out of the market, causing the economy to continue to spin downward.

On Black Tuesday, about $140 billion in assets disappeared almost overnight. Within six to eight months, more than 3 million people in the U.S. were unemployed.

In the summer of 1931, Bruce Cabot, a Las Cruces resident who grew up on a wheat farm in Texas, said he worked from sunrise to sunset in the wheat fields, cutting the crop for 25 cents a day.

"The wheat was chest high on us kids," Cabot said. "I made just enough money to buy me a new pair of shoes before school started. They cost $2.50."

Between 1929 and 1932, the income of the average American family decreased by 40 percent, from $2,300 to $1,500.

Necessities, such as food and clothing, became scarce, and luxuries were out of reach for most people.

"Due to the poor economy and tight finances, Great Plains farmers and ranchers still used antiquated agricultural methods and equipment more typical for the late 1800s," said Dave Lundy, co-curator of the Dust Bowl exhibit at the New Mexico Farm & Ranch Heritage Museum.

Adding to the terrible mix, the Great Plains suffered an extreme drought in the 1930s.

"With the drought, crops didn't make it, and the land was already vulnerable," Lundy said.

Though the terrain was accustomed to sporadic wind storms, the 1930s were battered by a large number of dust storms massive in size and intensity.

In 1933, there were approximately 70 dust storms on the Great Plains – about one every five days. Between 1932 and 1941, there were 379 dust storms in the region. In 1937, there were 134 storms in the first nine months alone, averaging a storm every two days.

"It would be the prettiest morning you ever saw until about 10:30 a.m., and then the dust started blowing in," Cabot said. "Momma put wet towels down on the cracks to keep the dust out of the house."

The day of the worst dust storm in U.S. history was named "Black Sunday," and occurred on April 14, 1935. The storm brought national attention to the matter.

"Storms like this one were called 'black blizzards,'" Lundy said. "This storm in particular put the size of the crisis into peoples' minds."

The storm started in Kansas and made its way southwest into New Mexico. It held a thick dust, and visibility was reduced to zero. Black blizzards were massive in size and their potential for destruction was the most threatening aspect.

Cabot said the tumbleweeds would collect against fences and the dirt would pile on top of them.

"Farmers would dig down and tie the old posts to a new post to hold the fence down because the wind and dust would carry them away," Cabot said. "People didn't farm; they lost all their wheat."

Lundy said farmers joked about not wanting to pay taxes on their land in New Mexico because half of it was now in Kansas.

In New Mexico, seven counties in the northeast suffered from severe wind erosion. With the increased amount of dust, predators were not able to hunt their prey.

New Mexico also suffered from a grasshopper plague.

"In 1937, New Mexico Gov. Clyde Tingley declared war on grasshoppers infesting Union County," Lundy said. "Poison was distributed and 'hopperdozers' were used to kill and catch the insects."

In southern New Mexico, areas along Picacho Avenue unofficially became known as "Little Oklahoma," crowded with migrants from the heart of the Dust Bowl.

"This isn't just an event that happened; this is a human story," Lundy said.

A DUSTY TRAGEDY

In the 1930s, a vast area of the South and Southwest was blanketed by dust, grit and grime. Poor farming practices and a severe drought made the land susceptible to extreme environmental conditions. Homes and farms in Colorado, Oklahoma, Texas and New Mexico were infiltrated with dust throughout the decade. People from New Mexico and the panhandle of Oklahoma fled to the Mesilla Valley. Shown right, in Clayton, N.M., farmers were literally up to their knees in dirt after severe storms rolled through northern New Mexico. Below, farmland was abandoned because the Great Depression left people with little money to farm, and the dust made it nearly impossible to do so.

HERZSTEIN MEMORIAL MUSEUM

LORETTO ACADEMY

The Loretto Academy, pictured above, was established in the 1930s by the Sisters of Loretto, who arrived to Las Cruces in 1870. The academy was the first school in southern New Mexico. Curriculum consisted of typical Victorian female pursuits. Students learned the basics, such as arithmetic, grammar, reading and spelling as well as home economics. Throughout the grades, penmanship, composition, elocution and physical culture were taught. The academy also emphasized the arts and offered lessons in instrumental and vocal music as well as painting and drawing. Harsh economic times and dwindling enrollment numbers closed the academy's doors in 1943.

NMSU LASC

GRANDVIEW ELEMENTARY MEMORIES

First-, second- and third-graders pose in front of their school in the mid-'30s. The school later became Bradley Elementary and was torn down in the mid-1980s.

JIM BRADLEY

PERMANENT FIESTA

Left, while aboard the USS New Mexico submarine, Jerean and Tom Hutchinson stand at the door of the galley. The galley is named for their festive restaurant, La Posta, right, a landmark in Mesilla since 1939.

LA POSTA

LA POSTA

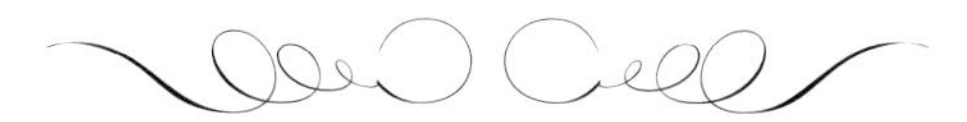

The year was 1939. Franklin Roosevelt was President of the United States, England and France declared war on Germany, the Green Bay Packers won their fifth NFL championship, "The Wizard of Oz" and "Gone with the Wind" reached the big screen … and Katy Griggs Camuñez turned 25 years old.

On the plaza in Mesilla, Katy wanted to open a "little chile joint." Her uncle, Edgar Griggs, a prominent Mesilla merchant, owned a building there. Katy wanted to rent it, but Uncle Edgar declined his niece's offer. However, because he loved his young niece and appreciated her vivacious personality, he offered to sell Katy the property for "one dollar, love and affection." With four tables on a dirt floor, her mother cooking in the back of the same room with no running water, Katy's La Posta Restaurant opened for business.

Through the years, La Posta became a favorite dining spot for locals and visitors alike. It was not unusual to find yourself dining next to a head of state or visiting dignitaries. Personalities such as Sam Donaldson, Val Kilmer, Sheryl Crow, Sam Elliott and George Foreman have dined at the restaurant. In fact, a few former Presidents have enjoyed La Posta "to go."

Katy operated La Posta until she passed away in 1993. In 1996, Katy's great niece, Jerean Camuñez Hutchinson, and husband Tom (Hutch), a retired Navy Captain, became the proprietors of La Posta. Together, the Hutchinsons kept alive the La Posta traditions Katy started more than six decades earlier, serving the same traditional recipes handed down from the Fountain, Chavez and Griggs families. They also have kept many of the same dedicated staff, some of whom have been with the restaurant for as many as 40 years.

The La Posta Compound, listed on the National Register of Historic Places, dates back to the 1850s. Over the years, it has housed many businesses including the Bean Saloon (run by Judge Roy Bean's brother), the Corn Exchange Hotel, where President Ulysses S. Grant stayed a few times, and the famous Butterfield Stagecoach line. In addition, notable personalities from the past like Billy the Kid, Kit Carson, Pancho Villa and General Douglas MacArthur frequented the property.

Finally, adding to its prominence and colorful history, Katy would be proud to learn her restaurant added a second location … well, sort of. In 2009, the USS New Mexico submarine named its dining facility "La Posta Abajo del Mar," or "La Posta Beneath the Sea."

RECIPE FOR SUCCESS

Katy Griggs Camuñez, center, started Katy's La Posta Restaurant in 1939. Her traditional recipes established a tradition to live on well after her passing.

LA POSTA

HUNTER "PREACHER" LEWIS

Hunter "Preacher" Lewis was instrumental in establishing the Episcopal church in the Southwest. While he was sick as a boy, he learned to knit and stuck with the hobby throughout his adulthood. Preacher knitted more than 2,000 baby baptism caps.

NMSU LASC

A FAITHFUL JOB

LEWIS ESTABLISHED 22 MISSIONS IN THE SOUTHWEST

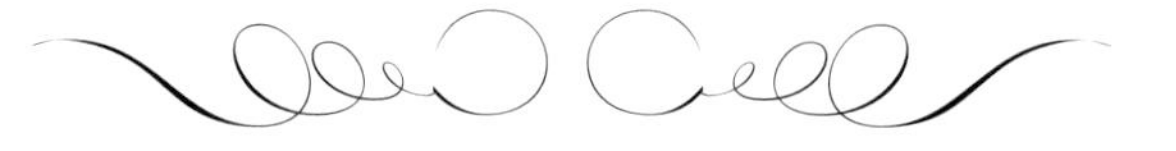

Hunter Lewis, commonly referred to as "Preacher," died on May 27, 1948. He was 79 years old; however, the reverend minister's legacy has far surpassed his lifetime.

Born in Virginia, Lewis came from a family of respected frontiersmen and was taught the value of hard work at an early age, working in the fields and dairy barn with his siblings.

On Sundays, the family attended Fine Creek Baptist Church because there was no Episcopal church close enough to attend. Lewis was baptized in 1879 at 10 years old.

His father, Henry, was a leader in the church, serving as Sunday school superintendent, a deacon and church moderator as well as choir director.

Lewis came to New Mexico in 1905, to head the Episcopal church.

It was a time when the West was still finding its way, and range wars and family feuds were not uncommon. Protestantism, one of the three major denominations of Christianity along with Catholicism and Eastern Orthodoxy, was laggard in comparison to the established Roman Catholic churches in southern New Mexico.

It has been said that Lewis "single-handedly walked the sands along the Rio Grande and established missions ... between the outskirts of El Paso and Albuquerque."

Though his habits were often referred to as "unconventional," Lewis was known for his devotion and loyalty.

But he wasn't the only one with unwavering faith. Some of his followers were so devoted to the preacher, they called themselves "Lewisites" instead of Episcopalians.

In "Journeys of Faith," a biography of Lewis by Lee Priestley, friends of Preacher call him cheerful and tell stories about the collection that financed his charities and the baptism caps he knitted.

In the preacher's obituary, it said he took up knitting as a boy while recuperating from chorea. In his lifetime, he knitted approximately 2,200 baby caps and 50 children's sweaters. He was also known for serving the needy through food drives.

"Lewis ... tirelessly served a vast mission field that over the next four decades would come to include 22 missions and as much as a third of the students at New Mexico's agricultural college," Priestley wrote.

During his lifetime, he is credited with building seven churches and ministering to more than 4,000 persons in Doña Ana and Sierra counties before his death.

GOVERNMENT CENTERS

Above, the Doña Ana County Courthouse opened in 1937. Former New Mexico Gov. James Fielding Hinkle took video footage from platform while community members watched from below during a dedication ceremony. The courthouse was relocated to Motel Boulevard in 2006. The Old Mesilla Court House in the 1930s is pictured to the right.

NMSU LASC

FIREFIGHTERS BANQUET

Doña Ana County firefighters celebrate their achievements with an annual banquet.

NMSU LASC

RAIN, RAIN GO AWAY

Previous to dams being built in the arroyos east of Las Cruces, rainwater from the East Mesa would cause destruction to homes, buildings and roads. Because a majority of the houses were made of adobe, walls would collapse. Cars would also be swept away. The city's poor drainage caused flood problems through the 1970s.

NMSU LASC

CAMP BROADWAY
AAA
TILE BATHS-LOCKED GARAGES

CLIMBING TECHNOLOGY

Left, workers install a utility pole at Stahmann Farms in 1935. Below, utility worker Earl Goddard practices climbing a utility pole.

NMSU LASC

TECHNOLOGICAL ADVANCEMENTS

Professor Jack Clark is caught taking a break in an electrical room of the New Mexico A&M mechanical engineering department.

NMSU LASC

YOU CAN'T BLOW THIS HOUSE DOWN

Especially in southern New Mexico, houses were made from adobe bricks that dried in the sun, above. The material was used because its components – sand, clay, water and some kind of fibrous or organic material, such as sticks, straw and/or manure – were cheap and abundant as well as durable.

NMSU LASC/BOB BURNS

THE HOUSE OF RALPH WILLIS GODDARD

Ralph Willis Goddard's children stand in front of his partially built home, far left. The photo to the right shows the home after it was complete. In the 1930s, homebuilding required careful planning because the practice was at least in part regulated by the Federal Housing Administration, which provided insured loan funding for home builders starting in 1934.

NMSU LASC

HORSE IS MAN'S BEST FRIEND

A.B. Cox admires his horse, Dusty, at the San Augustine Ranch in 1932. With few paved roads in the 1930s, horses were used to travel rough terrain.

JOHN YARBROUGH

MESILLA VALLEY AGRICULTURE

In 1939, well-known local cattle trader Charley Madrid, below left, poses during Field Day at Jornada Experimental Range, which served as a field research laboratory. Below right, farm equipment owned by Western Production Seed Corp. plows a field of hay.

NMSU LASC

NEW DEAL RESTRICTED COTTON FARMING

The Agricultural Adjustment Act of 1933 restricted agricultural production of crops, including cotton, in an effort to reduce a surplus and raise crop prices. This effort was part of the New Deal era and is considered the first modern U.S. farm bill.

NMSU LASC

STAHMANN FARMS

In a scene played out all over the country every year, someone with a friend or loved one in southern New Mexico gets a box in the mail, unwraps it, and finds a treasure of goodies made with pecans.

No one knows if Deane Stahmann had this pecan-gift-giving tradition in mind back in 1932 when he first planted pecan trees in the Mesilla Valley south of Las Cruces.

Neither did he likely envision the farms would be producing as many as 10 million pounds of pecans a year someday. The volume at Stahmann's helps New Mexico compete annually with Georgia and Texas for the title of top-producing pecan state in America.

Money may not grow on trees, but pecans certainly do, and Stahmann Farms grows more of them than just about anyone.

It wasn't long before they were making a dizzying array of snacks, candies and gourmet gift baskets too.

Demand in America has long been the bread and butter for Stahmanns, but in the the 2000s, demand from China and other overseas nations provided valuable new markets.

Those things could not even be imagined in 1925, when Deane arrived in 1925 with his father, William J. Stahmann. Their plan was simply to farm cotton. Deane's planting of the pecan saplings changed all that.

As the pecan trees grew, they began to alter the appearance of New Mexico Highway 28, the road that goes from Mesilla south to Anthony, N.M. Tourists make the trip in all seasons to look at the Stahmann pecan trees, and to visit the Stahmann's Country Store.

Some of those visitors may question unkempt weeds in the fields of trees. Those weeds have enabled the Stahmanns to nearly eliminate insecticides. The weeds are home to ladybugs, lacewing flies and other bugs that might seem to be annoyances if they were in your backyard. On Stahmann Farms, however, those insects take on aphids that love to attack the pecan trees.

Sally Stahmann-Solis, Deane's granddaughter, took over ownership of the farms when her father, Bill Stahmann, died in 2006. Sally worked directly with her father beginning in 1995, learning the business from him, as well as from many other longstanding employees.

After nearly 80 years, a Stahmann's pecan represents more than a tasty New Mexican snack. It represents Sally Stahmann-Solis, her father, her grandfather, her great-grandfather and every Stahmann Farms employee who has worked in the fields since those days Deane first planted pecan trees in the desert.

TRANSFORMING THE VALLEY

From a few saplings in 1932, Stahmann Farms became one of the largest pecan-producing operations in the world.

STAHMANN FARMS

WPA AND CCC PROGRAMS

During the Great Depression, New Mexico's poverty level went from bad to worse. President Franklin D. Roosevelt implemented the New Deal programs, which were designed to give immediate relief to those suffering while also revitalizing the economy. The Works Progress Administration (WPA) was the largest and longest lasting of the New Deal programs. Similarly, the Civilian Conservation Corps (CCC), shown above and below, which started in 1933, put young men to work. Its stated purpose was to "conserve the nation's endangered youth." Right, a sidewalk in the Alameda-Depot Historic District still has the WPA mark in 2011.

NMSU LASC/JOSH MAULDIN

WIDE OPEN SPACES

Popular hangouts in the 1930s included New Mexico A&M campus, below, and Dripping Springs, right.

NMSU LASC

WHITE SANDS NATIONAL MONUMENT

On Jan. 18, 1933, President Herbert Hoover declared 142,987 acres of white sand a national monument. More than 4,000 people celebrated the dedication of White Sands National Monument with an on-site picnic. Tom Charles, the monument's first custodian, was paid $4 a month. His primary responsibility was to count the number of guests.

NMSU LASC

NEW MEXICO A&M FOOTBALL

With the iconic Organ Mountains in the background, it's hard to mistake where this action was photographed as the New Mexico A&M freshman football team takes on its opponent, above. Below, the New Mexico A&M marching band performs during halftime at a college football game.

NMSU LASC

CELEBRATING AGGIE TRADITIONS

In addition to cheering for the New Mexico A&M football team, Aggie students also wore their pride on their backs with letter jackets, above left. During a New Mexico A&M homecoming game, Aggie fans lined up at the train station to "welcome" the Santa Barbara State Gauchos to the Land of Enchantment, above center. With slow-working doors, eager Gauchos started climbing out of the train windows. Continuing another tradition at the college, the Aggie marching band helped lead the annual May Day parade, above right, in the 1930s.

NMSU LASC

FFA STUDENTS CELEBRATE

Students at an FFA convention, above left, jam out at a New Mexico A&M event in the gymnasium. Center left, in 1937, a Maypole dance is held as part of the Water Carnivale at New Mexico A&M. The dance is one of the oldest Indian dances.

NMSU LASC

CELEBRATING IN LAS CRUCES

A reception in honor of New Mexico A&M president Hugh M. Milton was held in the gymnasium in the 1930s, above. More than a decade later, Milton Hall was named after the former president. Right, a patriotic parade in Downtown Las Cruces.

NMSU LASC

JOSE "CHOPE" BENAVIDEZ

Jose "Chope" Benavidez, the proprietor of the famed Chope's Bar & Cafe in La Mesa, strikes a dashing pose in this photo, believed to be taken in the late 1930s in downtown El Paso.

MARISA LUCERO

BATHING BEAUTIES

Queens for the Sun and Spring carnivals were selected as royalty of carnivals at New Mexico A&M each year. The Sun Carnival princess was selected by popular election of the student body, while the Spring Carnival queen was chosen by a panel of judges who chose a bathing beauty for the title.

NMSU LASC

FASHION TRENDS

Fashion in the 1930s paid attention to the shoulders, with exaggerated sleeves for men and women. The decade also saw new products being used, such as man-made fibers, especially rayon for dresses and viscose for linings and lingerie, and synthetic nylon stockings. The zipper also became widely used in the decade.

BURNS FAMILY/NMSU LASC

Mr. and Mrs. W. A. Broookreson
request the honor of your presence
at the marriage of their daughter

Louletia Inez
to
Kenneth A. Valentine

on Sunday, the twenty-fifth of August
nineteen hundred thirty-five
at four o'clock at
St. Paul's Methodist Church
Las Cruces, New Mexico

WEDDINGS OF THE '30S

Above, Kendrick Brookreson, Norma Miller, Kenneth A. Valentine, Louletia Brookreson, Louis Burleson, Mildred Brookreson, Richard Lundberg and Poal Brookreson celebrated the Valentine-Brookreson wedding Aug. 25, 1935. Another typical wedding from the 1930s, below, was of bride Carolina Loya and groom Luis Barrio, who were married on Oct. 3, 1934, in Las Cruces.

ALICE WARD/BARRIO FAMILY

MOTOR SECTION

1940-1949

WAR AND PEACE

WAR ON DISPLAY

By 1949, the idea of war was a not-so-distant memory and the ordnance department of White Sands Proving Ground put V-2 rockets they were testing on the other side of the Organ Mountains on display in nearby Las Cruces. In the earlier part of the decade, however, those V-2s were used by the Germans to deliver deadly blows on civilians in England and other parts of Europe as Germany sought world supremacy in World War II.

JEFFIE SCHATZABEL NEVAREZ

A World at War

As the leader of the National Socialist Party, Adolf Hitler shaped Germany into a world power that was above the law. His forces invaded Poland Sept. 1, 1939, causing Britain, France, Australia and New Zealand to declare war on Germany.

Proclaiming neutrality, America watched as Germany, and its ally Italy, took control of much of Europe and ventured into Africa. Even earlier, in 1931, Japan began invading Asian nations in its own quest for supremacy.

America remained neutral until Dec. 7, 1941, when Japan launched a surprise attack on the U.S. Naval base in Pearl Harbor, Hawaii. Japanese forces had crossed the Pacific undetected, and by 6 a.m., 183 Japanese bomber planes were headed for the U.S. Pacific Fleet.

They reached the base by 7:53 a.m., and began their attack on airfields and battleships. By the time the attack ended at 9:45 a.m., eight American battleships were damaged – five were sunk – as well as three light cruisers, three destroyers, three smaller vessels and 188 aircraft. The death toll: 2,335 American servicemen and 68 civilians. More than 1,000 were wounded.

It took less than 24 hours for the U.S. and Britain to declare war on Japan. And it took Germany less than a week to declare war on the U.S. Despite its attempts to remain neutral, the U.S. was immersed in the Second World War.

Ten hours after the Pearl Harbor attack, the Japanese Army, led by Lt. Gen. Masaharu Homma, attacked U.S. and Filipino forces on the Bataan Peninsula in the Philippines, which was a U.S. commonwealth at the time. Taken by surprise and not well-enough equipped to fight back, troops were able to stave off the Japanese siege for several months before being ordered to surrender.

Realizing there were more prisoners than could be transported, Homma ordered the already-famished soldiers to march 70 miles through the jungles of the Philippines to the shore where "hell ships" would take them to Japanese prisoner-of-war camps.

Many of those American forces were members of the New Mexico National Guard, said Monte Marlin, spokeswoman for White Sands Missile Range, which holds an annual Bataan Memorial Death March that attracts more than 6,000 participants in honor of the 78,000 soldiers who were forced to endure the grueling 70-mile march in 1942.

"New Mexico lost the most men per capita in World War II than any other state," she said, "and a lot of that is because of the Bataan Death March."

On the Home Front

In Las Cruces, with a census-recorded population of 8,835 in 1940, enrollment fell 30 percent at New Mexico A&M College, and nearby Fort Bliss in El Paso had 25,000 troops preparing for war.

The Civilian Conservation Corps, a New Deal program launched in 1938 to put young men back to work, had dissolved due to the war. The men had been trained with a military-like structure at camps throughout the U.S., including in Las Cruces.

The camp, located on present-day Melendres Street, was

1940
Young men from Pennsylvania trained at a local Civilian Conservation Corps camp, a program that was part of President Franklin D. Roosevelt's New Deal. The CCC was designed to put young men back into the labor force.

1941
County officials confiscated gambling paraphernalia and donated the scrap metal for the war effort, after the U.S. joined World War II.

1942
Patriotism ran high as organizations such as the Las Cruces Chamber of Commerce promoted the sale of war bonds to support American troops fighting in World War II.

1945
White Sands Proving Ground is established just east of the Organ Mountains on July 9. The "temporary" camp was created to test V-2 missiles obtained from the Germans.

1945
Exactly one week after the establishment of White Sands Proving Ground, July 16, 1945, the world's first atomic bomb is tested. Although the two projects were in close proximity to each other, they were totally separate endeavors.

NMSU LASC

1940s

Who's Who

Las Cruces Mayors

1938-44, '46-48, '49-53 .... Sam Klein
1944-46 .... Edwin L. Mechem
1948-49 .... James D. McElhannon

Postmaster

1938-56 .... Lena B. Sexton

New Mexico A&M Presidents

1938-47 .... Hugh M. Milton II
1947-49 .... John R. Nichols

Doña Ana County Sheriffs

1940 .... Jose M. Viramontes
1941-44 .... Miguel F. Apodaca
1944-48 .... Santos Ramirez
1948-50 .... A.L. Apodaca

New Mexico Governors

1939-43 .... John E. Miles
1943-47 .... John J. Dempsey
1947-51 .... Thomas J. Mabry

U.S. Senators

1933-49 .... Carl Hatch
1935-61 .... Dennis Chavez
1949-73 .... Clinton Anderson

U.S. Representatives

1935-41 .... John J. Dempsey
1941-47 .... Clinton Anderson
1943-55 .... Antonio M. Fernández
1947-49 .... Georgia L. Lusk
1949-51 .... John E. Miles

Las Cruces Public Schools Superintendent

1933-1954 .... Carl S. Conlee

By the Numbers

8,385 .... Las Cruces population (1940)
30,411 .... Doña Ana County population (1940)
$1,725 .... Average annual income
40 cents .... Minimum wage (1945)
11 cents .... Gallon of gas
3 cents .... First-class stamp
$3,920 .... Average home value
$30 .... Average monthly rent for a house
$850 .... Average price for a new car

In the News

Nov. 5, 1940: President Franklin D. Roosevelt becomes the first man to hold office for three terms after his 449-82 electoral college victory over Republican candidate Wendell Wilkie.

July 7, 1941: Finding it more and more difficult to maintain neutrality in the growing war in Europe, the United States occupies Iceland in an attempt to thwart a potential invasion by Nazi Germany.

June 4-7, 1942: With America fully in the war after the Japanese attack on Pearl Harbor, the Battle of Midway between the U.S. and Japan takes place at Midway Islands in the Pacific. Japan invaded the Aleutian Islands on June 7, making it the first invasion of American soil in 128 years.

June 21, 1943: While America is fighting a war in Europe, the Pacific and North Africa, race wars are under way in the U.S. Forty people are killed and 700 more injured after riots in Detroit and New York City's Harlem.

June 22, 1944: The Servicemen's Readjustment Act of 1944 (known as the GI Bill) is signed into law. Under the law, veterans are entitled to college or vocational education as well as one year of unemployment compensation.

April 12, 1945: Roosevelt dies from a brain hemorrhage and Vice President Harry S. Truman assumes the office. Truman will give the "go-ahead" for use of the atomic bomb as a weapon against Japan.

Jan. 24, 1946: Fifty-one nations gather for the first meeting of the United Nations.

April 15, 1947: Jackie Robinson becomes the first black Major League Baseball player when he joins the Brooklyn Dodgers.

July 26, 1948: Truman signs an order ending segregation in the U.S. military.

April 4, 1949: The North Atlantic Treaty Organization is formed. NATO includes the nations of U.S., Canada, Belgium, Denmark, France, Iceland, Italy, Luxembourg, Netherlands, Norway, Portugal and the United Kingdom. Its message was clear – attack one, attack them all.

1945
The footing of a steel tower is inspected after a successful test of an atomic bomb. The test leads to two more bombs exploding over Hiroshima and Nagasaki, Japan, on Aug. 6 and 9. The Japanese surrendered five days later, ending World War II.

1946
Las Cruces is incorporated as a city. Sam Klein was the city's first mayor, although Las Cruces had been incorporated as a town with a mayor since 1907.

1948
Las Cruces launches a bus line, the first line of public transportation for the burgeoning area.

1949
The body of Ovida "Cricket" Coogler is found. The investigation of her death uncovered corruption throughout New Mexico and dismantled illegal gambling operations from Las Cruces to Juárez, Mexico.

1949
A weeklong celebration was held to commemorate the 100th anniversary of the settlement of Las Cruces.

abandoned after many of the men in the CCC enlisted or were drafted to fight in World War II, said Deborah Dennis, executive director of Human Systems Research Inc.

"What we know about the Las Cruces camp is the young men were from Pennsylvania," Dennis said. "There was a mixing of populations, and it was the first time, for many, encountering Hispanics.

"What (the CCC) did was force young men to work out their differences and become a team. I've heard people say that one of the reasons we were successful in World War II was that many of the men came out of the CCC. They knew structure and discipline and had already worked out their social differences."

In 1941, after the CCC dissolved, the Department of War used the former CCC camp with a different purpose – to house prisoners of war.

German and Italian troops fighting in the German Afrika Korps and taken prisoner in North Africa were shipped to the Southwest because it had a similar climate to where they were captured.

"The first POWs were Italians and then Germans," Dennis said, "but they found that the two didn't mix well, so they built a second camp for the Italians (on a site that later became Young Park)."

The building that served as the CCC school was transformed into the Army headquarters that oversaw the POW camps under Capt. Clark Williams, Dennis said.

"The POWs sustained agriculture in the Mesilla Valley," Dennis said. "Farmers and ranchers would pick them up; they picked chile and cotton. Without POW labor, people wouldn't have been able to sustain (their farms). The government paid an incentive to the farmers to use them."

The treatment of war prisoners was questioned by some, even to the point of involvement by the American Red Cross. Dennis said the organization demanded the dismantling of a cage used for punishment.

Despite conditions, the POWs kept the area's agriculture industry alive and well.

A RACE TO THE FINISH

As the war forged on in Europe, Germany launched a final attack Dec. 16, 1944, in an attempt to capture Belgium, France and Luxembourg. The battle, known as the "Battle of the Bulge," lasted until Jan. 7, 1945, when Hitler reluctantly withdrew his forces.

U.S. troops continued on their way to Germany, crossing the Rhine River in March 1945, with the Soviets encircling Berlin by April 16, 1945. In April 20, to evade being taken prisoner by the Soviets, Hitler committed suicide.

A select group of German rocket scientists surrendered to the Americans, who were eager to learn the advanced technology created by those scientists. The Germans had developed the V-2 missile during World War II and used the warcraft to nearly obliterate London and other European targets in their quest for supremacy. At the time, the V-2 rocket was the world's first long-range missile and was the first unmanned aircraft to reach suborbital space.

A CLOSER LOOK

Bright Eyes was the first generation of optical equipment used to track missiles at White Sands Proving Ground. Las Crucen Clyde Tombaugh, famed as the discoverer of the planet Pluto, used his knowledge of astronomical observation techniques, optical design and photographic processes to develop this first fleet of specialized cameras.

WHITE SANDS MISSILE RANGE PUBLIC AFFAIRS OFFICE

"The Americans wanted it," said White Sands Missile Range Museum Director Darren Court.

When the Germans surrendered, the Americans finally got what they wanted. Earlier, they had intercepted components of V-2 missiles, but they needed German scientists, which included rocket scientist and aerospace pioneer Wernher von Braun, to teach them how to assemble and operate them. The question was – where could they assemble and test the rockets, yet allow the project to remain a top-secret mission? They found the perfect location in New Mexico, just east of the Organ Mountains.

Ranchers on the land, including the Cox family, were asked to temporarily lease their land to the federal government for the war efforts, and on July 9, 1945, White Sands Proving Ground was established.

"(The Germans') job was to assemble V-2s," Court said. "There were 300 railroad cars of V-2 parts and equipment backed up on the railroads from here to El Paso."

Learning about the V-2s helped the Americans advance not only in the area of defense, but also in the race to be the first to send a man into space.

"The V-2s allowed us to do experiments with the winds to determine how it affected humans at that height," Court said. "It was the beginning of something great."

Although the proving ground was meant to be temporary, the mission at the base became so important to testing and the future of space, that more military branches became involved, and the purpose was expanded beyond weaponry. Between 1946 and 1952, 67 V-2s were fired on the range.

Over the years, White Sands Proving Ground annexed adjacent lands, including the Alamogordo Bombing and Gunnery Range and the Trinity Site, the location of the first atomic bomb testing.

PRESIDENTIAL PILOT

Left, at 25 years old, Gerald Thomas, a junior-grade Navy lieutenant from Small, Idaho, piloted an Avenger torpedo bomber based on a Navy aircraft carrier. During the war, bombers attacked the Japanese in the Pacific. Thomas earned an Air Medal and later became president of New Mexico State University.

NEW MEXICO STATE UNIVERSITY LIBRARY ARCHIVES AND SPECIAL COLLECTIONS

FAR AND AWAY

While local residents such as Manuel Bustamante of La Mesa, below left, served in World War II in the European Theater, those on the home front, including businesses such as J.C. Penney Co., below right, promoted the sale of war stamps and defense bonds. The programs were used by the Department of the U.S. Treasury to help fund World War II.

ISELA ALVAREZ/NMSU LASC

PRISONERS OF WAR

Built at first for the New Deal-implemented Civilian Conservation Corps on present-day Melendres Street, this camp was transformed to house German POWs during World War II.

DEBORAH DENNIS, HUMAN SYSTEMS RESEARCH INC.

WHITE SANDS PROVING GROUND

Established in 1945, White Sands Proving Ground brought in American soldiers to assist with the testing of V-2 missiles obtained from the Germans during World War II.

NMSU LASC

READY TO SERVE

By the end of World War II in 1945, Doña Ana Red Cross surgical dressing supervisors joined 7.5 million volunteers to aid military personnel and their families.

ISELA ALVAREZ

ASSEMBLING THE BOMB

The plutonium core of the atomic bomb tested at Trinity Site was assembled in the master bedroom of the Schmidt/McDonald ranch house, above left. The ranch house was abandoned by its owners in 1942 when the Alamogordo Bombing and Gunnery Range took over the land to use in training World War II bombing crews. The team of scientists who were part of the top-secret Manhattan Project – which led to the world's first atomic bomb detonation – was led by J. Robert Oppenheimer, above right, who earned the nickname, "Father of the Atomic Bomb."

WHITE SANDS MISSILE RANGE PUBLIC AFFAIRS OFFICE/LAS CRUCES BULLETIN

THE DAY THE SUN ROSE TWICE

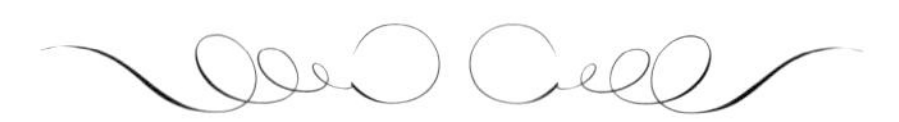

Before V-2 missiles were being assembled and tested at White Sands Proving Ground, an even more top-secret mission was being conducted in Los Alamos, N.M.

The Manhattan Project was formed in June 1942 to design and build an atomic bomb. It was considered a race with the Germans, who – according to intercepted intelligence – were designing their own bomb.

The project expanded over three locations in the United States – Oak Ridge, Tenn., where gas diffusion and electromagnetic process plants were built to separate uranium 235 from uranium 238; Hanford, Wash., where nuclear reactors were erected to produce plutonium; and Los Alamos, to design and build the bomb.

At Los Alamos, a group of scientists was being led by J. Robert Oppenheimer. It was believed that two elements – uranium 235 and plutonium – each could be used to produce atomic explosions, and the scientists came up with two designs, one with uranium 235 and another with plutonium.

Though the scientists decided the uranium 235 bomb did not need testing, they felt they needed to test the plutonium bomb because they were unsure of just how devastating the chain reaction would be. Of eight possible sites in California, Texas, New Mexico and Colorado, the Trinity Site in New Mexico was selected. Trinity was an ideal location because it was already controlled by the government and was relatively close to Los Alamos.

On July 12, 1945, two hemispheres of plutonium were delivered to the George McDonald ranch house – two miles from where the test would be administered. The team left Los Alamos for Trinity Site after midnight July 13, and assembled the plutonium core in the morning. The core was then taken to the test site and inserted in a mechanism under a 100-foot steel tower. The next morning, a crew raised the bomb atop the steel tower and detonators were attached.

At 5:29 a.m. July 16, 1945, the bomb exploded successfully. With a brilliant light, a shock wave and sound bouncing off the nearby mountains, observers as far as 10 miles away from ground zero said they felt a heat similar to that of the sun.

According to White Sands Missile Range reports, the shock wave broke windows 120 miles away and was felt as far as 160 miles away. Because of the need for high security, no information was released by the government until after the bombs were dropped on Japan. Army officials initially explained the situation by stating that a munitions storage area accidentally exploded at the bombing range.

The heat of the explosion vaporized the steel tower, melted the sand and turned it into a green glass. That glass, called Trinitite, covered much of the blast-created crater, which was 4 feet deep and 240 feet in diameter.

Once it was proven successful, a second atomic bomb – the first ever used in warfare – was exploded over Hiroshima, Japan, on Aug. 6, 1945. President Harry Truman made an announcement of what happened that same day. A third bomb was dropped on Nagasaki on Aug. 9, and by Aug. 14, the Japanese surrendered, ending World War II.

The inner workings of the Manhattan Project didn't stay confidential for long, as Soviets penetrated the secrecy of the project by 1949 and were on their way to building their own nuclear bomb – and ushering in the Cold War.

WEAPON OF MASS DESTRUCTION

Forming a mushroom cloud of radioactive dust and debris, the world's first atomic bomb was successfully detonated in the New Mexico desert on July 16, 1945.

WHITE SANDS MISSILE RANGE PUBLIC AFFAIRS OFFICE

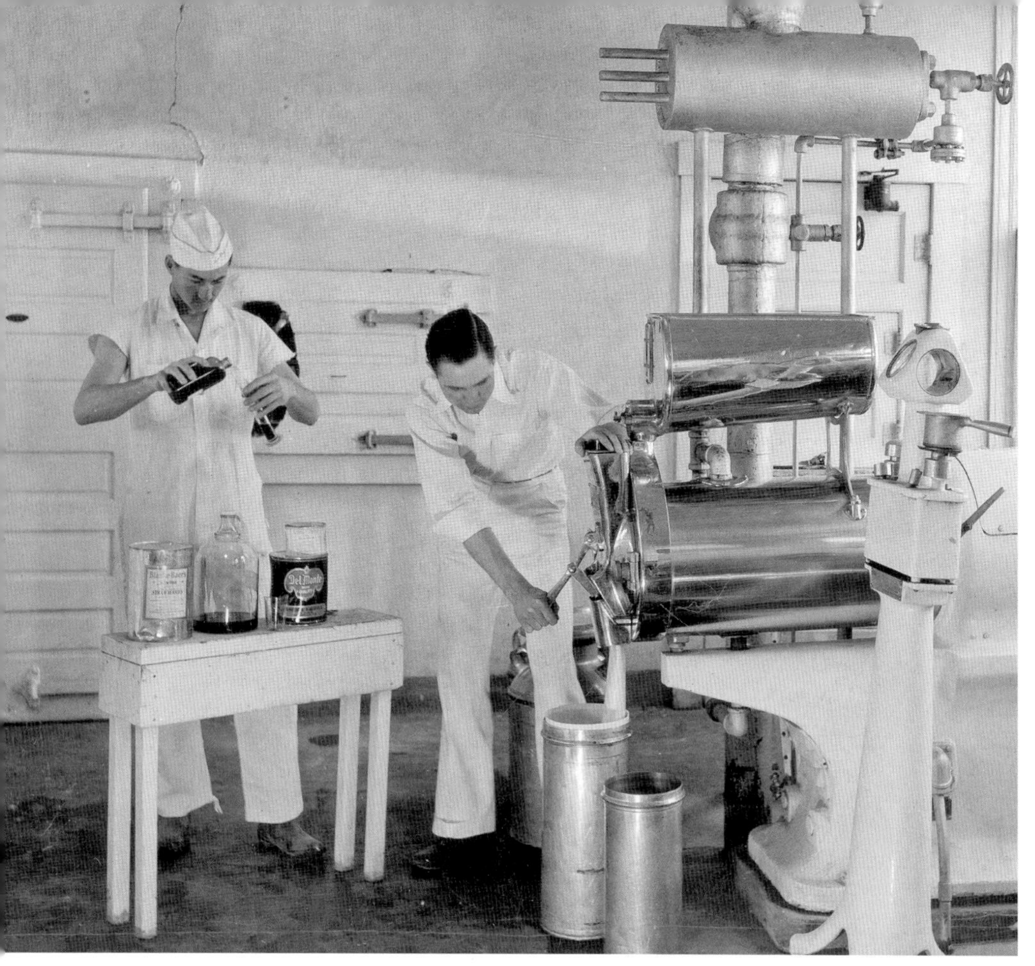

GOT CREAM?

Thriving even during the Great Depression, El Paso-based Price's Creameries expanded with processing plants, above right, into southern New Mexico during the 1930s and '40s. The company continues to provide dairy products in southern New Mexico, El Paso and Mexico.

NMSU LASC

SUSTAINED BY AGRICULTURE

Agriculture was still the main industry for Las Cruces in the 1940s. Close to the railroad, the Southwest Irrigated Cotton Growers had expansive sheds to temporarily store cotton bales before shipping them throughout the country. Though shops and businesses lined Main Street, areas surrounding the heart of the city were mostly farmland.

NMSU LASC

CELEBRATING CORONADO

Minnie Sutherland and May Baldwin ride in a carriage during the Coronado Cuarto Centennial parade, which celebrated the 400th anniversary of Spanish explorer Don Francisco Vasquez de Coronado's arrival in New Mexico in 1540.

NMSU LASC

A DAY AT THE SANDS

Transcending generations and decades, White Sands National Monument has always been a favorite family destination.

BARRIO FAMILY

CONTINUING A LEGACY

Annie Laurie Campbell poses in a photo with her son Martin Amador Campbell Jr. Annie Laurie married into the well-known Amador family in Las Cruces when she wed Martin Amador Campbell. The Campbells continued managing the historic Amador Hotel after the death of Corina Amador Campbell, Martin Amador's daughter, in 1936.

NMSU LASC

A NEIGHBORHOOD CELEBRATION

In the late 1940s, Jeffie Schatzabel, center, staring at her cake, celebrates an early birthday with seven Las Cruces neighborhood friends. An eighth child, peering through the screen door at right, longs to join the festivities.

JEFFIE SCHATZABEL NEVAREZ

MAIN STREET ACCOMMODATIONS

The Hotel Herndon on Main Street was one of several overnight choices for travelers as they passed through Las Cruces. Other lodging options in the Downtown area included the Campbell Hotel, below left.

NMSU LASC

A SOCIAL CENTER

Catering to the more affluent crowd in the 1940s, the Amador Hotel was successful as the social center of the town, competing only with the Las Cruces Country Club.

NMSU LASC

CHOW DOWN

Following World War II, consumer demand was at an all-time high, and customers frequently visited local retailers such as the Farmers Market & Supply Co., above and below. Companies such as Purina, which offered "chow" for a variety of animals in addition to Wheat Chex cereal, were flourishing due to the high volume of shoppers.

NMSU LASC

PREPARING FOR WAR

To fill the anticipated need for engineers as America got closer to joining World War II, the Engineering Defense Training program was launched in 1940. New Mexico A&M offered the workshops, left and below. Once the United States entered the war in late 1941, the program was renamed the Engineering, Science and Management War Training program.

NMSU LASC

ASPIRING ENGINEERS

Above, Goddard Hall, named for engineering pioneer Ralph Goddard, was the main classroom building for engineering students at New Mexico A&M in the fall of 1947. At right, students of New Mexico A&M engineering professor Dan Jett, top left, pose for a group photo. Jett served as dean of the engineering college from 1938-47. Jett Hall is named in his honor.

NMSU LASC/JIM BRADLEY

ROUGH RIDERS

The New Mexico A&M Rodeo Club in 1941 carried on the tradition of the Old West with style.

NMSU LASC

FALLEN HERO

Pecos Finley was a great basketball player for the Aggies in the late 1930s when they went to the NIT in New York City. He was killed in World War II in the Pacific.

NMSU LASC

FIELD TRIP

Mrs. Heath's kindergarten class took a field trip to see a Japanese war submarine on display on Main Street after World War II.

NMSU LASC

A NEW DEAL, A NEW SCHOOL

Using labor from the Works Progress Administration (WPA), a New Deal program designed to put laborers back to work on public works projects, construction on Court Junior High was completed in 1941.

NMSU LASC

WORLD OF AIRCRAFT

Students of the 1941 Air Craft Lab at New Mexico A&M proudly pose next to one of their finished products.

NMSU LASC

FOOD FOR THOUGHT

In 1941, agronomy students were hard at work understanding the science and technology of plants and their uses. With a war looming, their work was especially important.

NMSU LASC

LOS CONQUISTADORES

The Conquistadores Club, below, was established in 1937 to promote social life among Spanish-speaking students, to participate in intramural athletics and to give recognition to those members who were scholastically outstanding. By the 1940s, the cultural group had grown significantly.

NMSU LASC

TRAIL OF SUCCESS

Back row: Mary, John and Jim Ikard; front row: Winifred, Richard, Amzi and Catherine Ikard; Winifred and Amzi Ikard at their 50th anniversary; Marija and Vide Salopek; Harry and Mae Stout; Back row: Vide, Marija and Tony Salopek; middle row: Ann and John Salopek; front row: David, Frank and Tom Salopek.

IKARD/SALOPEK/STOUT

Ikard, Salopek & Stout

Early Generations of Las Cruces

The dusty trail from Anthony, N.M., to Las Cruces was unpaved and full of holes, but brought some of the brightest innovators, businessmen and pioneers to the Mesilla Valley. Among those who made an impact in the building of Las Cruces were the Ikard, Salopek and Stout families.

John Amzi Ikard arrived in the Mesilla Valley in 1923 as a 21-year-old cotton buyer from Chickasha, Okla. Amzi settled in Anthony and opened a mercantile. It was there he met his wife, Winifred Wareing, whose family came to the area in 1910 from Wiggin, England.

In 1938, Amzi started a propane distributorship and entered into a partnership with Sam Newsom, creating Ikard & Newsom Propane Company, which expanded throughout New Mexico and parts of Arizona. Jim Ikard, the eldest son, became president of Ikard & Newsom. In 1966, son John Ikard opened Ikards Furniture. In 1970, Jim and John helped found Citizens Bank of Las Cruces, and in 1988 they purchased Loretto Towne Centre. Catherine Odette and Richard Ikard are the youngest of the Ikard family.

FAMILY GATHERING

Back row: Frank, Tom and David Salopek; front row: Marija, Tony, Ann and John Salopek.

SALOPEK

Mary Ikard Salopek, Amzi and Winifred's eldest daughter, has served on several boards, including those of Las Cruces Public Schools, Citizens Bank, Memorial Medical Center Foundation and San Ysidro Church.

Mary married Tom Salopek, whose parents, Vide and Marija, came to the Mesilla Valley from Croatia in 1932. Their sons Tony, John, Tom, Frank and David were early agricultural pioneers and are best known for their vast pecan orchards, strong Croatian accent, height and work ethic. Developing raw land into farmland meant clearing mesquite, which was very labor intensive without modern machinery. Ann Hoffman is the only daughter; she resides in Albuquerque.

The Salopek family pioneers boast New Mexico Military Institute graduates, a Doña Ana County commissioner, a New Mexico state representative, an Elephant Butte Irrigation District president, a World War II prisoner of war, an Air Force pilot and many New Mexico State University and Texas A&M University graduates.

A multitude of complementary businesses have risen from the second generation sons and daughters, including fertilizer and beneficial bacteria sales, custom pecan farming, processing and sales, ranching and commercial roofing.

Kathy Salopek Stout, Tom and Mary's youngest daughter, married Barry Stout, whose grandfather Harry started his construction business in 1928. Harry Stout held one of the first New Mexico Contractor's licenses. Harry and his sons, Lester and Bobby, installed many of the original hardwood floors in the early homes of the Alameda area of Las Cruces. Bobby continued in his father's footsteps and assumed control of the hardwood flooring business in 1973. Bobby's wife, Elizabeth, is one of the oldest living direct descendants of General George Armstrong Custer. Harry and Mae also had a daughter, Ivogene Woods, who resides in Canutillo, Texas.

Barry and Kathy Stout still own and operate Stout Hardwood Floor Co. Inc. They restore many of the same floors Barry's grandfather, uncle and father installed many years ago and maintain the floors at facilities such as NMSU, the University of Texas at El Paso and Arizona State University.

The Ikard, Salopek and Stout families' drive and dedication to the growth and revival of historical landmarks, as well as their innovative business creations, have made them fundamental to the vibrancy of the Las Cruces community.

LEADING THE WAY

Father Henry Buchanan headed the Centennial parade, which celebrated 100 years of the establishment of Las Cruces in 1949. Buchanan performed the ceremony of the "Blessing of the Crosses." Three crosses were placed at the location where Las Cruces is believed to have originally received its name. As legend has it, a wagon train of pioneers was attacked and killed by Apaches, and their graves were marked by crosses. The location was also the site of an ancient Native American campground and had been pitted by treasure hunters. Many artifacts of the Apaches were found at that site, which was also close to sites known to have been occupied by the Mimbres and other ancient cultures.

NMSU LASC

ASSEMBLING AT THE ASSEMBLY OF GOD

The Las Cruces Assembly of God hosted the regional Assemblies of God Sunday School Conference in February 1942. The Assembly of God has maintained a strong presence over the decades, building a new church on the East Mesa in 2008.

NMSU LASC

SACRED SCULPTURE

A replica of Michelangelo's classic Renaissance sculpture, "La Pietá," was installed along present-day Amador Avenue with a ceremony on the land that housed the former Loretto Academy, which closed in 1947. After banker Frank Papen purchased the land for his commercial ventures, he agreed to retain the sculpture.

NMSU LASC

FOR UNITY AND CHARITY

The local court of the Catholic Daughters of America, now known as the Catholic Daughters of the Americas, work hard for their parishes and charities. The group was formed in 1906 in Utica, N.Y., and is now in 45 of the United States, as well as Puerto Rico, Mexico, Guam, the Virgin Islands and the Dominican Republic.

NMSU LASC

NOW PLAYING

The movie "Sealed Verdict," released in 1948, starring Ray Milland and Florence Marly, made its way to the Rio Grande Theatre on Main Street in March 1949. "Trouble Preferred," also released in 1948, was playing at the theater as well.

NMSU LASC

CROSSTOWN ENTERTAINMENT

The Mission Theatre in Mesilla Park, according to its 1948 advertisement in a New Mexico College A&M yearbook, was "the place of comfort and the best in entertainment." The theater was built in 1935 and was purchased by Jack Weiss in 1947. The theater closed in 1962.

1948 NEW MEXICO A&M YEARBOOK

STATE-OF-THE-ART VENUE

The State Theater on Main Street opened in 1940 with a gala grand opening just down the street from the Rio Grande Theatre. The new venue joined in a group of about 17,500 other movie theaters in the United States, as the concept grew in popularity. No longer used for movies, the State Theater is now occupied by the Las Cruces Community Theatre, which is working to restore the movie house to its original grandeur.

NMSU LASC

A ONE-STOP SHOP

Main Street was the center of the newly incorporated City of Las Cruces in 1946, with cafés and shops lining both sides of the busy thoroughfare. In addition to retail businesses, Main Street was also home to Mesilla Valley Electric Co., First National Bank and City Hall.

NMSU LASC

MEETING SHOPPERS' NEEDS

As shoppers strolled down Main Street, they could also drop off their laundry at Acme Cleaners and Laundry, above. Offering anything that anyone would need in terms of home décor, Las Cruces Furniture Co., right, was a successful business through the 1960s. The store was owned by the Klein family, including brothers Howard and Melvin "Sonny" Klein.

NMSU LASC

Cricket Coogler

With a small but growing population of around 12,000 in 1949, Las Cruces was a bustling community with plenty of drinking establishments, hotels, cafés and dozens of illegal gambling houses along the road from the city to Juárez, Mexico.

Young Ovida "Cricket" Coogler lived life in Las Cruces to the fullest. She worked at the Tortugas Café on Downtown Main Street, and her latest job was at the DeLuxe Café. After her shift, she often bounced around town to different bars where men – local residents, law enforcement and state officials – frequently bought her drinks, although she was a mere 18 years old.

Coogler's carefree life and frequent reckless decisions no doubt contributed to the reason behind her disappearance and death on April 1, 1949, but her murder is one that remains unsolved and leaves many questions unanswered.

"According to several accounts, she got into a car near Bowman and Church streets and was not seen alive again," said Paula Moore, author of "Cricket in the Web: The 1949 Unsolved Murder that Unraveled Politics in New Mexico."

"Three weeks later, her body was found in the desert north of the Mesquite cemetery."

HER LAST DAYS

Three days before she went missing, Ovida "Cricket" Coogler and her friend Josie Talamantes spent the day in El Paso, and Juárez, Mexico, and a sidewalk photographer took this snapshot of the two young women from Las Cruces. Coogler happened to be wearing the same suit when her body was found three weeks after her disappearance April 1, 1949.

PAULA MOORE

Through interviews and extensive research, Moore found that while Coogler's murder remained unsolved, the case uncovered corruption in the local and state government.

Doña Ana County Sheriff Alfonso Luchini "Happy" Apodaca quietly arrested New Mexico A&M College student and professional football player Jerry Nuzum, who studied at the college during the off-season and had been seen with Coogler the evening she disappeared.

Apodaca also arrested Wesley Byrd, a black man who frequented the Tortugas Café when Coogler was there.

Outraged by Nuzum's arrest because they were convinced the former Aggie football star did not kill Coogler, New Mexico A&M students submitted a petition to convene a grand jury, Moore said.

"It didn't go well," she said. "People would come in obviously fearful. The grand jury was unable to elicit much information when it came to Cricket Coogler, but what they did uncover were multiple illegal gambling operations with connections in Santa Fe."

From there, the grand jury orchestrated raids of the gambling houses in the county, and also uncovered corruption in the sheriff's office.

Not only had Apodaca been accused of torturing Byrd for a confession that was never given, the jury found that the sheriff made no move to investigate illegal gambling and had even delivered two slot machines to be used for gambling, as well as received a monthly kickback. According to Moore, the Doña Ana County grand jury submitted a list of 22 charges against the sheriff.

The torture charge became a civil rights lawsuit, and Apodaca and three others were sentenced to a year in federal prison.

The jury's report also mentioned eight other officials, including Judge W.T. Scoggin Jr., District Attorney T.K. Campbell, state police Chief Hubert Beasley, Las Cruces Police Chief Santos Ramirez, state patrolmen Carlos Salas and I.E. Salazar and Las Cruces policemen Reuben Flores and Vicente Lucero.

The crackdown on corruption became national news and was even mentioned in Time magazine and the New York Times. Campbell issued a 1949 statement of exoneration for Nuzum, but he was rearrested in 1951 to stand trial for Coogler's murder. His sensational trial ended when the judge ordered a verdict of not guilty.

The Coogler case also drew unwelcome attention to the state of New Mexico, causing mobsters who had purchased land in Santa Fe for casinos to look elsewhere for their gambling headquarters, Moore said.

"She was around people with money and power, and I think that gave her a heady experience," Moore said, "but I'm sure she never would have thought she could unfold so much. She was so young, and no one deserves what she got."

AUTOS AND AMMUNITION

As automobiles became more popular, auto parts stores, such as the national chain Western Auto Supply, popped up in the United States. In the 1940s, guns and ammunition also were available at the retail location.

NMSU LASC

FAST, SAFE SERVICE

Using products such as Bowes Seal Fast tires, local garages offered fast tire service. Right, local mechanics worked to repair cars involved in accidents.

NMSU LASC

THE LATEST IN AUTOMOBILES

Community members gathered to "ooh" and "aah" over the latest in automotive technology – the automatic transmission. Pontiac introduced the Hydra-Matic Automatic Transmission on its Streamliner model in 1948, with instructions on how to drive the car with its new feature.

NMSU LASC

THE YOU, YOU WANT TO BE

Popular Dry Goods Co. in Downtown Las Cruces offered a collection of Martha Manning Originals, a clothing manufacturer based in St. Louis. The dresses, according to a Martha Manning ad, are "scientifically fashioned to wish away pounds and years. You appear taller, slimmer, lovelier ... the you, you want to be, in a Martha Manning."

NMSU LASC

IT'S A YOUNGSTOWN

Promoting their "wondrous" steel cabinets, a Youngstown kitchen offered in the 1940s was depicted as neat, clean, modern and, above all, affordable.

NMSU LASC

MAYTAGS FOR LAS CRUCES

Maytag washing machines were back in production after the war in 1946, and Ikard and Newsom Inc. brought the dependable washers to Las Cruces. The first of the company's "automatic washers" were available in 1949.

NMSU LASC

NYLONS IN BLOOM

A sale on nylon stockings lured hundreds of Las Cruces women to Dunlap's White House on Main Street. By 1946, the nylons, which had been out of production because the newly developed synthetic fabric was used for defense materials, were back in high demand. There were similar scenes throughout the nation – thousands of women waited in line for a short supply of nylon stockings and would fight over them. The series of "disturbances" that were created by the shortage between 1945 and 1946 were dubbed "nylon riots." It took several months to meet the demand, leaving many women without stockings.

Nylon was invented in 1939 by an employee at Du Pont and was originally commercialized for women's stockings, but when America joined the war, all production of nylon went toward defense materials. Because of the shortage, women would pay up to $20 for a pair of stockings on the black market or draw seams on the backs of their legs to make it appear they were wearing them.

The need for nylons even inspired the song, "When the Nylons Bloom Again" by George Marion Jr. and Fats Waller.

NMSU LASC

PROUD TO BE AMERICAN

Army soldiers holding the American flag lead the way down Main Street during the Fourth of July parade in 1942. Patriotism was especially important, as America had recently joined the Allied Forces in World War II.

NMSU LASC

HUMBLE BEGINNINGS

On April 22, 1949, Las Cruces celebrated the centennial of its founding. Left, Teresita Viramontes, a freshman at New Mexico A&M, was named the Centennial Queen and was escorted by her brother, Aggie athlete Jimmy Viramontes. The young page in front was crown-bearer Rubén "Butch" Smith, who in the 1990s would be elected mayor of Las Cruces.

RUBÉN SMITH

SWIMSUIT COMPETITION

Tammy Graham was one of 11 contestants in the Centennial Queen Pageant held in 1949. Each group that entered the centennial parade was to sponsor a contestant for the pageant. The crown went to the young woman who raised the most money.

NMSU LASC

CENTENNIAL CELEBRATION

Much of Las Cruces turned out for the city's centennial celebration, which included a parade down Main Street. While Las Cruces was incorporated as a town in 1907 and as a city in 1946, the community was celebrating a different achievement. In 1849, Las Cruces was originally "laid out" by Army Lt. Delos Bennett Sackett, who found approximately 120 future Las Crucens to be part of the city.

NMSU LASC

STARSTRUCK

Women swoon over well-known 1940s actor Gilbert Roland as he takes a drink at El Patio Cantina in Mesilla. Opened in 1934 by Arthur Fountain – tending bar at left – a descendant of the legendary Fountain family. Roland, a native of Juárez, Mexico, is perhaps most known for his role in "The Cisco Kid."

EL PATIO

TENDING BAR

In the 1940s, Manuel Bustamante tends bar at Chope's in La Mesa. The bar and restaurant next door, still run by Jose "Chope" Benavidez's descendants, remain popular businesses.

ISELA ALVAREZ

GAMMIN' IN THE DESERT

Above, these cool teens – one proud to be a Las Cruces High School Bulldog – wore stylish clothes of the late 1940s. At right, a group of schoolgirls show off their trendy skirts.

BARBARA HUBBARD/MARY JANE GARCIA

1950-1959

THE MARCH OF PROGRESS

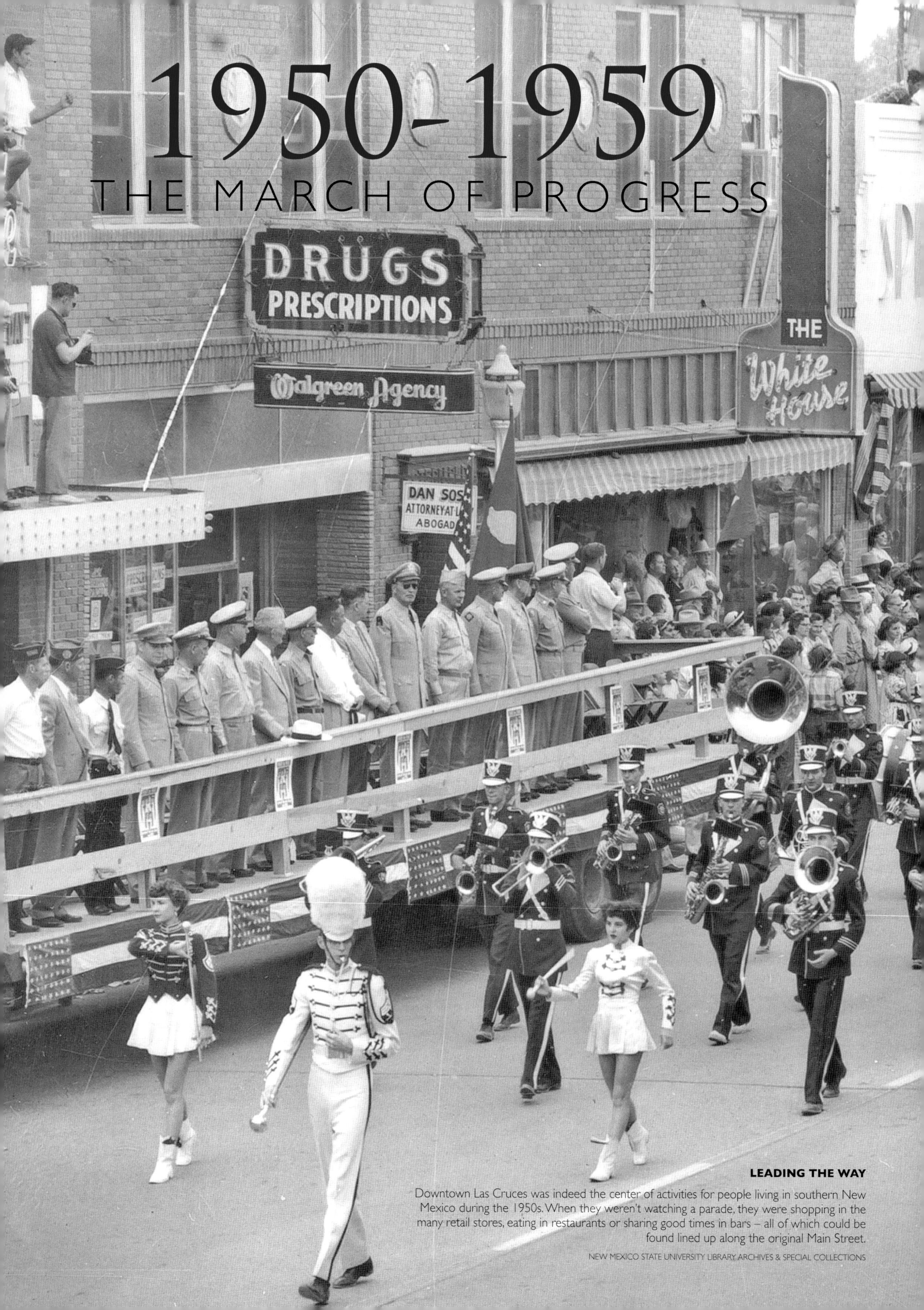

LEADING THE WAY

Downtown Las Cruces was indeed the center of activities for people living in southern New Mexico during the 1950s. When they weren't watching a parade, they were shopping in the many retail stores, eating in restaurants or sharing good times in bars – all of which could be found lined up along the original Main Street.

NEW MEXICO STATE UNIVERSITY LIBRARY ARCHIVES & SPECIAL COLLECTIONS

KARL'S
SHOES
SHOES

THE PLACE TO BE

Main Street was at its prime during the 1950s. Almost anything one needed could be found here, be it a dress at Woolworth's, a fine meal at the Boston Cafe or a movie at the State Theater.

NEW MEXICO STATE UNIVERSITY LIBRARY ARCHIVES

THE NEW WORLD BEGINS

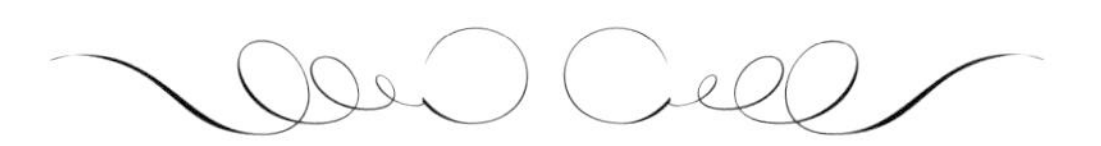

There was a time when Las Cruces and New Mexico State University were still worlds unto themselves, connected by Solano Drive, then just a dirt road.

Bob Porter, who went to what was then New Mexico College of Agriculture & Mechanic Arts from 1948-51, remembers the campus as a close community where everyone knew each other, which was possible considering there were only about 1,200 students attending.

But this was coming on the heels of the first boost of enrollment growth with many first-generation college students attending through the GI Bill. Porter, who would go on to head the New Mexico Farm and Livestock Bureau for many years, attended the agricultural college, which was then still the largest school.

Roland Thomas, son of Electrical Engineering Department Dean Melvin Thomas, lived on campus in a converted surplus Army barrack, and he said the children of faculty didn't intermingle much with the kids in town – Las Cruces was a three-mile drive away over dirt roads.

"The kids in town thought they had so much more than us because they had more things to do like going to the movies," Thomas recalled.

That was true – on Main Street in Downtown Las Cruces there were three movie theaters, as well as a number of restaurants, "a lot of bars" and retail stores, especially if one was looking for western wear, said Mary Jane Garcia. There was Popular Dry Goods Co. and Merry-Go-Round for clothes. Just as the railroad had previously established Las Cruces as the dominant community in the area, the Downtown bus station became a central arrival and departure place for those new college students.

With a population of more than 15,000, Las Cruces also offered a hospital. Memorial General Hospital opened April 1950 on the corner of South Alameda Boulevard and Main Street and was built by the city with a $250,000 federal grant.

Growing up in the small village of Doña Ana, Garcia attended Las Cruces Union High School, graduating in 1955. She recalls

1950
Memorial General Hospital opens on South Alameda Boulevard. The city was able to open the hospital through a $250,000 federal grant.

1952
New Mexico A&M men's basketball team makes its first appearance in the NCAA tournament.

1953
Work is completed on the Big Dome at the Evans Solar Facility in the Sacramento Mountains, which would become home to the Sunspot National Solar Observatory. The larger Vacuum Tower would not be proposed until 1958 and would take another 11 years to be built.

1954
Col. John Paul Stapp, "the fastest man on Earth," gets strapped into the rocket sled at Holloman Air Force Base before taking a 421-mph run on Sonic Wind 1.

1954
Las Cruces High School opens. Previously, students attended Las Cruces Union High School in a building at the corner of Alameda Boulevard and Picacho Avenue, which is now home to the Third Judicial District court. At the same time, area municipal and county school systems merge to become the Las Cruces Public Schools district.

NMSU LASC/NEW MEXICO MUSEUM OF SPACE HISTORY/U.S. DEPARTMENT OF TRANSPORTATION/WHITE SANDS MISSILE RANGE/JEFFIE SCHATZABEL NEVAREZ

1950s

Who's Who

Las Cruces Mayors

1949-53 .... Sam Klein
1953-55 .... Mike Apodaca
1955-61 .... James Neleigh

Postmaster

1956 .... Solomon G. Alvarez

NMSU Presidents

1949-55 .... John Branson
1955-70 .... Roger Corbett

Mesilla Mayor

1959-60 .... Albert Fountain

Doña Ana County Sheriffs

1937-40, '49-54 .... Jose M. Viramontes
1954-59 .... Frank Z. Romero

Las Cruces Fire Chief

1958 .... Juan Apodaca

New Mexico Governors

1947-51 .... Thomas J. Mabry
1951-55 .... Edwin L. Mechem
1955-57 .... John F. Simms
1957-59 .... Edwin L. Mechem
1959-61 .... John Burroughs

U.S. Senators

1935-61 .... Dennis Chavez
1949-73 .... Clinton P. Anderson

U.S. Representatives

1949-51 .... John E. Miles
1943-55 .... Antonio Fernandez
1951-57 .... John Dempsey
1957-64 .... Joseph Montoya
1959-69 .... Thomas Morris

Las Cruces Public Schools Superintendent

1954-64 .... Tom Mayfield

White Sands Missile Range Commanders

1947-50 .... Brig. Gen. Philip Blackmore
1950-54 .... Brig. Gen. George Eddy
1954-56 .... Maj. Gen. William Bell
1956-60 .... Maj. Gen. Waldo Laidlaw

By the Numbers

12,325 .... Las Cruces population (1950)
39,557 ... Doña Ana County population (1950)
$3,210 .... Average annual income (1950)
$5,010 .... Average annual income (1959)
75 cents .... Minimum wage (1950)
$1.00 .... Minimum wage (1956)
18 cents .... Gallon of gasoline (1950)
25 cents .... Gallon of gasoline (1959)
3 cents .... First-class stamp (1950)
4 cents .... First-class stamp (1959)
12 .... Schools in Las Cruces (1950)
16 .... Schools in Las Cruces (1959)
$1,510 .... Average new car (1950)
65.9 degrees .... Average temperature (1950)
66.4 degrees .... Average temperature (1959)

In the News

1950: Along with UN forces, the United States comes to the aid of South Korea after it is invaded by communist North Korea.

1951: Color television is introduced.

Dec. 5, 1952: A deadly layer of thick smog engulfs London, killing 8,000 people before it finally clears.

July 27, 1953: Armistice is signed, ending the Korean War.

December 1953: The first Playboy Magazine is published, with nude photos of Marilyn Monroe.

May 6, 1954: Roger Bannister is the first man to run the mile in less than four minutes.

July 17, 1955: Disneyland opens.

Sept. 9, 1956: In his first appearance on the "Ed Sullivan Show," Elvis Presley's hip gyrations are so disturbing that only his upper torso was shown.

Sept. 26, 1956: Work officially begins on the new national system of interstate highways.

1957: Dr. Seuss publishes "The Cat in the Hat."

Jan. 1, 1959: Gen. Fulgencio Batista flees Cuba, leading to Fidel Castro's takeover.

1955
At White Sands Proving Ground, a Nike Hercules prototype liquid propulsion system test triggers an explosion that caves in the wall of a reinforced concrete control room, killing one and injuring five.

1957
Work is completed on Interstate 10, making Las Cruces far less isolated from Texas and Arizona. Work on Interstate 25 heading north to Albuquerque from Las Cruces began soon after, but wouldn't reach all the way up to Wyoming until 1969.

1958
White Sands Proving Ground is officially renamed White Sands Missile Range.

1959
At Holloman Air Force Base, NASA begins training a 3-year-old chimpanzee nicknamed HAM (Holloman Aerospace Medical) for space flight. To his handlers, chimp No. 65 was known as Chop Chop Chang. A year and half later, he would be launched into space on a Mercury rocket.

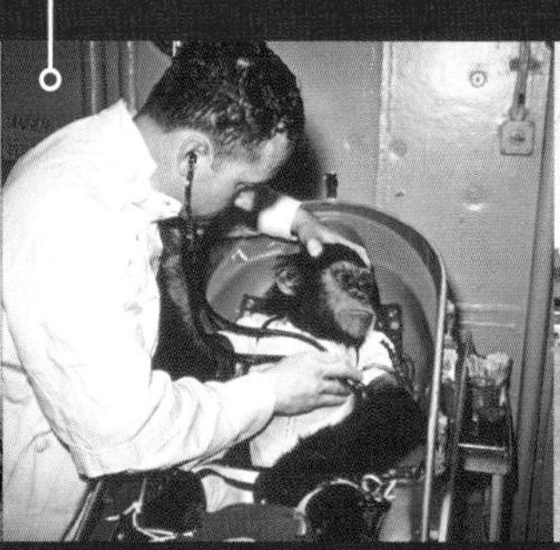

1959
Voters pass a state constitutional amendment to change the name of New Mexico A&M to New Mexico State University.

THROUGH HIS EYES

Astronomer Clyde W. Tombaugh, famous for his discovery of Pluto, looks through one of the telescopes he made in his backyard. He started his tenure as a professor at New Mexico A&M in 1955.

NMSU LASC

those days fondly – a Southwest version of the TV show "Happy Days." A young person with a pocket full of change could buy a comic book, lollipop and go see a movie.

While Downtown was the place to shop, cruising Main Street seemed to always lead to the Shamrock Drive-In restaurant on the north end, she said.

"Everybody went there," Garcia said of the Shamrock Drive-In. "Their tacos were really good."

On Sundays, after church let out, people would often take a trip to cross the one bridge into Juárez, Mexico, where there was plenty of shopping at the mercado for bargains on serapes and huaraches, or taking in the spectacle of the bullfight. The excursions would always be finished off by hitting the many nightclubs, such as the Crystal Palace and the Caverns.

"We had so much fun," Garcia said. "We were always planning on what to do Sunday."

A CROWN OF COTTON

In terms of agriculture in those days, cotton was king with Roundtree Cotton Co. on Picacho Avenue being the main shipper, Bob Porter recalled.

To pick the cotton, the farmer would bring in Braceros, who were contracted agricultural workers from Mexico.

After graduating from New Mexico A&M in 1951, Porter went to work for the Doña Ana County Farm Bureau as an assistant director during which he administered the Bracero Program for two years. The Doña Ana program was the largest with 6,000 Braceros during the cotton season. About 500 braceros were transported daily between Rio Vista, a processing center in Socorro, Texas, and Las Cruces. At the reception center, the braceros were medically examined and given time to clean up and rest from their trips.

However, once mechanization became available to pick cotton, the farmers quickly made the switch and the Bracero Program became history in about a year's time, Porter said.

Meanwhile, Las Cruces was beginning to grow. When Porter bought his first home, there were only three homebuilders to choose from – Dale Bellamah, C.B. Smith and Sons and Atlas Lumber. The lumber company had four home plans to choose from: A, B, C and D. "I chose D because I was so damn poor," Porter said.

A NEW DAWN

On the other side of the Organ Mountains, technology was progressing with White Sands Proving Ground and Holloman Air Force Base testing increasingly more advanced systems, especially those involving rockets. Laying the ground work for the space program, Holloman hosted animals that would be flown into space aboard early rockets, such as mice, dogs and chimps.

Back at New Mexico A&M, there was a new influx of students, this time the result of the GI Bill from the Korean War. Many of those returning veterans were from the school's ROTC program. Depending on the luck of the draw during registration, those male students registering first filled up the available Air Force ROTC program slots quickly, leaving the rest to take Army ROTC. Many of those in the Army ROTC didn't make it back home from the Korean War, while nearly all the Air Force ROTC members survived their tours of duty. As a result, many of them arrived more interested in the engineering program than agriculture and talk began about changing the school's name to New Mexico State University.

A DAY AT THE GIN

A popular hangout for teenagers in Doña Ana County was the cotton gin on the west side of town. Right, childhood friends Irene Barela and Mary Jane Garcia, who became a longtime state senator, would sit atop the bales with their friends. They would watch others jump from bale to bale in a contest see who could jump the farthest.

MARY JANE GARCIA

MISSILE DEVELOPMENT

Research at White Sands Missile Range included a full-scale, flight-type Army Sergeant missile installed for a transonic test program in the 16-foot propulsion wind tunnel at the Air Force Arnold Engineering Development Center in late 1959. The tactical missile was about 30 feet long.

U.S. AIR FORCE ARNOLD ENGINEERING DEVELOPMENT CENTER

TEST LAUNCH

An unguided Aerobee rocket takes off from Holloman Air Force Base. Not as heavy as the V-2, the Aerobee was used for upper atmosphere research.

NEW MEXICO MUSEUM OF SPACE HISTORY

OFFICERS' WIVES CLUB

The White Sands Officers' Wives Club visits Launch Complex 33 in 1951. Though military officers' wives clubs were originally social clubs, the organizations eventually evolved into volunteer organizations.

WHITE SANDS MISSILE RANGE PUBLIC AFFAIRS OFFICE

THE HEART OF LAS CRUCES

In the heart of Las Cruces, St. Genevieve's Catholic Church was the only Catholic church in Las Cruces for more than 100 years. Many Las Crucens – and their parents and grandparents – were baptized, given their first holy communion and married in the church. The church building was deemed unstable and was eventually condemned. It was demolished in the 1960s.

NMSU LASC

WHITE SPORTCOATS

Right, Albert and Henry Lucero, pose for the camera during a wedding at St. Genevieve's.

DOLORES CONNOR

FEAST DAY

Members of the San José Catholic Church celebrate Feast Day. A sanctuary in La Mesa, N.M., San José Catholic Church was constructed in 1853 and is listed on the National Register of Historic Places.

ISELA ALVAREZ

FIRST COMMUNION

Lorraine Bustamante takes her first communion at the San José Catholic Church in La Mesa in the early 1950s. In a tradition that is still carried on by some Catholics, she holds rosary beads and a prayer book, gifts she most likely received that day, and wears an elegant white dress and veil. In the past, communions were often occasions for large family gatherings that would last into the evening.

ISELA ALVAREZ

SCHOOL IS IN SESSION

Students at Holy Cross School in 1958 watch the priest perform a ceremony. Church schools would become some of the city's strongest private schools.

NMSU LASC/ALICE WARD

TEMPLE BETH-EL

The building that houses Temple Beth-El and the one that housed it in the past are simple, manmade structures, in which the congregation worships, studies, socializes and observes important events.

"It is wonderful to have a sanctuary, a social hall, a kitchen and classrooms," said Gerald Kane, Rabbi Emeritus of Temple Beth-El, "but the history of the dedication of a handful of Jews to raising their children in their tradition did not begin in any building."

Jewish families early in the history of Las Cruces began settling first as merchants. Over time, White Sands Missile Range and New Mexico State University brought more Jewish families to the area.

"Many of them traveled to El Paso's Congration B'nai Zion and Temple Mount Sinai as places to worship," Kane said. "Others wished to share with their children the precepts of Judaism in Las Cruces."

In 1953, the group established a Jewish school that met on Sundays. Teaching guides and curricula were gleaned from a trip to New York by one of the dedicated members, Kane said. To help establish the synagogue, a rabbi from El Paso traveled to the Mesilla Valley, consecrating on the first religious school class – 26 children – which met in the yards of two of the families.

At various times the religious school met at Branigan Library, the Corbett Center or at a space above the Popular Dry Goods store. For many years, congregants served as lay rabbis, performing b'nai mitzvahs ceremonies, officiating at High Holy Day services and doing whatever else they could to serve the growing Jewish community. It took about 20 years before those stalwart Jewish families were able to build a sanctuary/classrooms, then a social hall and kitchen. Later, separate classrooms were added.

"We can sense the pride these families had in the first building, even after we have to move on to the new building," Kane said. "The building on Parker Road, which currently houses Holy Family (Ecumenical Catholic) Church, will always be a symbol of the determination of a number of Jewish families to do their part for the growth of Judaism in general, and especially in Las Cruces."

Members of the Sisterhood were involved in fundraising. Deli dinners that became famous in Las Cruces led to what was known as "The Gala."

"It seems that the Jews, like Jews everywhere, knew that the way to the hearts of the townspeople was through their stomachs," Kane said.

"There are many people to thank for being such pioneers in establishing a Jewish community here. Many are still with us, no doubt kvelling at the traditions they established; many have moved on and remain in our memories as founding fathers and mothers of Temple Beth-El."

Past rabbis of Temple Beth-El have included Rabbi Joseph Klein, Rabbi Howard O. Laibson, Rabbi Cyril S. Stanway, Rabbi Emeritus Gerald M. Kane, Rabbi Paul Citrin and current Rabbi Lawrence P. Karol.

BUILDING ON SUCCESS

When Eddie Binns began studying civil engineering at New Mexico College of Agriculture and Mechanic Arts in 1955, the young man already had a lot of building experience under his belt from his youth working on houses in Portales and Roswell, N.M.

Realizing he had a knack for reading blueprints and understanding numbers, Binns chose to study civil engineering. When he arrived at what was then New Mexico A&M, the engineering faculty included all the originals – Daniel "Dad" Jett, Frank Bromilow and John Clark.

"The way civil engineering was taught then was much more broad-based," he said.

Binns would work 20 to 30 hours a week with homebuilder C.B. Smith and Sons in addition to his studies.

By the time he graduated in 1957, he had married a local girl – Bernice, a young lady whom he met when she was a waitress at the City Center Drug Store in Las Cruces, which also was the big political hangout in its day. The couple would have two sons and two daughters.

A MAN WITH A PLAN ... MAKE THAT PLANS

Eddie Binns, who would go on to become one of the main developers in the city, holds plans for a subdivision.

TODD DICKSON

He continued working for C.B. Smith, who took part in building several of the city's first suburban neighborhoods, including the Alameda Terrace subdivision with about 30 houses.

Homebuilding was also a lot simpler then, with few subcontractors. In 1958, builders decided to work together in areas such as government policies and home financing. C.B. Smith joined fellow former schoolteacher Lou Emerick along with Rupert Chisholm and Roy Moore to create the Las Cruces Home Builders Association.

One of the early victories for the association was changing how gross receipts tax (GRT) was charged, he said. Instead of charging GRT on every transaction during the building of a home, GRT was charged for the whole home upon completion, he said.

In 1963, Binns left C.B. Smith, where he been general manager.

"It was time for me to venture out on my own," Binns said.

Binns became one of the primary developers in Las Cruces. He started with apartments and modest housing developments near New Mexico State University. As the developments grew, he started other companies to supply the projects with concrete, rock and gravel, road building and homeowners insurance. He even became a licensed real estate agent and president of the Las Cruces Association of Realtors (LCAR). Binns also has sat on the boards of a local bank and El Paso Electric Co.

Binns has divested himself of many of the side businesses, including a winery he describes as a "hobby that got out of hand." But his main passion of building homes and commercial properties remains.

While many of his most recent developments are apartment complexes in the High Range area off Roadrunner Parkway, Binns said a housing development called Mesa Heights was the most rewarding to him. It included 100 homes and was intended for low-income, first-time buyers. These families could acquire the homes through "sweat equity" by helping to build their homes.

"I can't tell you how many times people from that project have come up to me and given me a big hug and say, 'Thanks to you I bought my first home for $12,000 and was able to sell it for $60,000,'" he said. "I'd have to say that has been the most rewarding project for me."

In 2011, LCAR bestowed upon Binns its prestigious Lifetime Achievement Award, which it had only given out twice before in its 50-plus-year history.

"That gives him the Triple Crown," said LCAR CEO Isaac Chavez. "He was LCAR president, Realtor of the Year and now Lifetime Achievement."

Binns, who was 77 at the time of the award, said he might retire in another 20 years.

BUILDING A FAMILY

Fay Hilley, Terry Hilley Jr., Glenda Hilley, and Terry "Ted" Hilley enjoy a quiet moment on a farm in northeast Las Cruces in 1953.

RAYMOND BUMGARNER

PACKAGING PECANS

Below, workers sort through pecans at Stahmann Farms before shipping to locations all over the United States. Pecans grown in the Mesilla Valley are valued for their color and flavor.

NMSU LASC

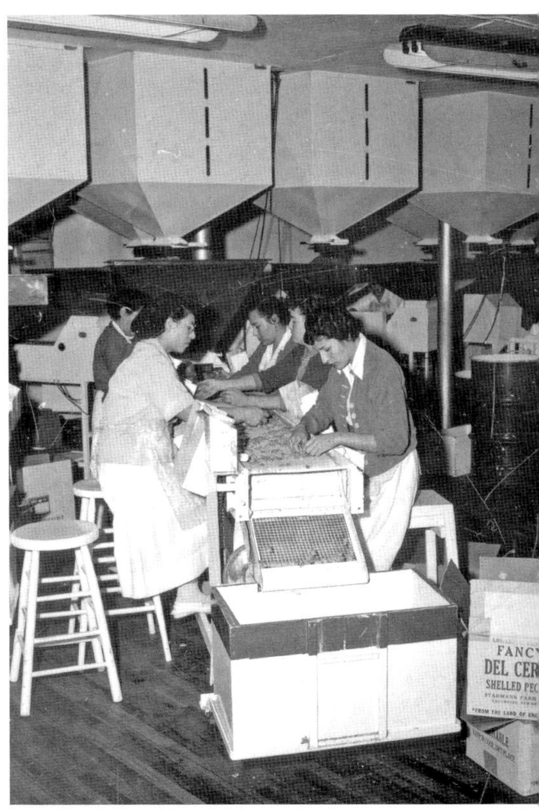

WATCH THE FLOOD

Rains would often bring flooding to the streets of Las Cruces, such as this one in the fall of 1955.

CITY OF LAS CRUCES

AGGIE RODEO TEAM

Competing for the Aggie rodeo team, Gary Schlothauer rides a saddle bronc at the Sheriff's Posse Arena, which was near the intersection of Hadley Avenue and Valley Drive.

JOHN YARBROUGH

THE ORIGINAL HADLEY HALL

Above, this 1953 postcard shows the original Hadley Hall, located at the top of the Horseshoe, which housed administrators. Left, the Rhodes Garret Hamiel dormitory was a place for young women to develop their social skills and make lifelong friendships.

NMSU LASC

PAINTING THE "A"

By the 1950s, whitewashing the "A" on Tortugas Mountain had become a strong tradition for university students.

NMSU LASC

FRATERNITY DANCES

The music changed, and so did the dances as rock 'n' roll made both fashion and dancing styles less formal.

NMSU LASC

GRADUATING CLASS

This group of graduates finished their schooling at New Mexico A&M College in summer 1950.

NMSU LASC

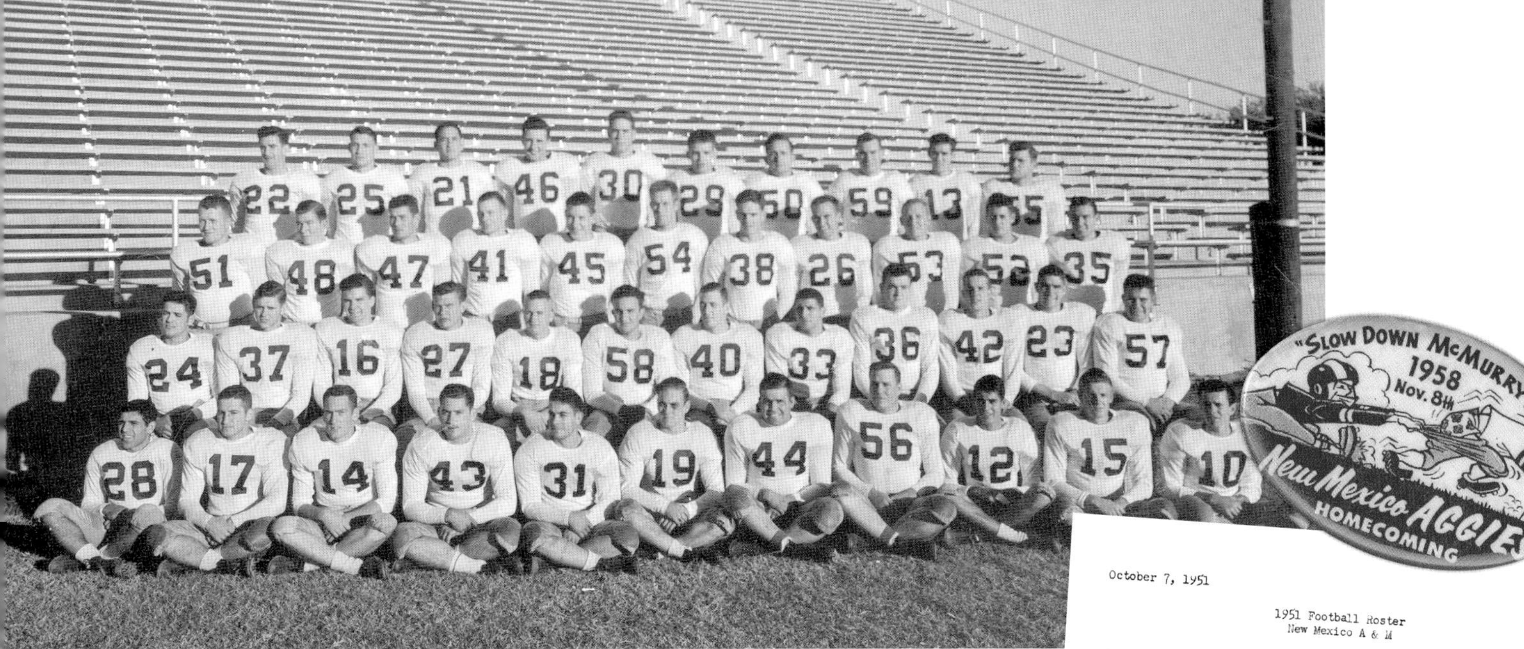

October 7, 1951

1951 Football Roster
New Mexico A & M

No.	Name	Pos.	Ht.	Wt.
10	Bradley, Jimmy C. /L	Halfback	5'7"	148
12	Robertson, Arthur J./S	Halfback	5'8"	145
13	Parsons, Russell L. /L	End	6'	165
14	Sanford, Charles W. /L	Quarterback	5'10"	160
15	Presley, Clark L. /L	Quarterback	5'9"	168
16	Aderhold, Jon R.	Guard	6'	165
17	Herbet, Al J.	Halfback	5'7"	160
18	Lujan, Lawrence S./L	Halfback	5'11"	165
19	Jacobs, Harold L.	Halfback	5'6"	155
21	Cervantes, Orlando /L	End	6'	170
22	DiCarlo, Al	Halfback	5'11"	185
23	Price, Ronald D.	End	6'	175
24	Navar, Macedonio /L +/S	Fullback	5'8"	180
25	Christie, Drew /L +/S	Guard	5'10"	170
26	Ward, Calvin Herb 2L	Tackle	6'	184
27	Carlson, Gordon W. /L +/S	Guard	5'11"	175
28	Tamuty, Don /L	Halfback	5'8"	150
29	Wicker, Clabe	Tackle	6'	185
30	Juen, Richard P. /S-/L	End	6'3"	185
31	Rice, Dawrance /L	Guard	5'7"	150
32	Armagnac, Raul	Guard	5'9"	184
33	Haiman, Fred	Halfback	5'7"	167
36	Brown, (Buster) J.H.	Center	5'11"	190
37	Hayes, Jimmy R. /L	Halfback	6'1"	184
38	Jeffers, Jaime /S	Center	6'1"	190
40	Gantz, Dale	Guard	5'10"	195
41	Graves, Jimmy /L	Tackle	6'3"	189
42	Reddick, H. James /S	Quarterback	6'	160
43	Duncan, Maurice /L	Guard	5'11"	190
44	Parkman, Wm. S. /L	Guard	5'8"	190
45	Boykin, Wm. Edward /L	End	6'2"	189
46	Jones, Fred /S	End	6'2"	185
47	Parker, Omer /L +/S	End	6'	174
48	Matthews, Gerald L. /S-/L	Center	6'	184
50	Pufal, Robert /S	Center	6'	190
51	Thompson, John A. /L +/S	Tackle	6'2"	225
52	Hill, Wm. Frank /L	Tackle	5'11"	210
53	Hill, Clay H. /S + /L	Tackle	6'	205
54	Andrews, Dick	Tackle	6'3"	200
55	Shaffer, Bill -/-L	Guard	5'10"	190
56	Paul, Leslie	Tackle	6'	207
57	Porter, Ben H. /L	Tackle	5'11"	228
58	Ortega, Joe	Guard	5'11"	210
59	Mounce, Bill /L	Guard	6'	200

Managers -- Roy Wolven
Charles Styron

Athletic Director -- George C. McCarty -- New Mexico A & M
Head Football Coach -- Joe T. Coleman -- TCU
Assistant Coaches -- Jim Patton -- Oklahoma A & M
Ray Evans -- Texas Western
Harvey Gabrel -- Texas Western

A TEAM OF WINNERS

The 1951 New Mexico A&M football team included Jimmy Bradley, who would become one of the winningest high school coaches in New Mexico. Below, the team would play at the original Memorial Stadium, the location of one of the busiest parking lots on the modern campus. The tower, below right, which served as the press box, became part of the College of Health and Human Services in the 2000s.

NMSU LASC

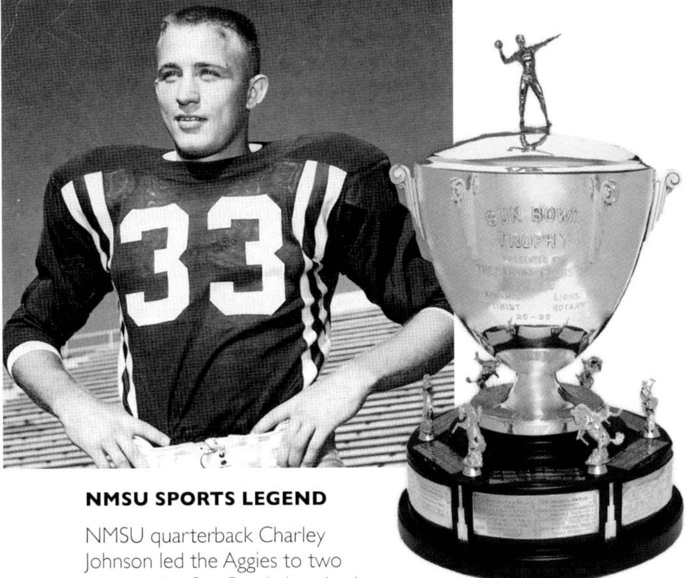

NMSU SPORTS LEGEND

NMSU quarterback Charley Johnson led the Aggies to two consecutive Sun Bowl victories in 1959 and '60. The 1960 Aggie footballers were undefeated at 11-0. Johnson went on to play 15 years in the NFL and was an All-Pro quarterback. Johnson's No. 33 is the only football jersey number to be retired by NMSU.

NMSU LASC

YOUNG AND OLD AT PLAY

Left, members of the Mesilla Park Reds in 1958. Below, the La Mesa Elementary School basketball players from the 1950s, are identified as Reymundo Guerra, Florencio, Raul T., Ricardo G., Silvestre G. and Sammy Telles.

MARISA LUCERO

LA MESA BLUE JAYS

Above left, the La Mesa Blue Jays semi-pro baseball team, in this photo from the 1950s, included, front row: Walter Lewis, Charlie Smith, George Garcia, J.L. Esslinger Jr., Chope Benavidez and Robert Benavidez. The little boy is unidentified. Second row: Roy Lewis, Armando Enriquez, Rudy Estrada, Chico Gonzales, "Chickie" Lopez, Junior Fernandez and J.B. Gutierrez. Back row: unidentified, Lauro Guaderrama, unidentified, Sammy Vargas, Joe Apodaca, "Doc" Humphries and unidentified. Above right, after more than a half century, several members of the La Mesa Bluejays baseball team gathered in the 2000s for a reunion. They are, left to right, Chalo Garcia, Luis Jimenez, Augustin Tellez, George Ybarra, Gonzalo Perez, Kiko Rivas, Lauro "Larry" Guaderrama, J.L. Esslinger, George Garcia, Manuel Leyva, Sal Gonzales, Johnny Acosta and Ruben Torres.

PATRICIA ESSLINGER/MANUEL LEYVA

EN ROUTE TO THE AGGIE HALL OF FAME

Williams Gym on the New Mexico A&M campus in 1953 was a training ground for future hall of famers. The Aggie basketball team that year featured, standing, Harry Guthmuller, Richard Juen, Kenneth Dann and James Brockman. Kneeling are Michael Daugherty, Coach Presley Askew and Lou Henson. Askew also coached baseball, and was named to the Aggie Hall of Fame in 1970. The Aggie baseball stadium is named for Askew. Henson later coached the Aggies for two highly successful stints – 1966-75 and 1997-2005 – and was named to the Aggie Hall of Fame in 1978. The Aggie basketball floor is named Lou Henson Court.

LOU HENSON

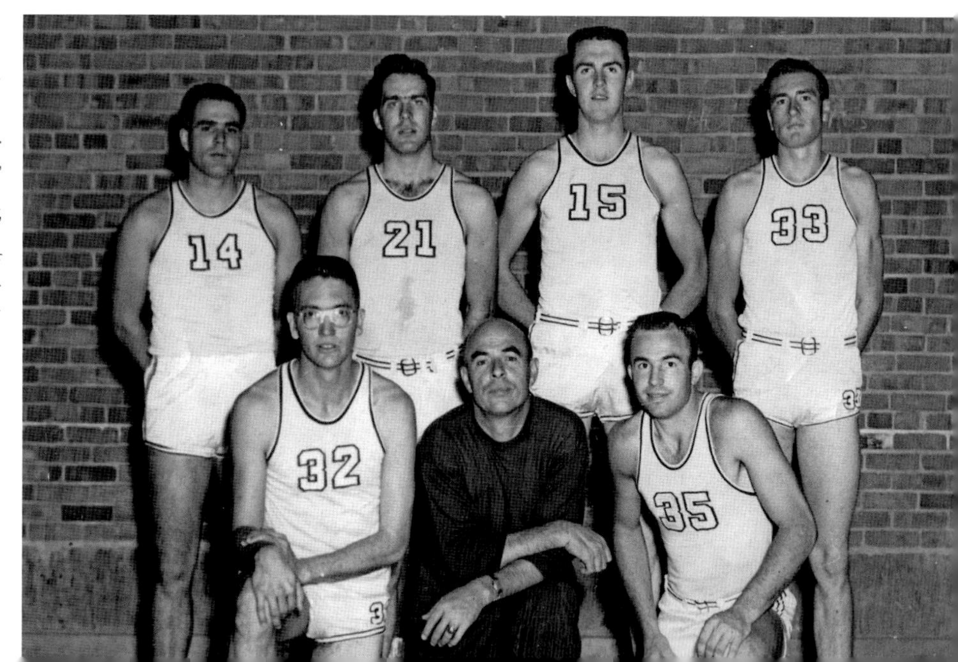

STUDENT LIFE

Above, left to right, Apolonio Melendrez, Reuben Vanegas, Moises Garcia and Arturo Garcia stand in front of Nuestra Señora de la Candelaria in Doña Ana. Priscilla Barrio gets ready to perform in the Las Cruces High School marching band. Irene Barela and Mary Jane Garcia sit outside of Las Cruces Union High School. Presley Askew Jr. gets ready to shoot in 1955.

MARY JANE GARCIA/BARRIO FAMILY/MARY JANE GARCIA/CROSSES

SECOND GRADE

Sitting in the second row, fourth from the left, in this MacArthur Elementary class photo is Dolores Lucero Connor, who later served as a city councillor from 2003-11.

DOLORES CONNOR

C.S. CONLEE

The 1955 Las Cruces High School yearbook The Crosses was dedicated to Conlee. "We dedicate this 1955 Crosses to a man who has served the Las Cruces School System for 21 years, Mr. C.S. Conlee. In 1933 Mr. Conlee came to Las Cruces as Superintendent of the Las Cruces Municipal Schools, and in 1937 he became Superintendent of the High School. Mr. Conlee served as Superintendent until July 1, 1954 when he retired.

NORMA JEAN GAYDER

WHITE SANDS SCHOOL

Right, first-graders are on their way to class at the White Sands School in 1953. Below, a song fest is held in the auditorium of the new elementary and junior high school at White Sands Proving Ground on the first day of classes.

WHITE SANDS MISSILE RANGE PUBLIC AFFAIRS OFFICE

SOUTH MAIN STREET

This aerial photo shows Downtown Las Cruces at the end of the 1950s. Visible in the photo are the original Doña Ana County Courthouse, Memorial General Hospital and the Sisters of Loretto Academy.

NMSU LASC

MEMORIAL GENERAL

The nursing graduating class of Las Cruces Memorial General Hospital in 1953. On the bottom row, second from right, is Dolores Archuleta, who would become a Las Cruces city councillor, serving from 2001 to 2009.

DOLORES ARCHULETA

DADDY BOB

Daddy's home from work – a classic scene from 1950s America. Bob Schatzabel, who worked for Prudential Insurance in Las Cruces in 1957, had recently earned the Distinguished Service Award from the Jaycees. Greeting him are his wife Sybil, oldest daughter Jeffie and his younger children, Patci and Skip. Schatzabel, a native of Brooklyn, N.Y., came to Las Cruces after World War II to go to college on the GI Bill. In 1947 and 1948, he was the starting quarterback for the Aggie football team. He remained an Aggie faithful, serving with the Aggie Alumni and Booster Association.

JEFFIE SCHATZABEL NEVAREZ

HERE ARE THE KEYS

Las Cruces car dealer Jeff Hooker hands the keys for a new 1959 Plymouth Savoy to Doña Ana County Sheriff's Deputy Max Corn. Hooker Motors was on Main Street, near the current location of My Brother's Place restaurant.

DAVID CORN

POLICE FORCES

The 1950s marked a growing professionalism in policing. With the addition of patrol cars, officers could be more mobile than the foot patrolman of old.

NMSU LASC

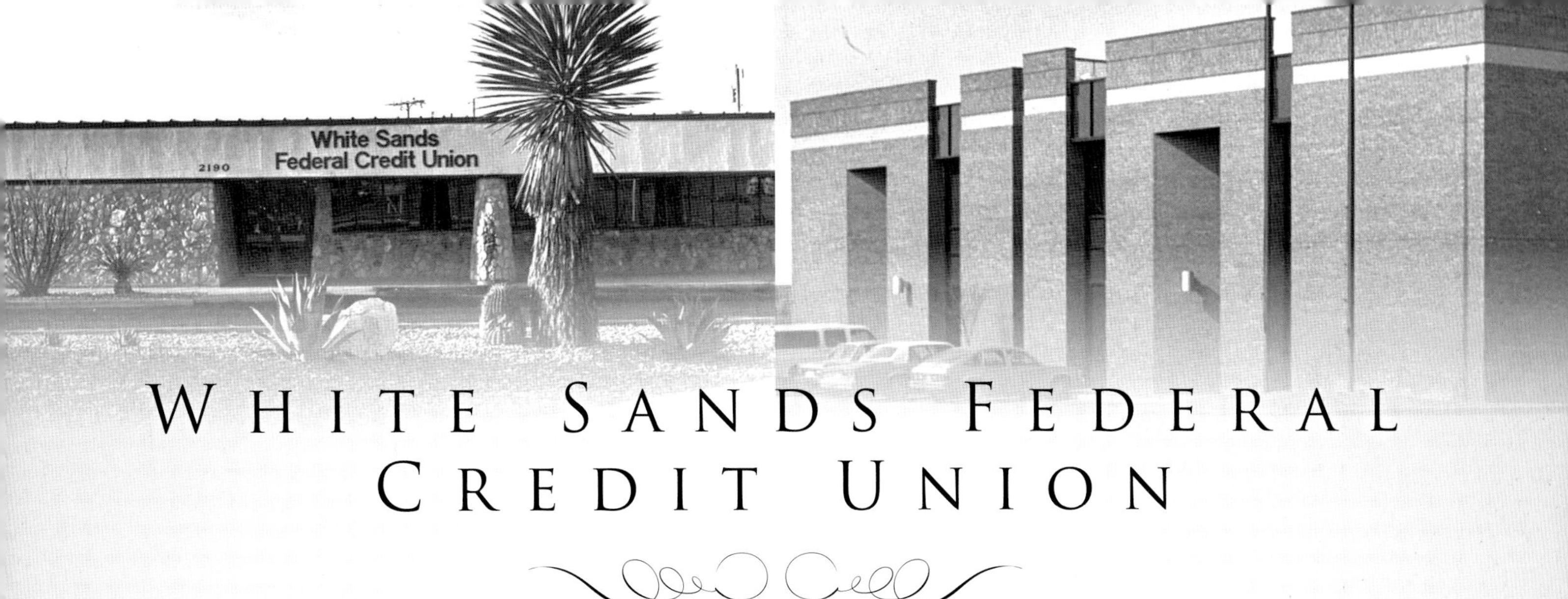

WHITE SANDS FEDERAL CREDIT UNION

White Sands Proving Ground was established in the New Mexico desert in 1945. A few years later, in 1952, a group of military personnel working there established White Sands Federal Credit Union.

The credit union started with a mere 17 shares and $85 in assets.

Over the next half century and beyond, the credit union continued to grow, and by 2011 had grown to more than $237 million in assets. Membership was more than 26,000.

Between 1952 and 2011, dedicated people made a lot of things happen to contribute to the growth.

In 1962, 10 years after its formation, the credit union hired its first paid employee, a part-timer.

Another decade later, in 1972, White Sands FCU hired its first full-time manager, Charles Eagle. The year ended with 5,783 members and assets up to $6.7 million.

By 1976, credit union membership had grown to 9,200 and assets to $14 million. In 1977, White Sands FCU merged with the employees' credit union of the City of Las Cruces and Doña Ana County. The same year, Memorial General Hospital's employees' credit union joined the membership. The additions grew White Sands FCU membership to more than 14,000. A year later, the credit union's first in-house computer facility was installed.

The national economic recession in 1979-80 had an impact on White Sands FCU. To combat inflation, the Federal Reserve Board clamped down on the money supply, which caused interest rates to rise and consumer spending and business borrowing to abruptly decline. White Sands FCU was paying 7 percent on share accounts in 1979. In 1980, the Depository Institutions Deregulation and Monetary Control Act was passed, which eliminated deposit interest rate limitations. White Sands FCU reached $22.6 million in assets.

In the mid-1980s, White Sands FCU added an ATM and VISA credit cards, as membership approached 19,000 and assets of $40 million. By 1992, White Sands FCU opened a second location, had more than 24,000 members and $81 million in assets.

In 1993, due to downsizing at White Sands Missile Range, the credit union saw its first decline in membership and assets. But by 1995, rapid growth shot membership up to nearly 30,000 and assets rose from $82 million to $140 million.

Remote and electronic services came in 1996, including a website with online banking and debit cards.

Accolades arrived in 2008, as Bancography Brand Value Index designated the credit union fourth best in the nation with assets less than $1 billion. A year later, White Sands FCU topped them all, earning the No. 1 ranking in the same category.

That small organization with $85 in assets in 1952 grew and prospered along with Las Cruces and the state of New Mexico, and became one of the most successful operations of its kind in the nation. In 2012, as New Mexico turns 100, White Sands Federal Credit Union celebrates its 60th anniversary.

IT GROWS AS IT GOES

White Sands Federal Credit Union began with a handful of military personnel and $85. A half century later, the credit union had multiple locations, tens of thousands of members and was ranked No. 1 in the country for its size.

WHITE SANDS FEDERAL CREDIT UNION

A MAIN STREET NIGHT OUT

Main Street Las Cruces lighted at Christmas time in the 1950s.

OLIVIA MCDONALD

IN SONG AND A JOYOUS MORNING

The Zeta Tau Alpha sorority, left, showcased their talent and beauty in their Styleshow, sponsored by local businesses. Right, at Christmastime, the young Flanagans enjoy real toys for real boys.

NMSU LASC

DRESSING UP AND SPINNING OUT

From a Mesilla fiesta to rockin' and rollin' at the roller skating rink to the Grandview Elementary School festival, Las Cruces has been a place honoring traditions and making new ones.

NMSU LASC

BLASTING OUT THE TUNES

Below, calling themselves the Varsity Eleven, this band from New Mexico A&M charged "only $125" for dances on campus. "The large instrumentation made it possible to produce the beauty and tonal balance that modern dance arrangements called for."

BARBARA HUBBARD

HANGING OUT

Above left, George Barrio and his brother Antonio on Antonio's first day of school at Lucero Elementary. Left, Doña Ana teens hanging out at Las Cruces Union High School. Bottom left, Doña Ana students, including Mary Jane Garcia, wait in front of Doña Ana Elementary School for the bus to Las Cruces Union High School.

BARRIO FAMILY/MARY JANE GARCIA

FRAT FELLAS AND 'MOM'

Members of the SAE fraternity pose for a group photo in 1951, accompanied by the beloved "Mom" Stevens, center.

BARBARA HUBBARD

MAKING A SPLASH

The Laabs Pool on Picacho Avenue was the main gathering place for young people on hot summer days. It was one of the first large outdoor municipals pools to be built in Las Cruces. By the 2000s, the pool systems had become too antiquated to maintain, so the building was razed.

BARBARA HUBBARD

FRIENDS, FASHION AND FUN

Left to right, Priscilla Gamboa poses in her '50s poodle skirt. 1955-56 officers of Future Homemakers of America at Las Cruces High School Ann Hedrick, Jean Kersey, Rita Gay Staten, Shan Stedronsky and Alice Valentine get all dressed up. A Mission Bell fashion model stands in front of "Josefina's Gate," a popular landmark in Mesilla. Louis, Carolina, Antonio and George Barrio, Priscilla Gamboa and Priscilla Barrio visit White Sands.

BARRIO FAMILY/ALICE WARD/NMSU LASC/BARRIO FAMILY

A TRADITION OF CARING

The heart and soul of a hospital is the people who work there, according to Paul Herzog, Chief Executive Officer of Memorial Medical Center.

Just walking through the halls you meet nurses who have worked with the hospital for 40 years, cardiologists who have been a part of medical advancements for 30 years and physical plant engineers who have seen the hospital add stories, new wings and complexes over three decades.

Dr. Bill Einig, who has served as both Chief of Staff and Chair of the board of directors during his 24 years at MMC, said, "We take good care of our employees, and they take good care of the community."

By 2011, MMC had served the people of Las Cruces and Doña Ana County for more than 60 years. It opened in 1950 as Memorial General Hospital at the corner of Alameda Boulevard and Lohman Avenue. When the community hospital was established, the county had a population of 40,000 residents.

In 1971, Memorial General Hospital moved to Telshor Boulevard, and in 1990 changed its name to Memorial Medical Center.

MMC provides inpatient and outpatient diagnostic and therapeutic services. It is home to the Southern New Mexico Family Medicine Residency Program, the only stand-alone community-based program in the state of New Mexico. As of 2011, it has had 63 family medicine residents, 32 of whom have stayed to work in New Mexico.

In the 1990s, the Ikard Radiation Oncology unit opened on campus. Within 20 years, MMC had a comprehensive Cancer Center that includes both Ikard Radiation Oncology and a Medical Oncology/Hematology department.

MMC built the HealthPlex on Northrise Drive in Las Cruces in 1999, providing outpatient surgery, lab and imaging services.

In 2010, MMC expanded cardiac services by adding a third catheterization lab and a dedicated 20-bed, clinician-designed Cardiac Care Unit to meet the growing demand to care for heart patients.

LifePoint Hospitals assumed the lease of MMC in 2004, but the buildings, Herzog said, are owned by the city and county.

"We have a unique relationship, a positive relationship with Doña Ana County and their health care department and the city of Las Cruces in working together to meet the needs of the community," Herzog said. "In many ways, Memorial has stayed a community hospital. It is a community asset. We really have a family atmosphere, ask anyone who works here, it doesn't feel like any other place."

The 2010 Census figures put the number of residents of Las Cruces and Doña Ana County at more than 200,000. MMC's 300 providers offer comprehensive care to all of those residents and many from the surrounding region. The MMC Team is always striving for their mission to "care for our community with compassion and respect."

NMSU LASC/MEMORIAL MEDICAL CENTER

ROADSIDE ATTRACTIONS

In order to attract travelers passing through town, Las Cruces businesses frequently employed clear and bold signage, often accented with neon lights. As of 2011, a group of history-conscious citizens were working on restoring and preserving the Amador Hotel. It's a shame that Molly's Diner still isn't around, or that gas isn't still just 26 cents a gallon.

NMSU LASC/JEFFIE SCHATZABEL NEVAREZ

A MAIN STREET STROLL

Bob Schatzabel strolls across Main Street in 1957. This view of Main Street looks south. Stopped at the crosswalk, at left, the pickup truck is an official Las Cruces Fire Department vehicle. At the right, a State Police car is parked up the street from White's Music Box, the oldest business to still operate Downtown by 2011.

JEFFIE SCHATZABEL NEVAREZ

SHAPING THE LANDSCAPE

The first "skyscraper" to create a skyline in Downtown Las Cruces was the First National Bank Tower. The brainchild of banker and visionary Frank Papen, the tower was built to create much-needed office space for companies associated with NASA and the space industry. Though NASA's presence in New Mexico isn't as large as Papen originally envisioned, the banker fared well for himself and his bank with other groundbreaking businesses, such as the Loretto Shopping Center, the first indoor, climate-controlled mall in New Mexico.

NEW MEXICO STATE UNIVERSITY LIBRARY ARCHIVES AND SPECIAL COLLECTIONS

1960-1969

PEACE, LOVE AND URBAN RENEWAL

A DECADE OF CHANGE

Quickly growing into the largest city in southern New Mexico, Las Cruces thrived with a population of nearly 30,000 in 1960 and anticipated steady growth ahead.

In the heart of Las Cruces, along Downtown Main Street, the Rio Grande Theatre played the latest movies from Hollywood, First National Bank of Doña Ana County served much of the community's banking needs, Las Cruces Furniture Co. had the latest in home décor and the Amador Hotel was still the place to be in the Mesilla Valley.

Martin Campbell Jr., who was born and raised in the hotel during the 1950s, remembers the time fondly. His grandmother was Corina Amador Campbell, who inherited the hotel after the death of her father, Martin Amador, and his wife, Refugio Ruiz de Amador.

"As a kid, I saw it as the social center in Las Cruces," he said. "The only other place to go was the (Las Cruces) Country Club. There were always various things happening at the hotel – many weddings and anniversaries."

Campbell spent his childhood in the hotel up until seventh grade, when he attended boarding school in Santa Fe through high school graduation. He didn't return to the hotel full-time until 1964, when he completed his military service.

By that time, the social center of the Mesilla Valley wasn't as vibrant as it had been just years before.

While all travelers passing through town between Dallas and Los Angeles were led through Main Street in the 1950s, the advent of the interstate system changed that path. Though the interstates that passed through the area were not yet completed, a truck bypass had been constructed west of Main Street. To accommodate travelers, motor hotels, such as the Ramada and the Palms hotels, sprung up in a different part of town. These additional accommodations also provided more venues for entertainment. Consequently, use of the older Downtown hotels began to decline.

"It made a big impact," Campbell said. "To me, we were frozen in time."

As Downtown Main Street businesses were beginning to suffer, First National Bank President Frank Papen had big plans for land just south of the Amador Hotel. Papen had taken the reins of the bank – which had a presence on Main Street since 1906 – with the vision to build the first motor bank in the area, in an entirely different location. He and other investors purchased the land that formerly housed the Loretto Academy immediately south of the Amador Hotel.

"It was the first drive-in bank (in southern New Mexico). It had marble floors, and the vault had the biggest door in southern New Mexico. I was a teller at the time," said John Papen, Frank Papen's nephew, who started working in the bank as teller in 1958. "When Mr. Papen pulled First National Bank (from its original location on Main Street), two-thirds of the merchants (on Main Street) told him he would go broke."

It was quite the opposite. Frank Papen took control of other banks, and First National Bank of Doña Ana County became the largest bank in southern New Mexico with branch offices in other locations around town, at White Sands Missile Range and in Anthony, N.M.

1960
An undefeated New Mexico State University football team earns its second consecutive Sun Bowl victory, beating Utah State 20-13. MVP quarterback Charley Johnson sets a Sun Bowl record for passing accuracy, completing 18 of 26 passes. NMSU finishes the season ranked No. 17.

1962
New Mexico Gov. Ed Mechem – from Las Cruces – signs a proclamation celebrating 50 years of New Mexico's statehood in 1962.

1962
The first drive-up bank in the area, First National Bank of Doña Ana County, opens its new location at 500 S. Main St. Bank President Frank Papen was the man behind the new project, which moved the bank from its northern Main Street location.

1963
White Sands Missile Range assists NASA in its Apollo program, which landed the first person on the moon.

1965
Papen brings the first climate-controlled mall to New Mexico. The Loretto Shopping Center included department stores, a grocery store and a cafeteria, contributing to the decline of businesses farther north on Main Street.

NMSU LASC /JEANETTE FOREMAN/STEVE PARRA

1960s

Who's Who

Las Cruces Mayors

1955-61 .... James F. Neleigh
1961-62 .... Edward R. Gutierrez
1962-63 .... Edward O. Noble
1963-74 .... Thomas J. Graham

Postmaster

1956-79 .... Solomon G. Alvarez

NMSU President

1955-70 .... Roger B. Corbett

Mesilla Mayor

1960-72 .... Nelson Clayshulte Jr.

Doña Ana County Sheriffs

1959-62 .... Alfredo H. Garcia
1963-65 .... Reyes Barela
1965-70 .... Rudolf Gonzales

New Mexico Governors

1959-61 .... John Burroughs
1961-62 .... Edwin L. Mechem
1962-63 .... Tom Bolack
1963-67 .... Jack M. Campbell
1967-71 .... David F. Cargo

U.S. Senators

1935-61 .... Dennis Chavez
1949-73 .... Clinton P. Anderson
1961-63 .... Edwin L. Mechem
1964-77 .... Joseph Montoya

U.S. Representatives

1957-64 .... Joseph Montoya
1959-69 .... Thomas G. Morris
1965-69 .... E. S. Johnny Walker
1969-71 .... Ed Foreman
1969-89 .... Manuel Lujan Jr.

By the Numbers

29,387 .... Las Cruces population (1960)
59,948 .... Doña Ana County population (1960)
$5,600 .... Average annual income
$1.00 .... Minimum wage
25 cents .... Gallon of gas
5 cents .... First-class stamp (1963)
6 cents .... First-class stamp (1968)
$2,600 .... Average new car
$12,700 .... Home value

In the News

Feb. 1, 1960: A nationwide campaign for civil rights is launched after four black students from North Carolina Agricultural and Technical College stage a sit-in at a segregated Woolworth's after they were denied service.

April 17, 1961: An unsuccessful attempt to overthrow Cuba's dictator Fidel Castro is made by U.S. CIA-trained Cuban exiles. Now known as the Bay of Pigs invasion, it takes just three days for the Cuban armed forces to defeat the exiles.

Feb. 20, 1962: American astronaut John Glenn becomes the first U.S. astronaut to orbit the Earth. He orbited the Earth three times, spending a total of four hours and 55 minutes in space.

June 17, 1963: Reciting the "Lord's Prayer" or other Bible verses in public schools is deemed unconstitutional by the U.S. Supreme Court.

Nov. 22, 1963: The country mourns over the death of President John F. Kennedy, who was shot during a motorcade through downtown Dallas. The accused sniper, Lee Harvey Oswald, while in police custody, was killed by Jack Ruby two days later on live national television.

Feb. 25, 1964: Cassius Clay, known to the world as Muhammad Ali, wins the World Heavyweight Championship after defeating Sonny Liston for the title.

Aug. 11, 1964: Race riots in Watts, a neighborhood of Los Angeles, begin, lasting five days. The damage: 34 deaths and property destruction exceeding $200 million.

June 29, 1966: The U.S. begins bombing Vietnam, and sends more than 385,000 troops into South Vietnam.

Oct. 2, 1967: Thurgood Marshall is sworn in as a Supreme Court Justice, becoming the first black member of the court.

April 4, 1968: Civil rights leader Martin Luther King Jr. is assassinated at a Memphis hotel by James Earl Ray.

July 8, 1969: After years of involvement in the Vietnam War, the United States begins withdrawing troops. More than 500,000 troops had been sent overseas to fight, and more than 58,000 were killed in the conflict.

July 20, 1969: Neil Armstrong and Edwin "Buzz" Aldrin become the first to set foot on the moon. The astronauts, along with Michael Collins, were part of NASA's Apollo 11 mission.

1965
Mayfield High School opens. The first phase of the building, costing $937,310, included 37 classrooms. With a new football team, the legendary Cruces-Mayfield rivalry is born.

1966
Lou Henson takes the helm of the NMSU men's basketball program, shaping them into one of the top teams in the nation.

1967
St. Genevieve's Catholic Church, a Downtown anchor since 1859, is torn down. A decision of the Diocese of El Paso, many Las Crucens felt as if "the heart of the city" was taken from them.

1968
The Pan American Center opens on the campus of New Mexico State University.

1969
The New Mexico Department of Game and Fish introduces oryx to the desert on White Sands Missile Range, to enhance the hunting experience. The antelope, which can weigh up to 450 pounds with antlers that average 34 inches long, are brought to the range from the Kalahari Desert in Africa.

A NEW VISION

Because of the bank's success, there was reason to think that retail businesses might also thrive in an area outside of Downtown. Across the street from the bank, land formerly occupied by the Loretto Academy was purchased from the Sisters of Loretto by the Franciscan Fathers in 1947.

The Loretto Corp. – created by Frank Papen and other investors to purchase the land – replaced the dilapidated building with the Loretto Shopping Center. Completed in 1964, the indoor, climate-controlled mall was the first of its kind in New Mexico. In its first phase of construction, Dunlap Department Store, Safeway grocery store and Furr's Cafeteria were among the first tenants to lease space in the mall, John Papen said.

"We used to eat at Furr's two or three times a week," he said. "Everyone went there."

Martin Campbell was a college student at New Mexico State University when the shopping center opened.

"There was a great amount of change," he said. "(Businesses on) Downtown (Main Street) almost immediately began to fail because a lot of consumers would go there. You could park, get out, get your grocery shopping done, clothes, everything. It was all right there."

Frank Papen seemed to be plugged in to the wants and needs of Las Cruces consumers. He was also aware of the needs of the burgeoning space industry and knew there was tremendous opportunity in the desert of New Mexico, John Papen said.

"He was friends with (New Mexico U.S. Sen.) Clinton Anderson, (chair) of the Senate Committee on Aeronautical and Space Sciences," John Papen said. "They wanted NASA to come to New Mexico, but there was no office space."

Frank Papen set out to fix that, he said. According to "Southern New Mexico Empire: The First National Bank of Doña Ana County," a book by Leon Metz, acquiring the Loretto Academy property was all part of Frank Papen's master plan. In 1966, a contract was approved for a $1.9 million, seven-floor office tower, Las Cruces' first and only "skyscraper." Three additional floors would come later in the construction process.

As the "new Downtown" began shifting south and Downtown business began declining in 1968, the idea of "urban renewal" and transforming Main Street into a pedestrian mall was born. Though the mall would not be completed until 1973, the plans were already well in motion in the late 1960s. There were similar plans in dozens of cities throughout the country.

Most businesses decided to "take the money and run," John Papen said. "They could have stayed and kept it alive, but they didn't."

The Campbells who ran the Amador Hotel weren't part of the pedestrian mall, but their business suffered as well.

"All of the bars on Main Street were closed (during urban renewal)," Campbell said. "You would think it would be good for us, but it brought in a rougher, less affluent crowd."

As businesses disappeared from the Downtown area, so did the people.

"It was like a ghost town," Campbell said. "Only a few people would show up, mostly homeless people. I watched (almost) every single business on Main Street go away."

The Campbells also "went away," eventually selling the Amador Hotel building to a group of investors who would create Citizens Bank of Las Cruces in 1970.

The business district shifted south to El Paseo Road, where more businesses would spring up around the Loretto Shopping Center.

"(Urban renewal) just snuck up on us," Campbell said. "It didn't seem like a big deal until it was a big deal, and then it was too late."

WELCOME TO CALHOUN COUNTY

The 1964 pilot "Calhoun: County Agent," starring Jackie Cooper and Barbara Stanwyck, was filmed in and around Las Cruces and Mesilla, but never aired. The process of writing and shooting the pilot is the subject of Merle Miller and Evan Rhodes' book "Only You, Dick Daring!"

NMSU LASC

TIME FOR CHANGE

Talks of urban renewal, a plan to transform the face of Downtown Main Street, began in the late 1960s. The plan would close the road to vehicular traffic to make way for a pedestrian mall. To prepare for a fresh Downtown, City Hall was demolished in 1967, right.

NMSU LASC

NO LONGER THE SOCIAL CENTER

The Amador Hotel was originally the social center of Las Cruces, below, a place for professionals and others to relax and socialize. However, during the 1960s, traffic just didn't come through the inn's doors as it once had. The owner of the hotel, Martin Campbell, finally sold the building, left, in 1970 to the Ikard family. James L. Ikard and Lewis E. Emerick were on the first board of directors of Citizens Bank of Las Cruces, which renovated and occupied the building when the bank started.

NMSU LASC

THE LAST DAYS

Downtown Main Street – from present-day City Hall near Lucero Street to Lohman Avenue – saw its last days of traffic during the 1960s, below. A plan for urban renewal turned Main Street into a pedestrian mall and, eventually, a ghost town.

NMSU LASC

LONE SKYSCRAPER

The 10-story First National Bank tower reshaped the Downtown landscape in Las Cruces when it was completed in 1967. Across Main Street from the tower and the bank was the one-stop shop Loretto Shopping Center. More businesses began popping up around the new shopping center and along El Paseo Road, luring customers away from Downtown Main Street. A drive-in movie theater can be seen in the center of this photo, just below the shopping mall.

NMSU LASC

GROUNDBREAKING BANKING

First National Bank of Doña Ana County President Frank Papen, right, helps break ground for his new banking location. The bank had been located in Downtown Las Cruces since its original opening in the early 1900s. When the new location opened in 1962 farther south on Main Street, it was the first of its kind in the area with four drive-up lanes and the largest vault door in southern New Mexico.

JOHN PAPEN

Moy Surveying Inc.

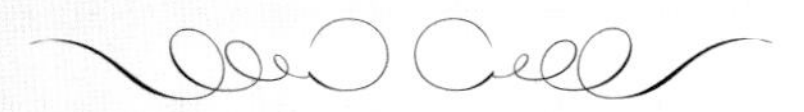

Jorge Moy, founder of Moy Surveying Inc., coined his own personal motto for himself and his company: "It is better to be right twice than wrong once."

His motto follows a principle he said has served him well his entire life: "I believe hard work will pay off in the long run."

Moy started as a surveyor in Las Cruces in 1958, and by 2011, his company was averaging 1,000 surveys per year in Doña Ana County.

Moy was born and raised in Chihuahua, Mexico. In 1957, Moy earned his professional license in Agronomy from the Escuela Particular de Agricultura in Ciudad Juárez.

When he came to Las Cruces, he started all over again, taking surveying classes at New Mexico State University. In 1963, Moy became an American citizen.

"I am blessed because all the people here have treated me very, very well," he said.

Throughout his career, he has done the survey work on some of the most important and iconic buildings in Las Cruces: the Pan American Center, Aggie Memorial Stadium, Corbett Center and the First National Bank Tower (which became the Wells Fargo Tower).

Over the years, Moy has surveyed nearly every building in the Las Cruces Public Schools.

In 1975, Moy earned his New Mexico surveyor's license and established a partnership, B&M Surveys. With B&M, Moy worked on the alignment of multi-rocket launchers for Boeing.

In 1984, Jorge started Moy Surveying Inc. One of his first employees, Kenny Valencia, and several others have worked there for 20 years or more. In 2009, he partnered with Henry Magallanez; both run the company and by 2011 they had 10 employees.

Moy's honors include: the 1996 Realtors' Choice Award, Las Cruces Association of Realtors; 2004 New Mexico Professional Surveyors' Surveyor of the Year award; 2004 Businessman of the Year from the Business Advisory Council of the National Republican Congressional Committee; honorary degree in civil engineering technology from Doña Ana Community College, 2007; and recognition for the degree from the New Mexico Senate, signed by Sen. Mary Jane Garcia, 2007.

Moy's professional associations include: the New Mexico Professional Surveyors; City of Las Cruces Utilities Commission; affiliate member, Las Cruces Real Estate Board; and the Advisory and Development Committee, Doña Ana Community College.

Jorge and Martha married in 1955 and have three daughters – Martha, Concha and Fabi. They also have two granddaughters and two grandsons. Moy said of all his accomplishments, he is most proud of the fact all three of his daughters are graduates of New Mexico State University.

SURVEYOR OF THE YEAR

Jorge Moy has surveyed some of the most important and iconic buildings in Las Cruces.

MOY FAMILY

NOVIOS

Jorge and Martha Moy were married in 1955. They have three daughters.

MOY FAMILY

STANDING OUT IN A CROWD

Miss New Mexico 1968, Karen Jan Maciolek of Albuquerque, entertains those around her as she poses for a photo during a visit to Las Cruces. Her pleasant personality earned her the Miss Congeniality award at the Miss America pageant, one of only two Miss New Mexico contestants to earn the honor. Only one woman from the Mesilla Valley has been crowned with the Miss New Mexico title – Ellen Growden of University Park in 1965.

NMSU LASC

ARTS FOR THE PEOPLE

Above, Joaquin Fore and Harlan McKay rehearse for the Las Cruces Community Theatre production of "The King and I." Right, Beth Ecklenker, John Hadsell, Andy Derenthal, Marina Horton and Patsy White take part in a Vaudeville production by the LCCT. Initially performing in the church yard of St. Genevieve's in 1963, members of the theater cleaned and refurbished the Fountain Theatre in Mesilla for their productions. The Fountain served the LCCT from 1964 to 1977.

JOHN HADSELL

MUSICAL GENIUS

Local musician Bob Burns took his show across the border in 1964, playing his trumpet at the Manhattan Club in Juárez, Mexico, right. He also played trumpet with the Ralph Marterie Orchestra, above, at the New Mexico State University Milton Student Center. Burns remains an active musician in the area, starting the City of Las Cruces "Music in the Park" series, as well as a monthly open mic night at the Rio Grande Theatre.

BOB BURNS

HAIL TO THE CHIEF

President John F. Kennedy, along with New Mexico Congressman Joseph Montoya, left, spent some time shaking hands of White Sands Missile Range personnel during his June 5, 1963, visit to the base. Five months later, on Nov. 22, the president was assassinated, and time stood still for many Americans.

WHITE SANDS MISSILE RANGE PUBLIC AFFAIRS OFFICE

ALL SYSTEMS GO

White Sands Missile Range played a key role in NASA's Apollo program by assisting with test launches and escape module landings, right. Kennedy promised America that a man would set foot on the moon by the end of the 1960s. Though he did not live to see it, the president kept true to his word when Neil Armstrong and Buzz Aldrin of the Apollo 11 mission were the first to set foot on the surface of the moon in 1969.

NMSU LASC

A PLACE TO CALL HOME

After a tumultuous journey from war-torn Indonesia to Holland, the Nicolitz family arrived safely in the United States in 1957. More than 50 years later, much of the family still resides in Las Cruces, including Wanda Nicolitz, bottom right. Not only would she have her own travel agency, but she would become the first lady of Las Cruces when her husband Bill Mattiace was elected mayor in 2003.

WANDA MATTIACE

STATE BOWLING TOURNAMENT

In the early 1960s, the New Mexico State Bowling Tournament came to Las Cruces. This Las Cruces team featured, clockwise from lower left, Charles Lucero, David Corn, Charley West, Fred Lemon and Bill Bohannnon.

CHARLES AND MARY ANN LUCERO

HOMES FOR SALE

Operating his real estate firm out of his motel lobby on West Picacho Avenue, David Steinborn plants a yard sign in a growing Las Cruces neighborhood. This would be the beginning of one of the southwestern United States' most successful real estate firms. Steinborn also became mayor of Las Cruces in the 1970s.

STEINBORN COLLECTION

SAINT PAUL'S "ELDERBERRIES"

The "Elderberries" of St. Paul's United Methodist Church included, front row: Muriel Steele, Jessie Gentry, Mabel Winsler, Callie Freeman and Mae Anderson. Back row: Katherine Jones, Oris Stith, Margaret Taggert, Jessie Patton, Ruth Kilgore and Lettie Buchanan. The Elderberries, usually 55 or older, provide a ministry and fellowship for older members of the church.

ALICE WARD, ST. PAUL'S UNITED METHODIST CHURCH

A NEW SANCTUARY

Construction began on the sanctuary of St. Paul's United Methodist Church in 1965. Heading into 2012, the church remained an anchor in Downtown on Griggs Avenue and Alameda Boulevard, and also hosts many secular events and concerts.

ALICE WARD, ST. PAUL'S UNITED METHODIST CHURCH

DEDICATED TO LAS CRUCES

Though he was vested in El Paso in 1929, Monsignor Walter Caffery spent much of his tenure serving the Las Cruces Catholic community.

JIM BRADLEY

THE HEART OF THE CITY

This photograph was taken the day before St. Genevieve's Church fell victim to a wrecking ball in 1967. "We were married in that church," said Mary Ann Lucero. "I became a Catholic in that church. I went to the last Mass in that church. I cried the whole time."

MARY ANN LUCERO

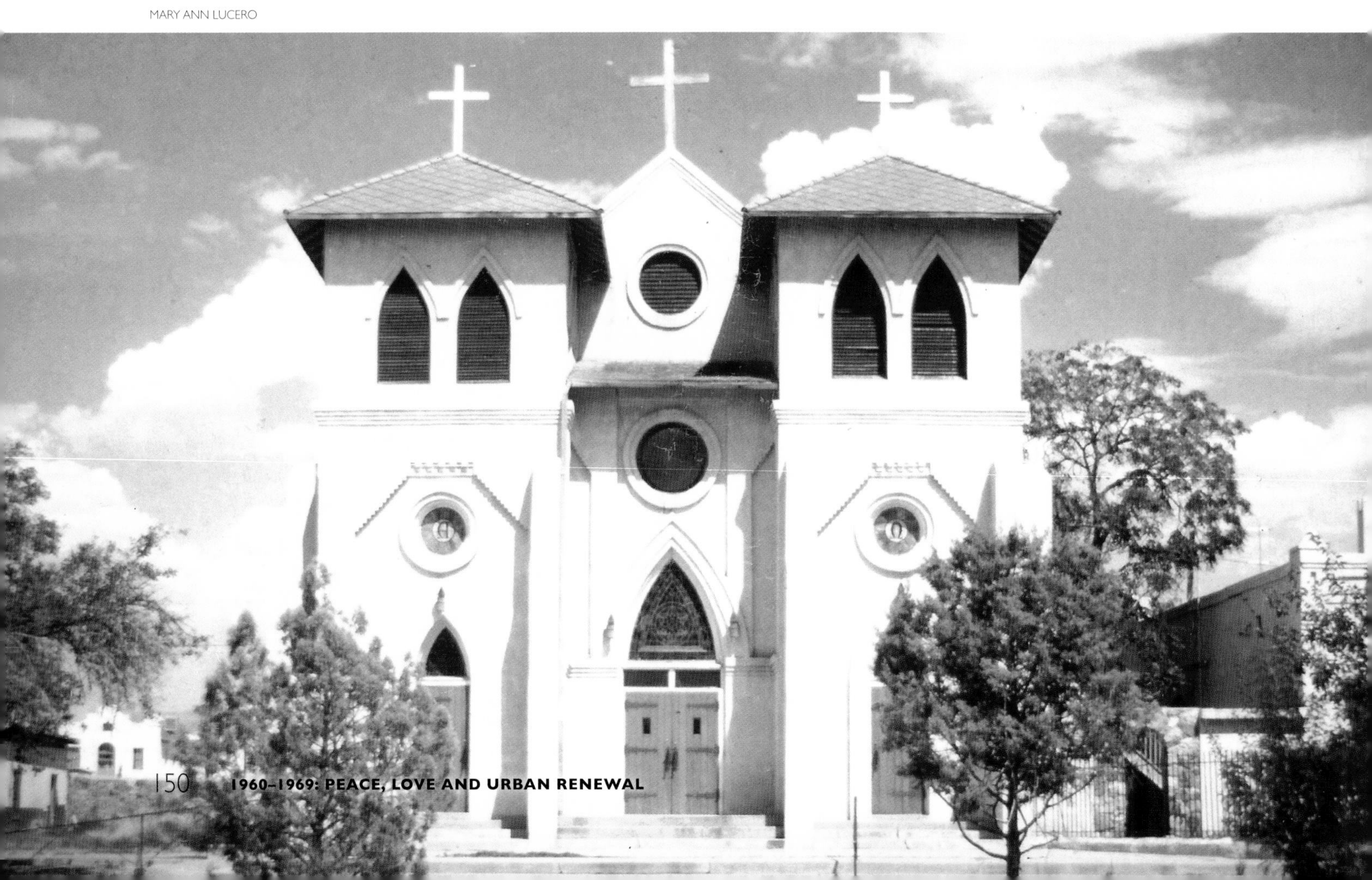

A CENTURY IN THE MAKING

In 1912, St. Paul's Methodist Church opened the doors to its new building, which cost $18,000, organ and all. The sanctuary's stained-glass windows were preserved when the building was dismantled and some were later installed in the El Calvario Methodist Church at 300 N. Campo St.

NMSU LASC/ST. PAUL'S METHODIST CHURCH

St. Paul's Methodist Church

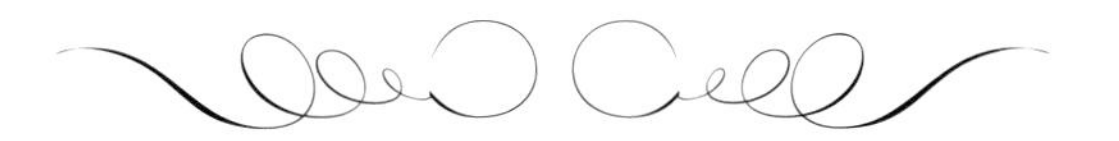

In the year 1912, when New Mexico was celebrating its new statehood, the congregation of St. Paul's Methodist Church was erecting a brick building on Griggs Avenue, just west of the Acequia Madre. This replaced the small Hendrix Methodist Episcopal Church South, built in 1889, which had been moved to the town of Berino. The cornerstone was laid on July 8, 1912, and, according to some records, the total cost of the building was $18,000, which included the $3,000 pipe organ at the front of the sanctuary. The building was completed by October 1912, in time to host the state meeting of the New Mexico Annual Conference of the Methodist Church.

Classrooms were added in 1925, making it possible to have several age departments instead of one multi-generational Sunday school. In 1949, an education wing was built which housed the entire children and youth departments as well as a Ladies Parlor.

In 1965, a new sanctuary, offices, youth department, kitchen and fellowship hall were built on property west of the 1912-49 building resulting in St. Paul's covering the entire Alameda Boulevard-Griggs Avenue corner. On Nov. 21, 1965, in a moving "Service of Transition," the congregation processed from the old building to the new sanctuary carrying the pulpit Bible and other articles of worship. In 1993, the old shingle roof was replaced with a new roof, assembled from large rolls of metal, and St. Paul's was nicknamed "The Copper Top Church."

Thousands have been part of St. Paul's, making possible local and global ministries. Highlights include cooperation with others to organize the Christian Day Nursery and Habitat for Humanity, participating in the Gospel Rescue Mission, supplying volunteers to rebuild in disaster areas, sending medical personnel to other countries and supporting worldwide mission projects. The church introduced St. Paul's Lambs class, a Sunday school learning environment for adults with developmental disabilities. In 1977, an early childhood program began as Mother's Day Out and is now St. Paul's Child Development Center.

The church has opened its doors to the community for such things as a bereaved parents support group, Growing Through Loss Conference, meeting places for other religious groups with no facilities, blood drives, music performances such as Voz Vaqueros Christmas concerts, La Casa events, the Victim Impact Panel and the Potters' Guild Empty Bowls fundraiser for El Caldito Soup Kitchen.

In coming years the church hopes to continue as a spiritual home for individuals and families and as a meeting place for groups from our community. St. Paul's United Methodist Church looks forward to a vital role in Las Cruces during New Mexico's second century.

More information on St. Paul's can be found in the book, "Through the Centuries, St. Paul's United Methodist Church, Las Cruces, New Mexico, 1869–2001," available at the church office.

COPPERTOP SANCTUARY

St. Paul's Methodist Church built this sanctuary on Griggs Avenue at Alameda Boulevard in 1965. In 1993, a new roof was added, earning the building its nickname, "The Copper Top Church."

ST. PAUL'S METHODIST CHURCH

YOU'VE GOT MAIL NOW

The University Park post office was a landmark on the New Mexico State University campus in the 1960s.

NMSU LASC

THE STUDENT CENTER

In the 1960s, students would "pig out" at the Milton Student Center. From the looks of things, hangin' at the student center was a blast.

NMSU LASC

RESEARCH PARTNERS

Started in 1946 to assist the research being done at White Sands Missile Range, the Physical Science Laboratory at New Mexico State University, below, has played an integral role in science and engineering at NMSU. The Clinton P. Anderson Physical Science Laboratory provided a home for PSL operations in the 1960s.

NMSU LASC

A FAVORITE PASTIME

Not only did the Milton Student Center offer places to eat and hang out, the basement also included a bowling alley. Milton Hall served as the student union until Corbett Center was constructed in 1968. Today, Corbett Center remains the student union, and underwent an $8.3 million renovation in 1996.

NMSU LASC

NEW HOME FOR BUSINESS

In 1968, construction was started on Guthrie Hall, the permanent home for the College of Business Administration and Economics, below. The building was named for Gwynne R. Guthrie, head of the department of commerce from 1925-69.

NMSU LASC

INAUGURAL COMMENCEMENT

The first commencement in the new Pan American Center at New Mexico State University, below, was held in 1968. The $3 million building was completed in 1968 and inaugurated on Nov. 30, 1968, with a 95-89 victory over Colorado State in men's basketball.

NMSU LASC

HANGIN' AT THE DORMS

Steve Parra relaxes by his 1967 Chevy Impala in the parking lot by the Women's Residence Center at New Mexico State University. The parking lot he stands in would eventually become the foundation for Corbett Center Student Union.

STEVE PARRA

Wooten Construction

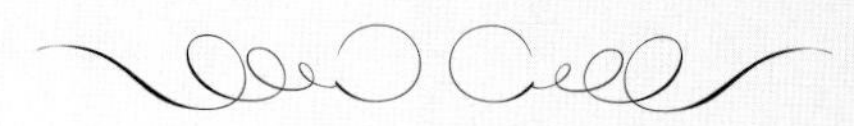

'DO IT RIGHT THE FIRST TIME'

Clay Wooten, center, looks over plans for the new officer's mess at White Sands Missile Range with U.S. military personnel in the late 1950s. At right, Clay Wooten in 2004.

WOOTEN CONSTRUCTION

Chances are, you've been in one of the hundreds of buildings built by Wooten Construction in the city of Las Cruces.

Founded in 1964 by Clay Wooten, the company has done more than 100 projects on the New Mexico State University campus alone, including four renovations of the Corbett Center.

In fact, Wooten Construction's work can be seen on three corners at the intersection of Church Street and Las Cruces Avenue: the old City Hall, the Post Office and the Bank of the West building.

And if you've been to the Doña Ana County Fairgrounds, that's some of Clay Wooten's earliest work. He helped construct the Air Force Radar Station that was first at the site.

Clay Wooten grew up during the Depression, working on the family ranch. At age 18, he found work as a carpenter in the Civilian Conservation Corps and, in 1938, he went to work for the Santa Fe Railroad. He came to Las Cruces in 1951 as a construction worker, and soon was a partner in a company with Rupert Chisholm. In 1964, he founded Wooten Construction, setting up his first office in the family home.

"My father's motto was 'Do it right the first time,'" said his son Ray Wooten, who worked with his father from the beginning and took over the family business in 1986.

Wooten Construction's first project was the Denison Office Building on North Main Street. In short order, the company began landing contracts for projects at NMSU and all of the public school districts in Doña Ana County. The company also built such structures as the Branigan Library, the District Court on Picacho Avenue, the Field of Dreams and the Doña Ana County government center.

In 2011, ownership of the business transferred to Ray's son, Ken Wooten, who worked in the sheriff's office for five years before joining the company full-time in 1994.

The business, Ken said, has been built on hard work.

Ray added, "We only work half a day, from six to six."

They are both grateful for the work that provided for the Wooten family and hundreds of employees over the years.

"This work gets in your blood," Ray said.

Wooten Construction is still based on the principles Clay Wooten passed down to his son and grandson.

"He was a Depression-era kid," Ray said. "He never spent money he didn't have, and he made sure all his projects were done right the first time. He'd say, there is only enough money to do it once so 'do it right the first time.'"

Today, Wooten Construction manages complex construction sites that involve the supervision of dozens and sometimes hundreds of people.

"You can't duplicate 50 years of experience," Ray said. "Because when you are talking about the construction business, it's all about experience."

ONE FAMILY, 50 YEARS OF EXPERIENCE

Clay Wooten's 1950 Chevy. Below, the renovation of O'Donnell Hall is one of many projects Wooten Construction has completed on the NMSU campus

WOOTEN CONSTRUCTION

FUTURE HOMEMAKERS

Gadsden High School elected Bernice Medina, Lorraine Bustamante, Evangeline Alaniz, Tonie Lucero, Irene Garcia and Rosemary Jacquez as Future Homemakers of America officers in 1966. The focus of FHA was home economics. After celebrating 50 years in 1995, the organization changed its name to Family, Career and Community Leaders of America in 1999.

ISELA ALVAREZ

HALL OF FAMER

Pervis Atkins helped lead the 1959 and 1960 New Mexico State University football teams to back-to-back Sun Bowl victories. In 2009, Atkins became the first and only NMSU player inducted into the College Football Hall of Fame, joining his coach Warren Woodson, who was inducted in 1989. Woodson led the 1960 team to a perfect 11-0 season.

NMSU ATHLETICS

STANDOUT TEAM

The 1962 Las Cruces High School baseball team, coached by Jim Bradley, included C.B. Rosas, third from left, who later played major league baseball. The baseball program also saw local success, earning state championships in 1961 and '64.

NMSU LASC

GRADUATION

Proud papa Bob Schatzabel, known as "Daddy Bob" by his children, stands with his oldest daughter Jeffie, on the day of her 1965 graduation from Las Cruces High School.

JEFFIE SCHATZABEL NEVAREZ

FORMIDABLE OPPONENTS

With a new school in Mayfield High School came a new football team to play Las Cruces High School. The rivalry became so intense that Yahoo! Sports Rivals High magazine named it one of the top 10 high school football rivalries in the nation in 2008. Now the game is played each year at Aggie Memorial Stadium where more than 20,000 rabid fans are usually in attendance.

NMSU LASC

TO INFINITY AND BEYOND

NMSU students join mathematician and amateur astronomer Walter Haas for a day at the NMSU observatory. Haas came to NMSU after teaching math at the University of Pennsylvania and University of New Mexico. Haas was mentored by Pluto discoverer Clyde Tombaugh, worked at White Sands Proving Ground and the Physical Science Laboratory.

NMSU LASC

Chimpanaut HAM's Space Exploits Recalled

the Rocketeer

Tim Frazelle Tops Men In His Class

NEW MEXICO

Albuquerque Journal

ALBUQUERQUE JOURNAL

Wednesday Morning, February 1, 1961

Chimp Survives U.S. Space Flight Test

Capsule Holding Animal Plucked From Atlantic

'Spy Satellite'

City Commission Eliminates Jobs Of Key Official

Space Chimps Blazed Trail For Astronauts

By Jane Thrall

JOURNAL STAFF WRITER

ALAMOGORDO — Heroes come in all sizes at the International Space Hall of Fame.

Images of Alan Shepard and John Glenn have their place in exhibits at the museum, inspiring awe from children who fancy themselves space explorers of the future.

But before Shepard or Glenn were blasted into space, a pair of smaller astronauts — astro-chimpanzees Ham and Enos — helped ensure the success of subsequent manned flights.

orbits covering more than 50,000 miles.

Not only was Enos' trip much longer in time and distance than Ham's, but the second chimp was used in not one but four behavioral tests.

But chimps — with genetic physiology that experts say is 99 percent identical to man's — have personalities as distinct as those of humans. And Enos, while perhaps even brighter than Ham, didn't have Ham's charm.

"Enos was better trained than Ham was," said Dittmer, the commissioned officer in charge of training primates for the Mercury program. "But since his flight was later than Ham's, he got

▲ The Albuquerque Journal's front page headline from Feb. 1, 1961 marks Ham's 16-minute suborbital flight. The 4-year-old chimp became a celebrity, appearing on the cover of Life magazine and even receiving a phone call from President John F. Kennedy.

▶ Astrochimp Ham, having just

SUCH A HAM

As NMSU and White Sands Missile Range conducted groundbreaking aerospace research, Holloman Air Force Base near Alamogordo was conducting tests of their own. Beginning in 1959, a 3-year-old chimpanzee named HAM, short for Holloman Aerospace Medical, began training at the base. On January 31, 1961, HAM was successfully launched into suborbital space, leading the way for Alan Shepard to take his shot at being the first American in space.

NMSU LASC

MORE THAN QUALIFIED

Students, including his son Alden, pictured right in the left-hand photo, of Clyde Tombaugh learned firsthand from the man who discovered Pluto. Though he only began teaching at NMSU in 1955, Tombaugh built his own telescopes in the 1920s when plans to attend college were ruined by hard times on the family farm in Kansas. His discovery of the solar system's most distant planet – despite controversy to "downgrade" Pluto's status from a planet to a dwarf planet – happened even before he had a formal post-secondary education.

NMSU LASC

UP CLOSE AND PERSONAL

Lucky friends of Clyde Tombaugh get a special view of the night sky atop the Alameda Boulevard telescope in 1963. While his most well-known contribution to astronomy is the discovery of Pluto, Tombaugh contributed greatly to Las Cruces in other ways. He also discovered hundreds of asteroids and taught astronomy at NMSU from 1955 until his retirement in 1973.

NMSU LASC

HIGHLIGHT OF THE FIESTA

Young women would don their hooped formal gowns in hopes they would be crowned queen of the Pan-American Fiesta, held each year on the Mesilla Plaza.

NMSU LASC

THE LAST PASSENGER TRAIN

The El Pasoan, one of the final passenger trains providing service from El Paso to Albuquerque, made a stop in the Las Cruces Depot on April 9, 1968. Its "big brother" Chief ended its service just a few days later. The end of passenger service in Las Cruces marked the end of passenger railroad service that spanned more than 100 years.

LAS CRUCES RAILROAD MUSEUM

A CELEBRATION OF CULTURE

At a 1960s event at TG&Y on North Main Street – later the home of Lowe's Fiesta Foods grocery store – participants performed traditional Mexican dances and music.

NMSU LASC

The Smith Family

Rubén Smith, who in 1991 would be elected mayor of Las Cruces, was born on a kitchen table in a house at 218 N. San Pedro St. His heart has been tied to the city's Downtown ever since.

Catarino and Josephine Gutierrez Smith had five children in all; in addition to Rubén were Albert, Grace, Jerry and Martha.

Their father, Catarino, and maternal grandfather, Alberto Gutierrez, could be considered among the first developers in Doña Ana County. Catarino was an active homebuilder and partner with Grace's husband, Steve Aguirre, in a concrete operation. Smith & Aguirre Construction Co. was still going strong in 2011. Gutierrez was a Las Cruces leader in purchasing plots and developing property. He established the first professional complex in the city for doctors and dentists.

"My grandfather was a Realtor before he even knew it," Jerry said.

Josephine was a pioneer in her own right, and in the mid-1950s was the first Hispanic female elected to the school board in Las Cruces. In that role, she was able to hand the diplomas to her first three children at their high school graduations.

The family left Downtown for a farm on Doña Ana Road north of the city. Rubén went to New Mexico State University, graduating in 1965 with an accounting degree. He then served in the U.S. Army.

MR. SMITH COMES TO LAS CRUCES

Catarino Smith Sr. and his wife, Luisa, with their children Eva, Catarino Jr. and Mary Lou.

SMITH FAMILY

Jerry, a self-described "turncoat," went to the University of New Mexico in Albuquerque. "I'm a Lobo," Jerry said. "After UNM, I went into the Peace Corps, to Brazil, in 1966. I got married and lived and worked in the Albuquerque and Santa Fe area before coming back home in the late 1970s."

He worked in the family businesses and worked as a real estate broker for about 25 years.

From 1982-91, Rubén served five terms as a state representative. In 1991, he became the first Las Cruces mayor elected directly by the citizens. Prior to that, mayors were selected by city council. Smith was mayor until 2003.

While in the Army, Rubén was the principal bassoonist in the North American Air Defense Command Band. He played bassoon classically in symphonies and saxophone with big bands. Jerry was also a saxophonist, and was a founding member of the Mesilla Valley Community Band.

This family love of music kept Rubén in tune with arts of all kinds. He was a president of the Doña Ana Arts Council and helped convert the old Branigan Library Downtown in to the Branigan Cultural Center. He worked tirelessly to save Court Youth Center, which would ultimately house Alma d'arte, a charter high school for the arts. In 2003, he was tapped to serve on Gov. Bill Richardson's cabinet as the first Secretary of the New Mexico Office of Cultural Affairs.

In 1972, while downtown streets were being covered with metal awnings during urban renewal, Rubén bucked the trends and created La Esquina. This pocket of downtown at Main Street and Las Cruces Avenue was built in an ancient Spanish motif.

Whether the subject is people or buildings or customs, Rubén has always lived with what he called a "respect for the old."

LIVING LAS CRUCES HISTORY

Alberto and Leva Gutierrez at their 50th anniversary, 1965. Josephine Gutierrez, an unknown baby, and Leva at 218 N. San Pedro St. Rubén Smith being sworn in as mayor of Las Cruces, surrounded by parents Catarino and Josephine, wife Elizabeth, and children Stewart and Cristianna in 1991. Leva and Alberto, circa 1915.

SMITH FAMILY

1970-1979

BRIDGE TO THE FUTURE

A NEW DOWNTOWN

With the urban renewal project near completion at the beginning of the 1970s, Downtown was prepared to welcome new businesses and customers with open arms. The newly completed pedestrian mall was inviting and soon provided a place for theaters, restaurants, churches and art galleries to make their home.

NEW MEXICO STATE UNIVERSITY LIBRARY ARCHIVES AND SPECIAL COLLECTIONS

SWEET SMELL OF SUCCESS

Taking a leisurely stroll through the Las Cruces Farmers & Crafts Market on Downtown Main Street is a familiar experience shared by many – including those who live in the Mesilla Valley as well as across the country.

A tradition rooted in humble beginnings, the Las Cruces Farmers & Crafts Market began in 1971 as a way for local farmers to sell their homegrown products to area consumers.

While still embracing this original concept, the farmers market has grown over the years to offer a little something for everyone.

A year after the market emerged, a group of local artists and craft vendors joined forces with the farmers to set up shop alongside the "yellow brick road" of the Downtown Mall, as long-time market attendee Dorothy Andress called it.

In 2011, Andress maintained the title of the longest-attending vendor at the market and has diligently set up her booth, selling crocheted and knitted items, among other crafts, since 1972.

"None of us in our wildest dreams ever thought it would take off like it did," Andress said.

In 2011, the Las Cruces Farmers & Crafts Market gained national recognition and was voted the No. 1 large market in the country by the American Farmland Trust.

The market attracts visitors from many different realms, Andress said. She has even had customers from Europe and other overseas countries.

Many things may have changed throughout the Mesilla Valley since the 1970s, but one constant has been the success the farmers market has seen.

Veteran patrons and newcomers alike can't help but love the atmosphere and variety the market provides for both the sellers and the buyers.

Artists Craig Dougherty and Jenny Yorston began selling their glass mosaic tables and sculptures in September 2011 and said they have noticed an increase in customer inquiries as well as sales.

According to Yorston, the market has provided an "excellent outlet" for getting to know and interact with the business community, which can be a challenge for those new to the city.

"The farmers market is a great opportunity to come meet new people, see beautiful things, try some awesome food and just enjoy the weather of New Mexico," Yorston said.

The market provides a welcoming atmosphere for all, whether looking for a family-friendly activity or taking that loveable canine for a stroll and the chance to stock up on tasty homegrown snacks or find that perfect unique gift is always a possibility at the farmers market.

Attracting hundreds of visitors every Wednesday and Saturday morning, local farmers and artisans have the opportunity to see their businesses expand with the ever-increasing customer base the market attracts.

"It's just a great outlet for my creativity; a great way to meet people and see things I've never seen before," Andress said.

"It's almost like an arts and crafts fair every week," Yorston said.

So what is it that has kept Dorothy Andress coming back year after year for 40 years?

"I just live for the moment, and it's been completely worth it for me to keep coming back," Andress said.

1970
Citizens Bank of Las Cruces, established by J.A. Ikard and his two sons, John and Jim, opened in the former Amador Hotel building. Ikard purchased the building from Martin Amador Campbell Jr. and renovated it using concrete block and frame additions to fit the needs of the new bank.

1970
The Aggie basketball team gained national attention for its most successful season to date, making it to the NCAA Final Four before falling to the eventual champion, UCLA.

1971
City of Las Cruces and Doña Ana County joined to build a new hospital on South Telshor Boulevard; moving the former Memorial General Hospital to its new location, where it is now known as Memorial Medical Center.

1971
The Holy Cross CraftFaire, now known as the Renaissance ArtsFaire, began at the Holy Cross Retreat Center.

IKARD FAMILY/LOU HENSON/NMSU LASC/RAFAEL TORRES/JIM HILLEY/LAS CRUCES BULLETIN/PICACHO HILLS COUNTRY CLUB

1970s

Who's Who

Las Cruces Mayors

1963-74	Thomas Graham
1974-76	Robert Munson
1976-80	Albert Johnson

Postmasters

Jan. 1, 1979	Richard Walter
Feb. 2, 1979	Al Hines (OIC)

NMSU President

1970-84	Gerald Thomas

Mesilla Mayors

1960-72	Nelson Clayshulte
1972-78	Roberto Frietze

Doña Ana County Sheriffs

1971-74, '79-82	Edward DiMatteo
1975-78	Antonio Gonzales

New Mexico Governors

1967-71	David F. Cargo
1971-75, '79-83	Bruce King
1975-79	Jerry Apodaca

U.S. Senators

1949-73	Clinton Anderson
1963-77	Joseph Montoya
1973-2009	Pete Domenici
1977-83	Harrison Schmitt

U.S. Representatives

1969-71	Ed Foreman
1969-89	Manuel Lujan Jr.
1971-81	Harold L. Runnels

By the Numbers

37,587	Las Cruces population
69,773	Doña Ana County population
8,115	NMSU enrollment (1970)
$7,395	Average household income
1.57	Number per household
36 cents	Gallon of gas (1970)
8 cents	First-class stamp (1971)
10 cents	First-class stamp (1974)
13 cents	First-class stamp (1975)
18 cents	First-class stamp (1978)
$3,900	Average price of a new car

In the News

May 4, 1970: Four students from Kent State University in Ohio were killed and nine wounded by National Guardsmen during a protest against the Vietnam War's spread into Cambodia.

Jan. 2, 1971: A ban on the television advertisement of cigarettes goes into effect in the United States.

Oct. 1, 1971: Walt Disney World opens in Orlando, Fla., expanding the Disney empire to the East Coast of the U.S.

June 17, 1972: The Watergate scandal begins when four men are arrested for breaking into the Democratic National Committee headquarters in the Watergate office building.

Jan. 22, 1973: The United States Supreme Court ruled in Roe vs. Wade that a woman cannot be prevented by a state from having an abortion during the first six months of pregnancy.

Aug. 9, 1974: President Richard M. Nixon resigns the office of the presidency, avoiding the impeachment process and admitting his role in the Watergate scandal.

July 4, 1976: The bicentennial of the United States is celebrated throughout the nation. The 200th anniversary included Operation Sail in New York City, as well as a Bicentennial Wagon Train that traveled the nation during the year, making a stop in Las Cruces on Feb. 17-18.

Nov. 26, 1976: Microsoft becomes a registered trademark, one year after its name for microcomputer software is first mentioned by Bill Gates to Paul Allen in a letter.

Aug. 4, 1977: The cabinet level Energy Department is created by Jimmy Carter.

Aug. 17, 1978: The first balloon, Double Eagle II, piloted by New Mexicans Ben Abruzzo, Maxie Anderson and Larry Newmanto crosses the Atlantic Ocean to come to rest in Miserey, France, after 137 hours of flight from Presque Isle, Maine.

March 28, 1979: An accident at the Three Mile Island nuclear power plant in Middletown, Penn., occurs. when a partial core meltdown is recorded. It is the largest accident in U.S. nuclear power history.

Nov. 1, 1979: The Chrysler Bailout is approved by the federal government. A $1.5 billion loan-guarantee plan is floated to assist the third largest car maker in the U.S.

1973
Protests erupted on the New Mexico State University campus due to student irritation with the strictly enforced curfews and rules against coed visits in the dorms.

1974
The new pedestrian mall in Downtown Las Cruces was completed as a result of urban renewal.

1976
Feb. 21, Fort Selden was dedicated as a state historical site to the sounds of a military salute fired by soldiers in Civil War uniforms.

1979
The new Thomas Branigan Memorial Library was built, moving from its former location on Hadley Avenue from 1935-1979, in what is now the Branigan Cultural Center.

1979
Picacho Hills Country Club opens a golf course designed by Joseph S. Finger.

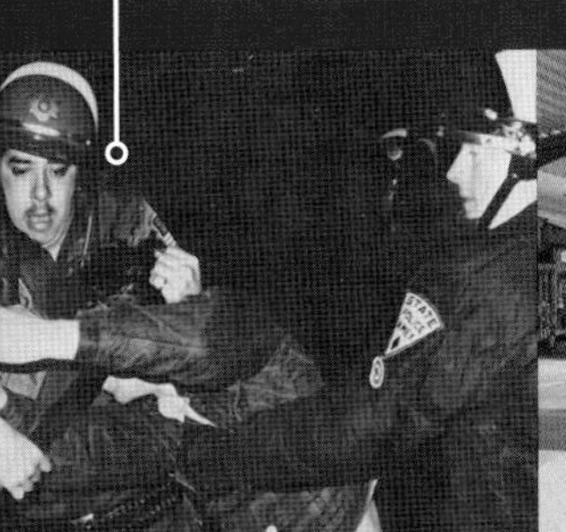

Citizens Bank

Citizens Bank of Las Cruces has "roots, not just branches, in the Mesilla Valley," according to President and Chief Executive Officer Justin Harper.

"All our funds are reinvested in Las Cruces," he said. "Our goal is to always remain strongly independent and to serve the community."

Founded in 1970, the bank's first board of directors included James L. Ikard and Lewis E. Emerick.

The first location was the original Amador Hotel building, which the bank restored and preserved as part of its commitment to Las Cruces and its heritage. In 1986, Citizens Bank moved into the Loretto Towne Centre at 505 S. Main St. The renovated bank office was the first phase of the center's redesign.

From the beginning, the majority of the directors have lived in Las Cruces, and some families have been with the bank from the beginning.

In those beginning times, the bank had assets of $4 million. Forty-one years later, Citizens Bank had grown to six locations and assets of $385 million.

Part of the growth, Harper said, is rooted in meeting customers' expectations of convenience and service. Citizens has met some of those by adding locations, but also with technology, by installing 33 ATMs (including one in every PicQuik) and providing mobile phone banking.

"It's about customer service," he said. "As we look toward the next 10 or 15 years, people will be doing more banking via computers and phones. We will have the technology to meet that demand."

But technology doesn't override personal relationships, Harper said. If customers have an issue they need to resolve with the bank, they don't need an email or an 800 number. They can simply talk with a real person, by phone or face-to-face.

The relationships benefit from continuity. The bank has grown along with the community, and several employees have served the community for 20 years or more.

According to Ruth Christopher, chief financial officer and vice president, who has been with the bank 27 years, the mission of Citizens Bank is to provide and deliver the best financial services the first time, every time.

That mission helped Citizens Bank become the largest and oldest locally owned bank in the city. Keeping it local and reinvesting in the community has helped the bank grow to the point where it now serves more than 18,000 customers.

No matter how sophisticated things get, for Harper, the bank's philosophy is simple: treat everyone fairly — the way you would want to be treated.

ORIGINS OF A LEGACY

Key figures in the early days of Citizens Bank of Las Cruces include: Lewis and Sarah Emerick, Jim and Gloria Ikard, and John Ikard and his mother, Winnie Ikard. The top image is of the Amador Hotel, which the bank restored and used as its first location in 1970.

CITIZENS BANK OF LAS CRUCES

A PLACE FOR THE SENIORS

Below, the Robert Munson Senior Center has served as the senior community focal point since 1977. The center's structure is overseen by the city's Public Services Department and administered by the Senior Programs Administrator and Center Manager. Within this structure are the volunteer, nutrition, long-term care and transportation programs.

NMSU LASC

COMING IN FOR A LANDING

Above, the Las Cruces International Airport, formerly known as the Las Cruces Crawford Airport, is located eight miles west of Las Cruces on Interstate 10, overlooking the Mesilla Valley. In the 1970s and into the 1980s, the airport was a major hub for Zia Airlines. In 2011, the airport is used by general aviation, New Mexico State University and private charters.

NMSU LASC

A TOURIST'S DELIGHT

The plaza and gazebo in the town of Mesilla were refurbished in 1978 to better accommodate residents and the growing number of visitors. The plaza is also home to many cultural and historical activities, the most prominent of which are the Cinco de Mayo and Diez y Seis de Septiembre Fiesta celebrations.

NMSU LASC

THE LIBRARY'S NEW HOME

Right, volunteers gather for the groundbreaking of the Thomas Branigan Library. Above, construction continued for more than a year. Below, dedicated on Dec. 9, 1979, the completed building serves Las Cruces as its public library.

NMSU LASC

STEINBORN EXPANDS

Above, developer David Steinborn cuts the ribbon on his real estate firm, marking the merger with Al Socolofsky, operating as Socolofsky-Steinborn Real Estate. The company is currently known as Steinborn & Associates Real Estate under the new ownership of John L. and Amy Hummer.

NMSU LASC

AMADOR HOTEL GETS A FACE LIFT

The Ikards make the Amador Hotel the new home of Citizens Bank of Las Cruces, refurbishing it to better fit the needs of the bank in 1970. Above left, the original hotel lobby, and left, the bank lobby after being refurbished. All of the original antiques from the Amador family were preserved.

NMSU LASC

ONE BIG PAINTING

One of several historic tank murals, the Don Juan de Oñate water tank, painted by renowned New Mexico artist Tony Pennock, was dedicated in February 1973 as the first official manmade project of the national Bi-Centennial Commission.

NMSU LASC

BUILDING FAMILY, BUILDING BUSINESS

Lenny, Leroy "Lee" and Barney Rawson, circa 1940. Lenny and Barney, 1948. Joan and Barney Rawson with sons young Lee and George at home on Thomas Avenue in 1962. Barney, Ellen and Lenny Rawson, 1954. George and Barney stand with Nicole, Morgan, Philip, Simon and Ben Rawson, 1988.

RAWSON FAMILY

THE RAWSON FAMILY

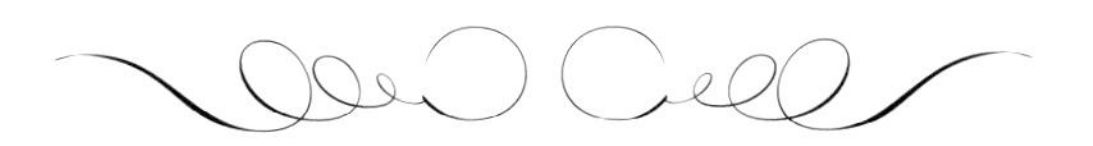

In a quest to seek relief from the aches and pains of arthritis, Leroy "Lee" Clifford Rawson packed up his wife Ellen and three children in 1945, left their home in Moline, Ill., and headed for the warm, dry climate of Tucson, Ariz.

On the way, the family stopped in Lordsburg to visit relatives. Lee stepped out of the car into the warmth of the New Mexico sun, immediately felt less pain and decided, at that moment, this was where he wanted to live.

Lee, a salesman by trade, began his new life as an entrepreneur in Lordsburg, opening a restaurant and a painting business, with his wife by his side. As the businesses grew, so did the three Rawson children. In the span of three years in the late 1940s, the two sons, Carl, nicknamed "Barney," and Lenny, joined the New Mexico National Guard. Lou Ellen, the youngest, left for college in Albuquerque. The boys were immediately activated into the Korean War and moved from Lordsburg to El Paso, where they were stationed at Fort Bliss. Shortly afterward, Lee and Ellen, wanting to be closer to their sons, packed up once again and moved to Las Cruces in 1950. The community embraced the Rawsons, and Las Cruces became their permanent home. In 1952, Lee started Lee Rawson and Sons, which set the foundation of future businesses in Las Cruces for years to come.

Barney married Joan in 1952. They had two sons, George and Lee, nicknamed for his grandfather. In 1961, when the boys were young, Barney expanded Lee Rawson and Sons into the building business. With a passion for helping youth, Barney focused on training local young men to be builders. About a dozen of these men went on to become leading builders in Las Cruces. As Barney's own sons began to mature, their entrepreneurial skills began to develop. Just as their father and grandfather before them, they opened their own businesses.

The elder Lee passed away in 1970. George Rawson and his wife, Yvonne, started Rawson Construction in September 1972. They changed the name to Pueblo Builders, Inc., and, in 1978, Yvonne became the first female licensed contractor in Las Cruces.

George and Yvonne, along with two other partners, created the landmark development Sonoma Ranch, a beautiful subdivision surrounding a golf course in Las Cruces. As New Mexico turns 100 in 2012, Pueblo Builders will celebrate 40 years in business.

In 1973, the younger Lee Rawson opened his business, Las Cruces Door, now Rawson Builders Supply, Inc., a supplier, subcontractor and contractor of residential and commercial specialty building products for Las Cruces.

Both Lee and George have been active public servants. Lee served as a state legislator for 22 years and serves on New Mexico's State Investment Council. George helped start Builders Trust of New Mexico in 1979 and later served on the New Mexico State Board of Finance for eight years.

In 2007, Joan and Barney were in a head-on collision while visiting their hometown of Moline. Joan was badly injured, but after a long recovery, survived. Barney, however, was killed instantly. As one could imagine, Barney's death was a tremendous loss to the Rawson family and to Las Cruces. However, while reflecting on the effects of his father's death, George said, "We became refocused on our family business, and we have become stronger."

Joan, George and Lee, with five generations of family in Las Cruces, described their legacy in the community: "Quietly working to make a difference in the lives of others and our community."

The Rawsons believe faith in the Lord Jesus Christ, dedication to family and hard work have been the foundations for their success. They will always be grateful for the support given to them by the people of Las Cruces.

BREAKING BARRIERS

Albert Johnson, a Las Cruces city councillor during the early 1970s, was elected mayor in 1976. Johnson was the first black mayor in the state of New Mexico. Johnson died in 1984 at 49 of leukemia. A memorial park was dedicated to Johnson at the intersection of North Main Street and Picacho Avenue in 1985.

NMSU LASC

SITTING IN THE GOVERNOR'S MANSION

Born in Las Cruces in 1934, Jerry Apodaca, seated above, was elected governor of New Mexico in 1974, the United States' first Hispanic governor since 1918. In 1978, President Jimmy Carter appointed Apodaca as chair of the President's Council on Physical Fitness.

NMSU LASC

A MIXED-GENDER CLASS

The spring 1974 cadet class for the Las Cruces Police Department listens intently to their instructor. In 1972, Congress passed an amendment to the Civil Rights Act of 1964, prohibiting state and local agencies from job discrimination based on gender. Police departments around the nation were required to hire women for jobs on an equal basis with men.

NMSU LASC

LORETTO CENTER

Loretto Shopping Center, Las Cruces' first indoor shopping mall, was built on Main Street just a block south of Downtown. It featured ample free parking, department stores – such as JCPenney and Dunlap's – TG&Y, Jerry's Pet Store, Safeway, Levine's and many other stores in the 1970s. Most of the store entrances faced a covered, air-conditioned interior public area, naturally lit by skylights. Like so many other malls around America at the time, Loretto Shopping Center quickly became the place to be and be seen. Business quickly declined with the opening of Mesilla Valley Mall in 1981, and the Ikard family purchased the defunct mall and created the Loretto Towne Centre, which in 2011 houses several government agencies, incuding the Las Cruces Public School administration and the New Mexico Motor Vehicle Devision.

NMSU LASC

NEW HOSPITAL

Above, Memorial General Hospital moved to its location off South Telshor Boulevard in 1971 and changed its name to Memorial Medical Center in 1990. Right, the hospital advisory board in 1971. Below, a rendering of the new hospital prior to construction.

NMSU LASC

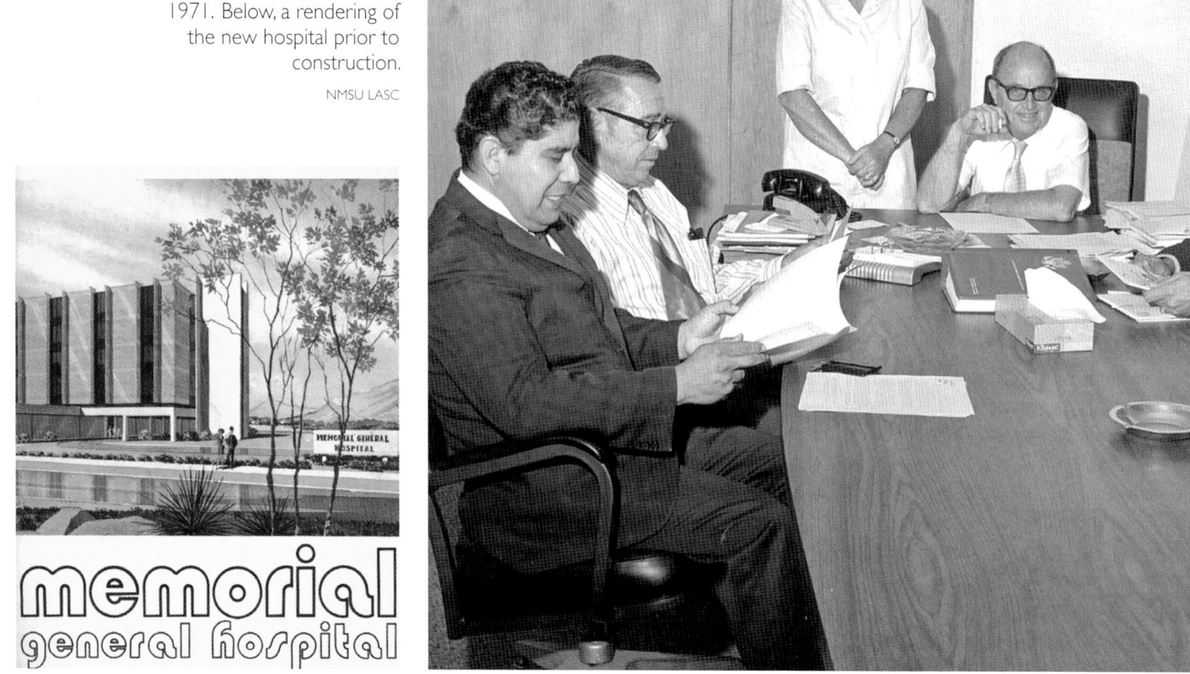

UP TO THE CHALLENGE

When her husband and Solar Electric co-founder, Ralph Garza, died in 1989, Mary A. Garza faced a steep challenge. She and her employees responded to the challenge, dramatically growing and improving the company.

SOLAR ELECTRIC

SOLAR ELECTRIC COMPANY

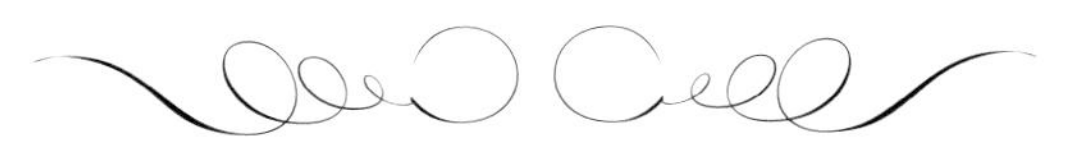

Mary A. Garza and her husband, Ralph, founded Solar Electric Company in 1979 "with a pickup and a pouch," as Mary recounts. By 2011, Solar Electric had become one of the most prosperous electrical contracting companies in southern New Mexico. However, when Ralph Garza died suddenly in 1989, Mary would have to prove herself to banks and bonding agencies in order to keep the business going.

"Being in a man's field, succeeding would be an added challenge," she said.

The first line of business was to gather the nine employees and reassure them. The only option for Solar Electric was to continue the business, as well as address employees' concerns should they decide to continue their journey with the growing company. Solar Electric would sustain its commitment to its employees. This meeting resulted in a deeper commitment from each and every employee.

Ralph and Mary A. Garza

Since then, the firm's bonding capacity increased from $25,000 to more than $6.6 million. Solar Electric has employed more than 40 people. The company has been awarded numerous government contracts at White Sands Missile Range because of its commitment to excellence in the field of analytical data, work quality and time performance.

Mary has earned an exceptional reputation for being fair, forthright, and a person committed to her word. Her many strengths in business have enabled her to establish herself and Solar Electric with remarkable distinction in business at both the local and national levels.

The many awards and achievements Mary has attained include: the 2003 Hispanic Small Business of the Year for New Mexico, 2002 Top 50 Women-Owned Business of New Mexico, 1999 U.S. Small Business Administration Award of Excellence, 1998 U.S. Small Business Administration Award of Excellence, 1995 Top 25 Women-Owned Business in New Mexico, 1993 U.S. Hispanic Business Woman of the Year for the nine-state Region II, 1991 Employer of the year Award by Jobs for Progress Board of Directors, and Honored Member, Who's Who Worldwide

Through her involvement in the Rio Grande Minority Council, Mary Garza has helped mentor women- and minority-owned businesses in southern New Mexico. Mary personally guides applicants through the process of becoming business owners and helps give them the necessary tools to succeed.

"I believe in giving back to the community," she said. "I love to see new businesses succeed."

"Customer first" is the foundation for Solar Electric's success in addition to providing quality and timely service.

"Maintaining a solid reputation in southern New Mexico is also key," she said, adding that providing incentives for employees to succeed professionally and share in the company's success is also important.

"The employees are the ones who make a company."

The early projects of Ralph Garza and Solar Electric are still up and working, she said. Ralph installed the traffic signals and lights on University Avenue and El Paseo Drive as well as the first traffic signal in Truth or Consequences.

Mary is a graduate of a business college and is the mother of two children: David, a graduate of University of California at Berkeley, and Melinda, a New Mexico State University graduate.

THE FLOOD

A flood in September 1972 left Las Cruces residents swimming in their houses and cars. Up until this time, there were little to no drainage systems throughout the city, leaving it susceptible to floods such as this. After consistent flooding problems, studies began at New Mexico State University and within the city to determine flood relief plans. In the mid-1970s, the Army Corps of Engineers built a 7-mile dam, located east of North Telshor Boulevard, upon which walkers and joggers can frequently be seen enjoying the view during their exercise.

NMSU LASC

BOWMANS BUILD LEGACY

What do you do when one of your children is in need? If you're Bob and Wanda Bowman, you do whatever it takes. If that means picking up and moving halfway across the country, to a place you'd never been before, that's what you do.

That's how the Bowmans, in 1971, found themselves moving from St. Louis, Mo., to southern New Mexico, with its climate better suited to their son Kurtis' health.

Turns out southern New Mexico's business climate was well suited to the Bowmans' talents as well.

In 2011, they celebrated their 40th year in business in Las Cruces.

It all started very humbly. The first year in Las Cruces, they joined with Bob's brother John to purchase La Fiesta TV and Music Center. Bob was an engineer and put his skills to work repairing televisions. Wanda sold organs and gave music lessons on the side.

The Bowmans had the vision to continually diversify their business, moving gradually toward furniture.

Soon they were selling appliances and Curtis Mathes televisions, for many years recognized as the highest quality TV brand.

In 2003, when many people their age would have been eyeing retirement, the Bowmans leapt into their biggest venture to date, becoming licensees of the new Ashley Furniture HomeStore in Las Cruces.

Five years later, in 2008, New Mexico Woman magazine named Wanda one of the top 25 businesswomen in the state.

A unique opportunity arose in 2010, when one of the Bowmans' longtime customers was elected governor of New Mexico.

Susana Martinez became the first elected Hispanic female governor in U.S. history. She was also the first governor in U.S. history to hire Wanda Bowman to furnish the governor's residence.

The Bowmans consistently give back to the community.

They founded the Families in Need furniture program. They have an annual All I Want for Christmas giveaway. Surplus furniture is donated to Habitat for Humanity's ReStore. Every October, during the Tough Enough to Wear Pink campaign, Ashley Furniture HomeStore opens its doors to Las Colcheras Quilters Guild, who create pink quilts for cancer patients.

"Having outstanding employees has made it a success for us," Wanda said. "And we have a very strong faith in God. That probably has as much to do with our success as anything else."

Another key to their success has been family. Their three children, Kathleen, Kurtis and Paul, despite moving to other parts of the country, have long been supportive of their ventures. Paul returned to Las Cruces and has served for many years as general manager of the Ashley Furniture HomeStore.

"We love Las Cruces," Wanda said.

THROUGH THE YEARS

At top: Ashley Furniture HomeStore's management team in 2011 features Lou Hendren, director of sales and marketing; Paul Bowman, general manager; Ernesto Chacon, customer service manager; Wanda Bowman, CEO; Annette Ortiz, CFO. Above: Bob and Wanda Bowman at the Curtis Mathes store in Las Cruces. The 2003 ribbon cutting of the Ashley Furniture HomeStore. Wanda Bowman, saleswoman and music teacher, in the 1970s at La Fiesta TV and Music Center.

BOWMAN FAMILY

PAN AMERICAN CENTER: A MILESTONE AT NMSU

When former Aggie men's basketball coach Lou Henson began shaping the program into a top NCAA participant in 1966, playing games in the Las Cruces High School gym was no longer acceptable.

The only gym on the New Mexico State University campus at the time, Williams Gymnasium, was long past its heyday.

"It only seated about 1,800 and had concrete bleachers, and that was it," Henson said about Williams Gymnasium.

LCHS could double the crowd base with about 3,000 seats.

Together with the help of architects Rem Alley and Fred Day, the trio began the planning of a 13,000-seat arena.

"The new gym helped us recruit, and it was one of the best facilities in the area," Henson said.

HOME OF THE AGGIES, AND MUCH MORE

The NMSU Aggies started playing basketball in the Pan American Center on a parquet floor requested by Coach Lou Henson. The center also played host to concerts by acts as diverse as Pearl Jam, George Strait and Earth Wind & Fire.

NMSU LASC

Henson said a lot of people thought the Pan American Center was built for $3.5 million, when in actuality it was only $3 million.

"It's what we had to work with, and we could do it because the water levels allowed us to berm up the sides. You couldn't do that anywhere else," Henson said.

Named for its location right off Interstate 25, otherwise known as the Pan-American Highway, the Aggies were proud to have a place to call their own, and thus began the record that proved it.

The first 10 men's basketball games played in the Pan Am were home-team wins, and 1970 marked the Aggies' most successful season as of 2011.

That year, the Aggies advanced to the NCAA Final Four before falling to that year's eventual tournament champion, UCLA.

The players on the men's and women's basketball teams, the volleyball team and the community were all ready for the upgrade.

"We never heard anything negative about building it. Everyone knew the need for it, and we just went with it," Henson said.

On Nov. 30, 1968, the new Pan American Center opened its doors to much Aggie success and established itself as an up-and-coming venue for the entertainment industry.

Some of the biggest names in concert history were ushered through the doors of the Pan American Center under the wing of Barbara "Mother" Hubbard.

Hubbard was the event coordinator of the Pan Am for more than 30 years and said "it would be easier to list the big names that didn't come through the doors than list those that did."

As the Aggies' fan base grew and event requirements changed, so did the Pan American Center. It received a face-lift with a renovation in 2006 – a project costing $22 million.

THE PAN AMERICAN CENTER

The Pan American Center was open for business in 1968 and has been home to men's and women's basketball, volleyball, entertainment and graduation ceremonies.

NMSU LASC

BARBARA HUBBARD
A LAS CRUCES LEGEND

When the wind blew a southern belle in a beat-up Dodge pickup truck down Interstate 10 in the spring of 1957, only fate would know it was bringing one of the best and longest reigning entertainment gurus into Las Cruces.

Born and raised in Benton, Ark., Barbara "Mother" Hubbard put herself through college waiting tables at a local restaurant near her alma mater, Henderson State University.

After receiving a master's degree in education and teaching at Arkansas State University, Hubbard decided it was time to move west.

"I had such bad allergies, and I was tired of the weather so I just got in the truck and didn't stop until I hit Las Cruces," Hubbard said, laughing.

As luck would have it, former school Superintendent Thomas Mayfield heard of her arrival, and within the evening, Hubbard had a new job.

"(Mayfield) called me up, said he was coming to interview me, and didn't care that I wasn't even dressed (up) for it," Hubbard said.

When the Pan American Center opened its doors in 1968, Hubbard had received her second master's degree from New Mexico State University and was asked to become the center's business administrator.

One might say the rest is history. Who else can say they have played gin rummy with John Wayne, let the Doobie Brothers wash underwear in her sink or let U2 borrow her truck?

None other than Barbara Hubbard, who served as the Pan Am events coordinator for more than 30 years, scheduling major artists such as Bon Jovi, John Mellencamp, Dolly Parton, Rod Stewart, Bill Cosby, Gloria Estefan, Reba McEntire and Elton John, just to name a few.

Hubbard's favorite act "has to be the first one I ever scheduled, Bob Hope," she said.

Describing his performance at Pan Am, Hubbard said they had built the "USS Hope" in the center of the stage and invited war veterans onboard to welcome Hope onstage.

"There wasn't a dry eye in the audience that night," Hubbard recalled.

Hope, in fact, was the one who dubbed "Mother Hubbard" as the queen of Pan Am entertainment.

Even though Hubbard "retired" in 1996, as of 2011 she remains executive director of a national talent scholarship program she started with Hope, which has created 16 endowments at NMSU.

"It's my way of tying education to the entertainment world," Hubbard said. "I want to give the kids a shot to make it who otherwise wouldn't have the opportunity."

THEY ALL LOVE BARBARA

Barbara Hubbard is all smiles with country legend Reba McEntire, above left, and rockin' out backstage with KISS, above right.

BARBARA HUBBARD/NMSU LASC

LOVE AND BASKETBALL IN LAS CRUCES

Family gathered at New Mexico State University's Fulton Center to celebrate Lou and Mary Henson's 50th wedding anniversary. Front row: Front Will Edison, Zach MacAdam. Second row: Danny Heinrich, Lou Henson, Mary Henson, Claire Edison, Haley Edison. Back row: Catie Wojciehowski, Kristy Rutter, Lindsey Henson, Evan Rutter, Lisa Rutter, John Rutter, Lori Henson, Fred Heinrich, Leigh Anne Edison, Coit Edison, Laurie MacAdam, Lacey Henson. At right, Lou and Mary shortly before their Dec. 29, 1954, Las Cruces wedding.

HENSON FAMILY

THE LOU HENSON FAMILY

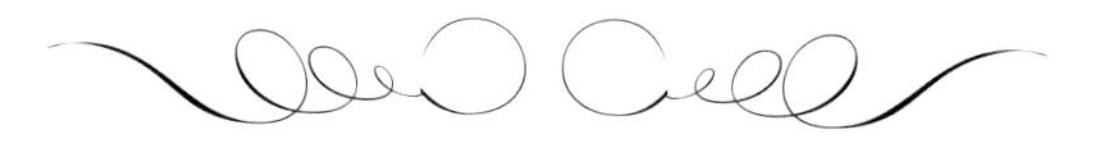

One of basketball coach Lou Henson's most memorable teams was known as "the Miracle Midgets."

But Henson may owe his biggest debt to the Jolly Green Giant.

In the summer of 1952, Henson, then a junior college basketball player in Oklahoma, took a job working for the Green Giant Company in Lanark, Ill. There he met a farm girl, Mary Brantner.

At the end of the summer, Henson headed to Las Cruces, N.M., to play basketball for the New Mexico A&M College Aggies and their new coach, Presley Askew. On the court, the Aggies were subpar, finishing 7-12. Off the court, he continued his long-distance courtship with Mary, eventually convincing her to head southwest.

On Dec. 29, 1954, Lou and Mary were married in Las Cruces.

"All of our children were born here," Mary said. "And I drug them to all the games."

The Hensons were instant fixtures in Las Cruces. Lou went to graduate school, and by 1956 was an assistant coach at Las Cruces High School. Soon the kids started coming. Lou Jr. was born in 1957. Lori arrived in 1958, by which time Lou was the head coach at LCHS. He promptly led the Bulldogs to three consecutive state championships. After the second one, in 1960, Lisa was born.

Lou left Las Cruces in 1962, at age 30, to become head coach at Hardin-Simmons College in Abilene, Texas. He returned in 1966, this time to coach the New Mexico State University Aggies. And in 1967, Lou and Mary's fourth child, Leigh Anne, was born.

Success on the court, on the campus and in the community would culminate in the glorious year of 1970. That March, the Aggies made it to the NCAA Final Four. That May, Lou received NMSU's Distinguished Alumnus Award.

After five more solid seasons, and three more NCAA tournament appearances, Lou left to coach the University of Illinois of the Big Ten in 1975, for 21 successful seasons.

In 1996, Lou and Mary returned to Las Cruces, ostensibly to retire.

But when the Aggies parted ways with coach Neil McCarthy, athletics director Jim Paul offered the job to Lou, who reluctantly accepted for a year, with the stipulation he wouldn't be paid. A salary was required to make it official, so Lou earned a dollar a year. Seventy-seven cents after taxes.

One season became eight, and Lou led the Aggies to four more 20-win seasons and another NCAA trip before retiring in 2005 with 779 victories. Add in his high school wins and the total is 924.

In May 2005, at NMSU's graduation ceremony, Lou and Mary were both presented with honorary doctorates, for their service to the university and Las Cruces. In another honor, New Mexico Hwy. 28 was named the Lou Henson Highway.

Mary, a breast cancer survivor, became involved with the NMSU Aggies Are Tough Enough to Wear Pink campaign in 2009, helping raise millions in funds for research and awareness of the disease.

In 2011, the Las Cruces Association of Realtors recognized Mary and her three co-chairs of the Pink campaign as Citizens of the Year. Lou had received the same honor in 1971. The bookended awards, 40 years apart, neatly illustrate the lasting impact Lou and Mary Henson have had on Las Cruces.

GO AGGIES

The Aggies' investment in the Pan American Center paid off. During its first three seasons at the new arena, the Aggie men's basketball team earned the longest home-win streak in program history. Below, Aggie cheerleaders sporting the latest cheer style of the '70s, with a shorter dress length and vests on the men sporting Pistol Pete, the Aggie's mascot.

NMSU LASC

A CHAMPIONSHIP TEAM

Below, the Lou Henson-coached men's basketball team of the 1969-70 season made it all the way to the NCAA Final Four, where NMSU lost to eventual champion UCLA in the first round of the Final Four. However, NMSU earned third place by defeating St. Bonaventure 79-73 in the consolation game.

NMSU LASC

LONGSTANDING PRESIDENT

Gerald Thomas, appointed president of New Mexico State University in 1974 when campus enrollment was 8,155 students, retired in 1984 with an enrollment of 12,500 students. Sixty-eight percent of all the graduates earned degrees during his tenure. Gerald Thomas Hall, which houses the College of Agricultural, Consumer and Environmental Sciences, was named in his honor.

NMSU LASC

STADIUM STORIES

Above, the old Aggie stadium was demolished just before the new Aggie Memorial Stadium, right, was built in 1978. The first game played saw the Aggies defeat rival University of Texas at El Paso 35-32. As of 2011, Memorial Tower is the only remnant of the former stadium and is a part of the College of Health and Social Services.

NMSU LASC

HOMECOMING MEMORIES

Members of the Zeta Tau Alpha sorority cheer for the Aggies while preparing for the Homecoming game of 1979.

NMSU LASC

A CLEAR SHOT TO 'A' MOUNTAIN

Left, an aerial view of the NMSU campus, showing the Pan American Center standing alone prior to the building of Aggie Memorial Stadium. NMSU was at the edge of town, with no development to the east until the early '70s, when Las Alturas was created on the eastern side of Interstate 25.

NMSU LASC

THINGS TO CELEBRATE

Campus life was full of change in the 1970s. Students, both men and women, were finding their voices to speak out about issues that were previously not recognized. Some controversial topics included the environmental movement, anti-Vietnam protests, the Watergate scandal and women's issues.

NMSU LASC

THE WOMEN'S MOVEMENT

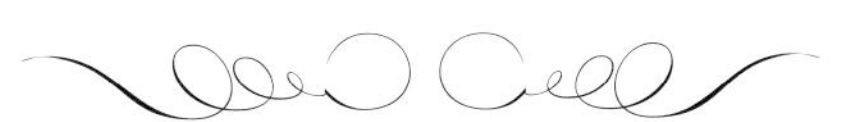

In January 1973, two New Mexico State University professors decided to gauge student interest in a topic that was gaining momentum in the national spotlight: women's studies.

At the time in Las Cruces, there were no rape crisis centers, domestic violence shelters or women's health clinics. Access to contraception was close to impossible for young women in the area. When professors Sherry O'Donnell and Charles Duval first stepped into the two-week, interim class, they were shocked to find the class filled to standing room only.

Throughout the course of the class, students were given a safe environment to discuss the issues and experiences women in society were facing, and the opportunity to come up with potential solutions on a local level.

"It was life changing for many of us who went on from the class to form 'consciousness raising groups' who met weekly throughout the city," said Nancy Barnes-Smith, who was a student in the class.

Barnes-Smith said the energy and commitment of those groups resulted in convincing the university to allow for the first rape crisis center and domestic violence shelter, housed in a small apartment in Rhodes Hall on the NMSU campus in 1975.

"What young women take absolutely for granted today just wasn't our reality back then," Barnes-Smith said.

STAND UP AND SPEAK UP

Many look back on the 1970s as a time of political awareness. When controversy in the nation arose, New Mexico State University students were never shy to make their opinions known. Issues such as war, equality and integration were heard.

NMSU LASC

Doña Ana Community College

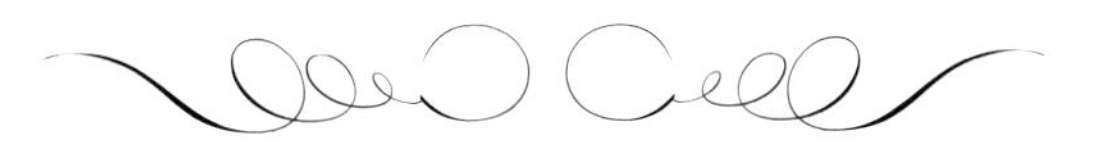

From its origins as a workforce training center with just a few hundred students, Doña Ana Community College has grown to six locations serving nearly 10,000 students in 37 academic and degree programs – 3,300 of these students also take classes online.

DACC was founded in 1973 as the Doña Ana County Occupational Education Branch. During the first years of its existence, classes were held in World War II barracks on the New Mexico State University campus, at Memorial General Hospital, and in high school classrooms.

Within a few years, it was renamed Doña Ana Branch Community College and in 1978 established its first campus – later called the central campus – along Espina Street southwest of NMSU.

In the late 1980s, the college's mission was expanded to include preparing students for university studies. As a result, in the decade between 1985 and 1995, enrollment increased 528 percent.

A series of two-story buildings were added to the central campus, but that location soon filled to capacity. The college launched a series of strategic plans to build new facilities in the highest population growth areas in the county.

The Sunland Park Center was opened in 1997 and the Gadsden Center in Anthony, N.M., in 2001. Construction of two other centers – one in Chaparral and the other in Hatch – was under way in 2011.

In the first decade of the 21st century, DACC dropped the word "branch" from its name. The college also built a new, state-of-the-art campus off of Sonoma Ranch Boulevard on Las Cruces' East Mesa. The energy-efficient buildings are designed to blend in with the desert landscape and the Organ Mountains. DACC's East Mesa Campus began to serve as the administrative headquarters in 2011.

DACC was a founding partner in the Early College High School, the first of its kind in New Mexico. ECHS students take dual-credit courses throughout high school and will be able to receive a high school diploma, an associate's degree and credit toward a bachelor's degree upon graduation. This concept began with The Bridge, a nonprofit organization composed of local businesses and educational institutions.

As DACC approaches its 40th birthday in 2013, it does so with a strategic vision to improve the lives of the people of Doña Ana County with relevant and effective educational opportunities.

DACC is an active community partner. It is a catalyst for positive economic development and plays a leading role in developing and supporting a workforce of qualified workers.

A JEWEL IN THE DESERT

Doña Ana Community College's East Mesa campus was designed to blend with the desert. Administrative headquarters moved there in 2011.

DACC/WILLIAMS GROUP

ORGAN MOUNTAIN FOOD CO-OP

MOUNTAIN VIEW MARKET

In 1975, a group of health-conscious New Mexico State University students decided to pool their resources and create a buying club so they could purchase whole foods at bulk prices. Together, they could order enough to make it worthwhile for the Tucson, Ariz., Co-operative Warehouse to send a truck to Las Cruces.

Quickly, the operation became so large it was more practical to open a store. They transformed a little home at 1309 E. Foster Road, just east of Solano Drive, into the original Organ Mountain Cooperative.

In 1980, the co-op moved to the corner of Picacho Avenue and Valley Drive. They shared the space with a restaurant started by four co-op members called Desert Rose Cafe. A poster from this era reads: "A Store with Character: Where Mutual Aid is More Important Than Profit, and Each Member is an Owner ..." Many long-term co-op members hearken to this location and its restaurant as a sort of golden age.

In 1984, the co-op moved to another Foster Road location, just south of the current location. Staff from the time reminisce about the exciting development of having a real walk-in cooler for the first time, catapulting the co-op into the 20th century.

In 1993, the co-op moved just a short leap away to the Idaho Crossings Center at 1300 El Paseo Road. When the store moved to the Idaho Crossings location, it was renamed Co-op Market, and soon thereafter, members voted on a new name: Mountain View Market. In 2001, the co-op expanded from its 3,500-square-foot section into an 11,000-square-foot space.

In 2007, the market partnered with a member to create a demonstration garden in Mesilla to encourage local food production. In 2008, a Growers' Market was opened in the parking lot to promote and support locally-grown produce and local food production which served as a vending outlet for local farmers and gardeners. In October 2011, the market acquired an existing Mesilla farm to provide fresh, local produce.

Also in 2011, the co-op created and designed its own unique, interactive website, which enabled Internet delivery services.

Education and outreach programs are ever-expanding, reaching at-risk children, senior church groups and all points in between. Mountain View Market continues to work toward achieving its goals for creating a beacon of sustainability, empowering employment, local economic stability and promoting the cooperative model.

The co-op's product emphasis continues to be on wholesome, high-quality natural foods. Additionally, the co-op works to educate consumers about foods and nutrition and to promote local and organic products and producers. Mountain View Market also networks with other cooperative businesses to encourage an economic environment that benefits all consumers.

YOU'VE COME A LONG WAY, BABY

Mountain View Market, originally the Organ Mountain Food Co-op, grew into its modern store from humble, 1970s beginnings in a small house in Las Cruces. At top is the header from one of the Co-op's 1980s newsletters.

MOUNTAIN VIEW MARKET

A FRIENDLY FACE

Formed in 1977 by Bobby Stephens, Save Mart is one of Las Cruces' oldest locally owned grocery stores.

JOHN YARBROUGH

HERE COMES THE PARTY

Below, Albert Fountain and his father, Arthur Fountain, who opened El Patio Cantina in 1934. They would sometimes bend the rules and drink past the legal curfew into the wee hours of the morning.

NMSU LASC

A DESERT BEACH

White Sands has been a popular family destination since its introduction as a National Monument in 1933 by President Herbert Hoover. Pictured above is the Elston family enjoying White Sands on a hot day in the summer of 1972.

BOBBIE MONTANA

FAR OUT, MAN

NMSU student Steve Parra kicks back with his custom-built home stereo system. The 1970s gave birth to the electronic revolution, in the 1980s the first home computers and video games gained popularity.

STEVE PARRA

DOWN, SET, HIKE

A 1973 football camp at NMSU for grades 7 through 12, run by Aggie coach Jim Bradley, who later coached several Mayfield High School championship teams. Several students, including Mike Bradley, pictured center row fourth from the left, forgot their shirts that day. Mike Bradley went on to become the MHS football coach.

JIM BRADLEY

SCHOOL LIFE

Above, the 1971-72 La Mesa Elementary School basketball team. Below, the 1975-76 Court Junior High band. At the time, Court Junior High, built in 1941, was the only junior high school in Las Cruces, and added a music wing in 1952.

NMSU LASC

BLUE & WHITE DYNAMITE

A Court Junior High School pep rally in 1975 cheering on the football team on their upcoming game.

NMSU LASC

FASHION

Monumentally famous for being the disco era, the 1970s were filled with bright colors, bell bottoms and Saturday night fever.

NMSU LASC

DRUM MAJOR MARCHES ON

Lynli Brown was drum major for Gadsden High School in 1978.

ISELA ALVAREZ

1980-1989
STAYING STRONG

HISTORY IN THE MAKING

The Mesilla Valley was on the front lines of a battle over water rights with Texas, but that didn't get in the way of people continuing to enjoy the mainstay traditions of the area, such as the famous Whole Enchilada Fiesta. With the help of Roberto Estrada, pictured third from right, who makes one big enchilada every year, the fiesta began in 1981 and quickly evolved as one of the area's most-anticipated annual events.

NEW MEXICO STATE UNIVERSITY LIBRARY ARCHIVES & SPECIAL COLLECTIONS

A Legal Nightmare

"Thou shall not covet thy neighbor's water" became the 11th commandment in the Mesilla Valley throughout the 1980s when El Paso ambushed New Mexico with the beginning of a three decade-long battle over water rights to the Rio Grande.

Preparing for nearly two years before filing suit, the El Paso Public Service Board and the Houston law firm Vinson & Elkins were ready to challenge New Mexico's ban on groundwater exportation – even if it took Supreme Court action.

Since the 1940s, the export ban had given New Mexicans a false sense of security about their water usage and was a keystone to El Paso proving their case.

El Paso charged that groundwater was a commodity and, therefore, unconstitutional to have such restrictions on state-to-state commerce.

In 1986, six years after the initial suit was filed, the issue came to a head in a small, crowded conference room in the Department of Agriculture at New Mexico State University.

Throughout the course of that year, the proceedings lasted 54 days, with historian and co-author of "One Hundred Years of Water Wars in New Mexico: 1912-2012" Linda Harris there for every minute of it.

"There were so many different entities to be considered. Livelihoods were at stake on both sides," Harris said.

Harris, who worked for the New Mexico Water Resources Research Institute at the time, was in charge of covering the case and providing the public with information about the proceedings.

Longstanding hostilities between New Mexico and Texas became evident and, according to Harris, Las Cruces and the surrounding areas would be the most affected by groundwater redistribution.

In Las Cruces, bumper stickers could be seen bearing the phrase, "Thou Shall Not Covet Thy Neighbor's Water," and residents had the attitude of "how dare they do this," Harris said.

New Mexico was not going to go down without a fight. State Engineer Steve Reynolds knew what he was doing and was "essentially the judge and jury of the case," Harris said.

"He was the most powerful water official in the state," Harris said. "He was legendary."

Reynolds had been at his post for the past 20 years and was also

1980
Mesilla Valley Mall was built, becoming the premier indoor shopping mall in Las Cruces, taking the title from what was formerly known as Loretto Shopping Center, where most area residents did their shopping.

1980
Friday, Sept. 5, lawyers for El Paso filed suit in Albuquerque against the state of New Mexico, which would become a three-decade-long battle over groundwater rights in the southern region.

1981
Mesilla Valley Transportation opened its first operating fleet, a small business hauling refrigerated and perishable goods throughout the borderland area.

1982
NASA's space shuttle Columbia makes a landing from its third mission to space, STS-3, the only mission to land at White Sands Missile Range.

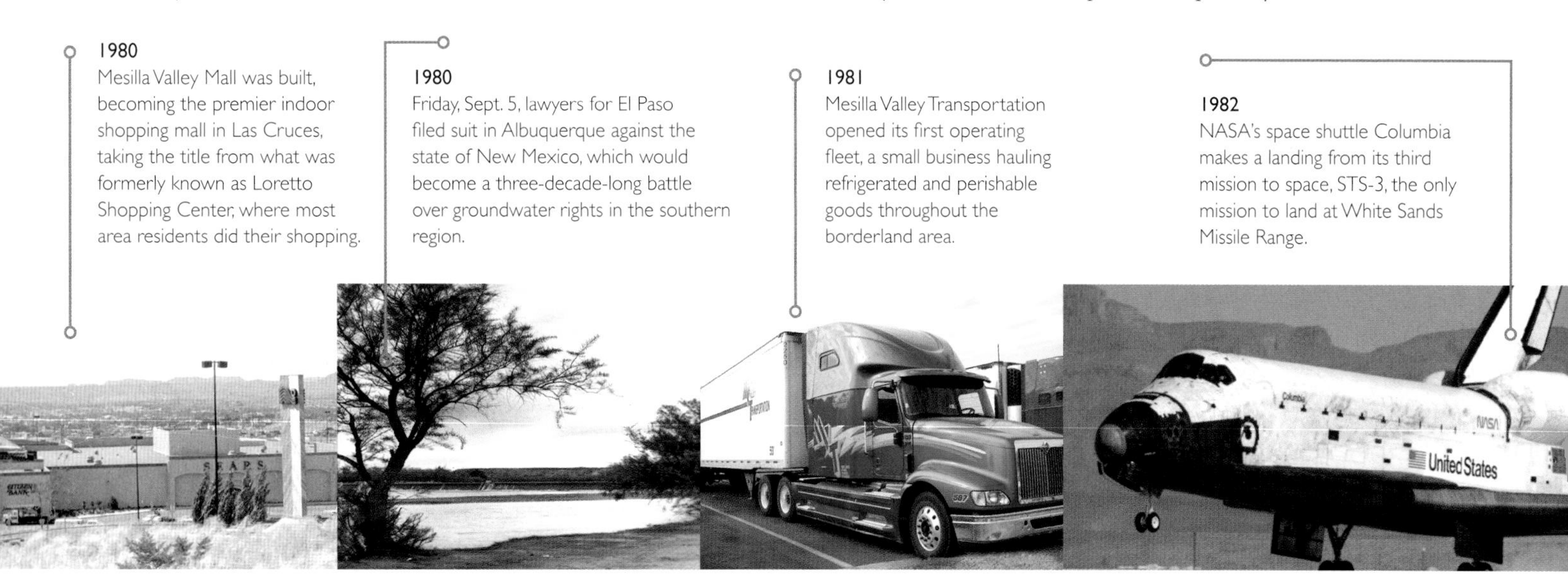

NMSU LASC/WATER RESOURCES RESEARCH INSTITUTE/MESILLA VALLEY TRANSPORTATION/WHITE SANDS MISSILE RANGE PUBLIC AFFAIRS OFFICE/CASA DE PEREGRINOS/LAS CRUCES BULLETIN/LORI CONN/TODD DICKSON

1980s

Who's Who

Las Cruces Mayors
- 1980-82 .... Joseph Camuñez
- 1982-87 .... David Steinborn
- 1987-89 .... Herculano Ferralez
- 1989-91 .... Tommy Tomlin

Postmasters
- Oct. 14, 1980 .... Bill Halm (OIC)
- April 4, 1981 .... Victor G. Duran
- April 30, 1986 .... Bennie Matlock (OIC)
- Nov. 22, 1986 .... Robert Bejarano

NMSU Presidents
- 1970-84 .... Gerald Thomas
- 1984-94 .... James E. Halligan

Mesilla Mayors
- 1978-86 .... Mary Leslie
- 1986-90 .... Rosalie Rader

New Mexico Governors
- 1979-83 .... Bruce King
- 1983-87 .... Toney Anaya
- 1987-91 .... Garrey Carruthers

U.S. Senators
- 1973-2009 .... Pete Domenici
- 1977-83 .... Harrison Schmitt
- 1983-2011 .... Jeff Bingaman

U.S. Representatives
- 1969-89 .... Manuel Lujan Jr.
- 1971-81 .... Harold L. Runnels
- 1981-2003 .... Joe R. Skeen

Las Cruces Public Schools Superintendents
- 1972-82 .... John Stablein
- 1982-89 .... William "Bill" Floyd
- 1989-2001 .... Jesse L. Gonzales

By the Numbers

- 45,086 .... Las Cruces population (1980)
- 96,340 .... Doña Ana County population (1980)
- 75,301 .... White
- 50,204 .... Spanish origin
- 1,597 .... Black
- $17,710 .... Average household income
- 1.83 .... Number per household
- $3.10 .... Minimum wage (1980)
- $3.35 .... Minimum wage (1981)
- $1.25 .... Gallon of gas (1980)
- 18 cents .... First-class stamp (March 1981)
- 20 cents .... First-class stamp (Nov. 1981)
- 22 cents .... First-class stamp (1985)
- 25 cents .... First-class stamp (1988)
- $7,210 .... Average new car (1980)
- 12,347 .... NMSU enrollment (1980)

In The News

Feb. 13, 1980: A "miracle on ice" occured at the Winter Olympic Games held in Lake Placid, N.Y., when a team of U.S. amateur ice hockey players defeated the all-star Soviet Union team.

May 18, 1980: Mount St. Helens volcano in Washington State erupts, killing 57 people. The blast was estimated to have a power 500 times greater than the Hiroshima atomic bomb.

Jan. 20, 1981: The inauguration of Ronald Reagan as the 40th president of the United States occurs in Washington, D.C.

March 30, 1981: President Ronald Reagan survives an assassination attempt, shot in the chest in Washington, D.C.

April 12, 1981: The first launch of the space shuttle from Cape Canaveral and the Kennedy Space Center occurs as Columbia begins its STS-1 mission.

June 18, 1983: On a successful Challenger space shuttle mission, Sally Ride becomes the first American woman to travel into space. On that same mission, Guion Bluford is the first African-American to travel into space.

Dec. 11, 1985: General Electric Corp. agrees to buy RCA Corp. for $6.28 billion in the largest corporate merger ever outside the oil industry.

Jan. 20, 1986: Martin Luther King Day is officially observed for the first time as a federal holiday in the United States.

Nov. 9, 1989: The Berlin Wall, after restricting traffic from East and West Germany for 38 years, begins to crumble when German citizens are allowed to travel freely for the first time.

1982
The Roman Catholic Diocese of Las Cruces was established, adding Lincoln, Chavez and Sierra counties, which had all previously been served by the Roman Catholic El Paso Diocese.

1982
Casa de Peregrinos was established by sister Martha Carrigan with the backing of the local Catholic churches. It was meant to fill a need as an emergency food bank for those in need.

1983
Young Park was adopted as the Renaissance ArtsFaire's new home, a big enough area to house the near 25,000 crowd the Faire now attracts.

1984
College Heights Christian School became incorporated as the Mesilla Valley Christian Schools and held its first high school graduation in May 1985, with a single student.

1984
Amateur paleontologist Jerry MacDonald brought national recognition to the Robledo Mountains for excavating thousands of trackways that can now be found at the New Mexico Museum of Natural History and Science.

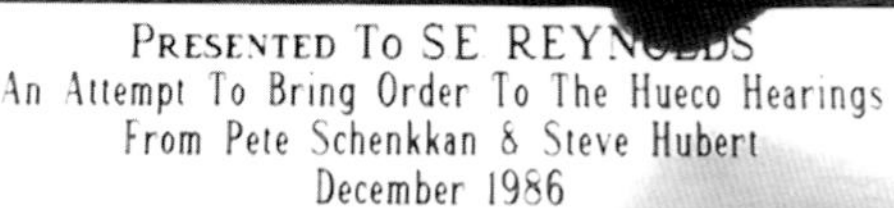

WATER WOES

Left, State Engineer Steve Reynolds pumps water following the Elephant Butte spill of 1985. Center, El Paso attorney Pete Schenkkan and Elephant Butte Irrigation District attorney Steve Hubert gave this gavel to Reynolds to replace the pocket knife he was known to bang on the table, calling the water hearing to order. Right, Reynolds poses next to his favorite souvenir, the "Viva Milagro Beanfield" T-shirt, after the 1988 movie "Milagro Beanfield War," directed by Robert Redford, was filmed in Truchas, N.M. The plot centered around one man's struggle to defend his small beanfield and his community against much larger business and state political interests.

LINDA HARRIS

named co-defendant in the case.

In July 1982, the U.S. Supreme Court ruled that groundwater was to be considered an article of commerce, and its transfer across state lines could not be restricted.

"It was like saying if you grow peanuts in New Mexico, you can only eat the peanuts in New Mexico," Harris said.

Reynolds and the state acted quickly by enacting new laws that allowed the transfer of water on a case-by-case basis, ensuring the protection of the citizens and agriculture involved.

In the hearings that began in 1986, both sides used statistical population growth projections to help their case, with El Paso citing their water needs on the grounds that there was simply no other option. Getting it from the Rio Grande was economically and logistically the plan that made the most sense.

Groundwater reservoirs from the Rio Grande were not easy to identify, as their locations crossed between both state lines and, sometimes, right down the middle.

Doña Ana, Otero and Lincoln counties, NMSU, the Elephant Butte Irrigation District and citizens of Las Cruces all rallied to protest El Paso's suit, citing decreasing public welfare, property value and water quality as their main platform.

After 54 days, more than 30 witnesses and 13,000 pages of testimony, Reynolds denied all of El Paso's well applications. As stated in Harris' "One Hundred Years ..." Reynolds' ending declaration was simple: El Paso wouldn't get the water, because it did not need it.

The fight was not over, and in 1988 El Paso appealed New Mexico's decision in a U.S. district court and failed.

As new leadership emerged in El Paso, Las Cruces and New Mexico, both sides began to compromise out of exhaustion from legal proceedings. In 1990, Reynolds died while still in his post of State Engineer.

Several water disputes have erupted since then, and Harris said there were "no winners and no losers, no matter whose water it is."

"From a conservation standpoint, (the case) was a blessing in disguise," she said.

Resulting from the case, both sides realized the need for better conservation of a scarce, yet vital resource in the desert environment.

Harris said at the end of the case, many participants were given T-shirts that read, "Water Hearing Survivor 1986-1987."

LEASBURG DAM

Groundwater rights to the Rio Grande became a large controversy in the early 1980s.

LINDA HARRIS

DEVELOPING LAS CRUCES

In 1963, David Steinborn moved to Las Cruces and began a respected and well-known real-estate endeavor, known as Steinborn & Associates Real Estate. Steinborn also served three terms as mayor of Las Cruces from 1982-87.

NMSU LASC

A GROWLIN' DAY

Las Cruces City Council decided to take a walk on the wild side with this mountain lion all smiles at Mayor Joseph Camuñez' desk.

NMSU LASC

A REPUBLICAN WIN

Above, before being elected the 27th governor of New Mexico in 1987, NMSU graduate Garrey Carruthers' previous jobs included being the special assistant to the U.S. Department of Agriculture and the director of the Water Resources Research Institute, as well as chairing the Republican Party of New Mexico. Below, upon hearing word of winning the gubernatorial race in 1987, Carruthers and his wife, Cathy, celebrate with supporters, including Sen. Pete Domenici, Rep. Manuel Lujan and the media in Las Cruces.

NMSU LASC

TO INFINITY AND BEYOND

In the late 1980s, after retiring as CEO of Eastern Airlines, Col. Frank Borman, far right, moved to Las Cruces. He was best known as commander of the 1968 Apollo 8 mission, leading the team of American astronauts to orbit the moon. Upon arriving in New Mexico, the lifelong pilot became equally associated with earthbound vehicles as majority owner of the Borman AutoPlex of Las Cruces.

NEW MEXICO MUSEUM OF SPACE HISTORY

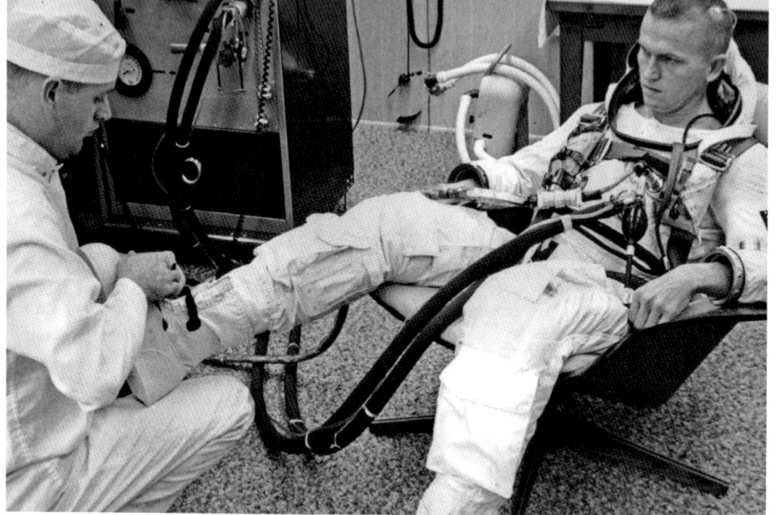

TIME TO RIDE

Paul Bowman with his dad, Bob, and a new '88 Mazda RX-7 convertible.

PAUL BOWMAN

A NEW ERA IN HOME TECHNOLOGY

Home computers became popular in the 1980s, as they were marketed for individual use and affordable for the average consumer.

NMSU LASC

A FAVORITE PASTIME

The advent of cable networks in the 1980s exploded the use of television. The ABC, CBS and NBC broadcast networks no longer had a monopoly on viewers, and the '80s were considered the golden age of television dramas.

JORGE LOPEZ

MAKING MEMORIES

In 1983, Sony marketed the first Betamax video camera, similar to the one New Mexico State University student Jeanne Gleason is sporting, below.

NMSU LASC

A RARE SIGHTING

According to New Mexico State University, nearly 800 journalists, left, gathered to see NASA's Space Shuttle Columbia land at White Sands Missile Range's Northrup Strip on March 30, 1982, at the conclusion of the third shuttle mission. The area would later be renamed White Sands Space Harbor. Columbia completed 27 successful missions before being destroyed during re-entry into Earth's atmosphere on Feb. 1, 2003. All seven crew members were killed during the disaster.

NMSU LASC

SPACE SHUTTLE COLUMBIA

The Space Shuttle Columbia landed at the missile range's Northrup Strip on March 30, 1982, at the conclusion of the third-ever shuttle mission. The area would later be renamed White Sands Space Harbor.

WHITE SANDS MISSILE RANGE PUBLIC AFFAIRS OFFICE

GO AND TEACH

The Diocese of Las Cruces was established in 1982, with the Most Rev. Ricardo Ramírez as its bishop. The diocese serves all of southern New Mexico.
DIOCESE OF LAS CRUCES

DIOCESE OF LAS CRUCES

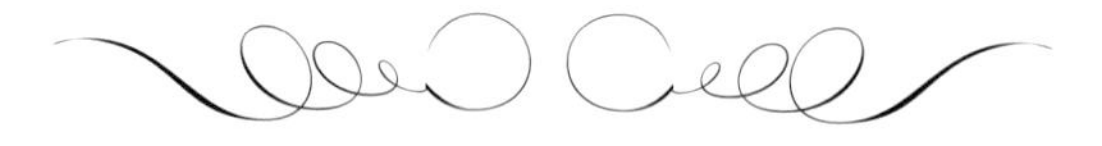

The Roman Catholic Diocese of Las Cruces was founded in 1982, and for its first 29 years had only one bishop, the Most Rev. Ricardo Ramírez.

The diocese extends across all of southern New Mexico from Arizona to Texas. It has an area of approximately 45,000 square miles.

The Diocese of Las Cruces was created out of parishes once part of the Archdiocese of Santa Fe and the Diocese of El Paso. Some parishes in the diocese have a history that began when the area was part of Mexico and under the supervision of the bishop of Durango, Mexico.

By 1852, there were churches at Doña Ana, Mesilla and Las Cruces. The only resident priest was at Mesilla's San Albino Catholic Church, and until 1859, he visited the other two churches – Nuestra Señora de Candelaria de Doña Ana and Santa Genoveva de Las Cruces – to administer sacraments.

Ramírez grew up in Bay City, Texas, and was named Auxiliary Bishop of San Antonio in 1981 by Pope John Paul II. He became the first bishop of the Diocese of Las Cruces on Oct. 18, 1982.

Throughout his three decades as the leader of the church in Las Cruces, Ramírez emphasized social justice. His 2001 pastoral letter, "Speaking the Unspeakable," on the issue of domestic violence, received international attention.

He also became involved in such issues as immigration, poverty, the plight of migrant workers and conditions in the colonias, undeveloped and sometimes illegal subdivisions in rural areas.

Bishop Ramírez helped to either create or sustain several important traditions in the Diocese, including the annual Mass on top of Tortugas Mountain on the Feast Day of Our Lady of Guadalupe, the Border Mass, which is concelebrated with the Bishops of Juárez and El Paso at a fence in the border town of Anapra and the Mariachi Mass and Conference. The latter is also an example of the Bishop's support for the arts throughout the diocese.

The bishop also celebrates Mass every October at the summit of Mount Cristo Rey, which is part of the Sunland Park parish of San Martín de Porres.

In the early years, it was not uncommon for the bishop and members of his pastoral center staff to log as many as 60,000 miles per year on their cars as he made his annual visit to each and every parish. In recent years, the diocese has employed its own distance learning network to save on travel costs.

The bishop has served on more than a dozen national and international committees, most notably as Commissioner of the United States Commission on International Religious Freedom.

A member of the Congregation of St. Basil, Ramírez invited several of his brother Basilian priests to serve in the diocese.

On Sept. 12, 2011, Bishop Ramirez, in accordance with church norm, offered his resignation upon the occasion of his 75th birthday. In time, the Vatican will select the succeeding bishop, and another era will begin in the diocese.

ALL SMILES

The man on the left, former New Mexico State University Board of Regents President Rudy Apodaca, and former president of the Farmers & Merchants Bank, Dallas Johnson, pose with pageant winners gathered at Mesilla's Double Eagle Restaurant in 1981.

NMSU LASC

FAITH TAKES GROUND

Below, the Most Rev. Ricardo Ramírez became the first bishop of the newly established Roman Catholic Diocese of Las Cruces Oct. 18, 1982. Deeply committed to social justice, including the cause of religious freedom, he served two terms on the U.S. Commission on International Religious Freedom. Later, he served on the U.S. State Department Advisory Committee on Religious Freedom Abroad.

NMSU LASC

A GOOD COWBOY

If you're a cowboy, you know it's a good day when you're on the ranch with a good horse at your side, as John Yarbrough was on this day in 1987.

JOHN YARBROUGH

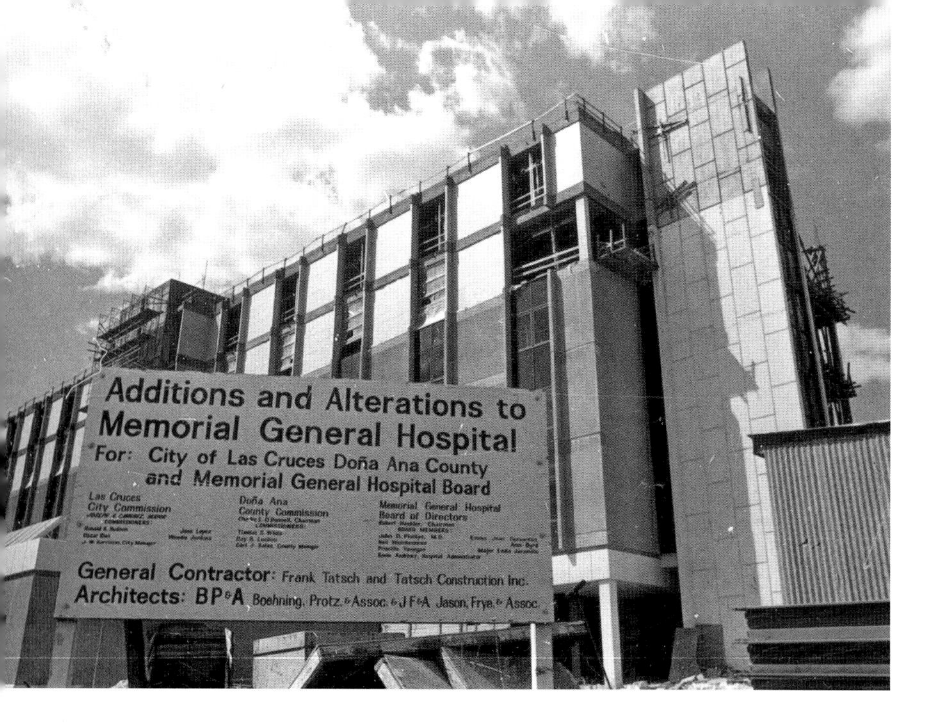

A GLIMPSE OF THE FUTURE

In 1985, New Mexico was one of the first states to adopt the MainStreet program. As a result of urban renewal in Las Cruces that began in 1968, the northern portion of Main Street was shut down, above. The pedestrian mall continued to struggle for popularity, but was an inviting place to hang out, below. Some familiar buildings were built during the 1980s, such as Mesilla Valley Mall, bottom left, and additions and alterations were made to those already standing, such as the Memorial General Hospital, top left, and the Armijo House, middle left.

NMSU LASC

THE ALLEN FAMILY

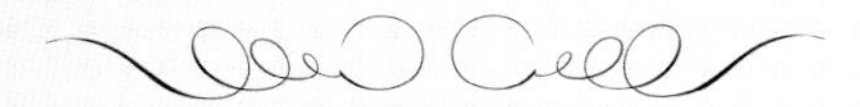

Their office walls are decorated with movie posters, and guests are invited to sit in stadium-style seating while they wait to speak with a member of the Allen family, owners of Allen Theatres, a business with roots as deep as New Mexico itself.

In 1912, the same year New Mexico joined the union, Frank B. Allen opened the Allen Opera House in Farmington, N.M. His sister played the organ while guests were treated to silent films into the 1920s.

In 1949, Russell Paul Allen, son of Frank Allen, built the second movie house in Farmington, the Totah. The decision wasn't easy.

"We lived in a one-bedroom apartment above the original Allen Opera House," said Larry Allen, son of Russell P. Allen. "Dad told us we could build a new house or another theater, but we couldn't afford both. So we built another theater."

Larry Allen, third-generation owner, said early steps such as this one, and his father's commitment to advanced technology, paved the way for the family's success in the theater business.

"Dad put stereophonic sound in the Totah so we could play 'Ben Hur' and 'The Ten Commandments' in the proper sound," Larry Allen said. "He invested $25,000 – a lot of money at the time, a year's worth of profit."

Allen Theatres continued to expand. In 1982, Larry Allen and his brother Lane bought the theaters in Las Cruces, venturing away from the original location and doubling the number of screens to manage. In 1998, the Allens introduced stadium-style seating with their newest theater, the Telshor 12 in Las Cruces. Larry Allen called multiplex theaters "the game changer" in the movie theater business at the time. By 1999, the circuit had theaters in 10 New Mexico towns, for a total of 74 screens.

Digital projection was introduced to cinema in 2003. The Allens knew the future of movies had been changed forever.

In 2007, Allen Theatres installed new Christie digital projectors and Doremi servers in Las Cruces, Farmington, Roswell, Hobbs, Clovis, Alamogordo and Gallup.

"We were part of the first 3,400 screens in the country to convert," said Russell G. Allen, vice president of operations who was named after his grandfather and is the son of Larry Allen.

As New Mexico turns 100 years old, the family runs and owns theaters in 10 New Mexico towns, for a total of 95 screens. New Mexico was the 47th state to join the union, and Allen Theaters continues its connections to the Land of Enchantment, being the 47th largest movie theater company in the U.S.

GENERATIONS OF ENTERTAINMENT

Larry Allen, Asa Allen, Heather Gandy and Russell G. Allen operate Allen Theatres, a family-owned business since 1912.

ALLEN FAMILY

THE ORIGINAL RUSSELL

Left, Russell Paul Allen, second-generation owner of Allen Theatres, as a boy in Farmington, N.M. His son Larry and grandchildren would continue and expand the family business. Right, a flyer promotes the 1989 grand opening of Allen Theatres' Cinema 8 in Las Cruces' Mesilla Valley Mall. Those screens were replaced in 2009 by the Cineport 10, also at the mall.

ALLEN FAMILY

THE ORIGINAL ALLENS

Frank and Augusta Allen pose for a photograph with their son Russell Paul Allen.

ALLEN FAMILY

A TRADITION LIFTS OFF

Rising early enough to inhale the crisp, still, pre-dawn mornings of New Mexico are what balloonists all over the state live for – that, and the view.

In the early 1980s, the Mesilla Valley was familiar with a lively group of balloon pilots who came together to form the Greater Mesilla Valley Aerostat Ascension Association, a club that has banded balloonists in the area together throughout the past 30 years.

At the backbone of the club, and at nearly all of the ballooning events in southern New Mexico, were Bob and Ona Fern, whose well-known dynamic personalities were the life of the ballooning party.

A LOT OF HOT AIR

Left, Ona Fern lands her balloon on Elephant Butte next to unsuspecting sailor, Bob Fern in 1978, right, the Ferns take off one early summer morning in the Mesilla Valley.

BOB AND ONA FERN

"The camaraderie between the pilots and balloonists at this time was very close. We all looked out for each other," Ona Fern said.

Fern fell in love with "Queen Celeste" – a brightly colored, checkered-patterned balloon – in 1977, when a friend from El Paso took her for her first ride.

"I saw there were women pilots and said to myself, 'Hey, I can do that,'" Fern said.

It seemed "Queen Celeste" was made for Fern, who said it was designed with women pilots in mind, with a smaller basket and envelope.

In fact, balloonist Carol Davis flew the "Queen Celeste" to new heights, achieving a world record when she reached an altitude of 22,000 feet in 1974.

After several fateful moments – including landing "Queen Celeste" on Elephant Butte Lake next to catamaran sailor Bob Fern the first time they laid eyes on one another – ballooning had the Ferns' hearts.

Her famous words, "Hey sailor, wanna exchange rides?" on that first fateful meeting led to the couple's marriage, and the ride of their lives to become some of the leading balloon enthusiasts in the area.

"Queen Celeste" and the Ferns made headlines again in 1978 when they had the balloon tethered at a party in Dripping Springs, and a strong gust of wind knocked Ona Fern out of the basket, ripping the tether loose and leaving an inexperienced passenger at the helm.

Fortunately, the passenger knew enough about ballooning to navigate all the way to White Sands by the next morning, making it the first balloon flight over the Organ Mountains.

Bob Fern said these trial-and-error days helped set the standard for current ballooning and piloting laws.

"Now there's tests and guidelines and inspections to pass," Bob Fern said. "It's not so easy to get your pilot's license anymore."

Ballooning in the Mesilla Valley was uncommon and somewhat unorganized, so in 1978 the responsibility was handed over to Ona Fern.

"Back then, I hardly knew how to fly a balloon, much less run a race," she said.

Starting in 1981, ballooning jumped on board with The Whole Enchilada Fiesta, marking the prelude to the popular Labor Day Weekend throughout the early '80s.

In 1986, the club had grown to include more than 50 balloonists from the area, who launched into several pilot competitions, including the Hare and Hound Race, the Black Jack Convergent Navigational Task and the Chile Drop.

A FAMILIAR FACE IN THE PARK

In the heat of the summer of 1986, Peter Wolf Toth came to Apodaca Park to create "Dineh," one of more than 70 large Native American sculptures he has carved around the world, including one in each of the 50 United States. The statue and base at Apodaca Park are 20 feet tall.

SID GRAFT/JESSICA GRADY-MAULDIN

OPEN SPACES

Above, new to the area from New York City, teenager Steve Calderazzo discovered the many outdoor sports the Mesilla Valley had to offer in 1986.

NATISHA HALES

THE WHOLE ENCHILADA FIESTA

Above left, what would Las Cruces' Whole Enchilada Fiesta be without the creation of the world's largest enchilada, crafted every year by Roberto Estrada, of Roberto's Mexican Food, who in 1981 made a flat enchilada measuring about six feet in diameter. The fiesta began in 1980, known as "Vaquero Days," to capture and recognize the Hispanic and Cowboy culture in the area, and has since been recognized as one of the top 100 events in the U.S. and the third largest in New Mexico.

NMSU LASC

CAMPUS JOURNALISM

Emily Davis, Jim Hilley, Todd Dickson, Karen Islam, Kathy Clem, George Andrejko, Glen Warchol, Greg Vigil, Gil Sarabia, Jeff Renegar, Donna Chilton, Minerva Carrillo, Bruce Halvorson, Terry Mullen, Doug DesGeorges, Loretta Lopez, Steve Schroats, Joel Rickman, Michelle Stephens, Anna Maria Perez, Steve Eckles and Kim Linder pose for the 1981 Roundup staff yearbook photo.

BARBARA HUBBARD

HOMECOMING HEROES

New Mexico State University Homecoming queen and king winners pose for the camera with a stadium full of Aggie fans in 1980.

NMSU LASC

THE LAMBDA CHIS

The Lambda Chi fraternity jams to a rock 'n' roll song at Greek Sing during Greek Week, a tradition at NMSU in which the fraternities and sororities compete for glory during a series of events and games.

GEORGE ANDREJKO

ALL IN THE FAMILY

COAS Bookstore owners Mike and Veronica Beckett, center, maintain more than 275,000 books with the help of sons Brandon and Brett Beckett.

BECKETT FAMILY

COAS BOOKSTORE

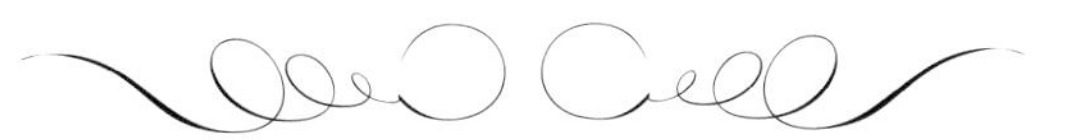

"The story I heard was there were so many books that the house was literally splitting," Mike Beckett said. "I have a memory of getting under the house with my dad and putting up bricks. Finally my mom said we had to get the books out of the house."

And so Mike's dad, Pat Beckett, motivated by his wife, Becky, opened the first COAS Bookstore near the corner of Lohman Avenue and Solano Drive in Las Cruces in 1983.

The bookstore traveled around the city to several locations before opening Downtown at 317 N. Main St. in 1991. The Becketts also owned a COAS Bookstore in Las Vegas, Nev., throughout the 1990s. A second Las Cruces location on Solano Drive was opened in 2005.

COAS is the kind of bookstore one expects to find in a city such as Chicago or Seattle. With more than three-quarters-of-a-million books in two locations – not to mention rare and out-of-print books, movies, music, games and more – a person could spend months combing the shelves and still not see everything there is to see.

For years, Pat worked as an archaeologist at New Mexico State University. He collected archaeological books and built his own library by buying and selling books from other collectors. Eventually, the collection was straining the foundation of the family home.

There are at least two explanations for the store's unusual name. His father founded a publishing company, the Center of Anthropological Studies, in the 1970s. However, the story Pat later told Mike is that a "coa" is the Aztec Nahuatl word for "digging stick."

As of 2011, the store has a new logo and a recently streamlined Internet sales operation, www.coasbooks.com. The aggressive marketing and e-commerce efforts are just part of staying competitive in a changing economy, said Mike Beckett, who with his wife, Veronica, has owned COAS Bookstore since 2007.

Mike and Veronica introduced much-needed efficiencies to the business. Veronica does all of the office administration and bookkeeping for what has turned out to be a fairly complicated business. Now that their sons Brandon and Brett have joined the business, they have, in turn, streamlined operations even more.

The success of the bookstore, at a time when many booksellers are being hard hit, is due to the determination of four generations of the Beckett family.

"My grandfather built bookcases for this store, and I helped him," Mike said. "Everyone in our family grows up making bookcases. My father built bookcases and my sons have built bookcases."

For many years, his sister Kristy Lambert also worked for the family business.

Brandon, an international business student at NMSU in 2011, has launched a palm tree logo and marketing campaign for COAS Bookstores, and also manages the stores' Facebook page.

Brett, who earned a bachelor's degree in aerospace engineering at NMSU, completely revamped COAS' Internet store, which sends books to almost every country in the world. Brett discovered a way to lower many costs, allowing COAS Bookstores to stay competitive on the Internet.

COAS Bookstores in Las Cruces have comfortable nooks where customers can relax and read – a feature added by Veronica.

Mike Beckett puts the COAS philosophy this way: "We just want to be a good, honest, standup business."

PRIDE AND PASSION IN PINK

Dressed in pink are members of the Lou Sisbarro family: daughter Nicole Ikard, Lou Sisbarro, Pat Sisbarro and son Dan Sisbarro. They stand with members of the Las Cruces Fire Department in front of the pink firetruck Lou acquired to help promote breast cancer awareness. Pat, a founding co-chair of the NMSU Aggies Are Tough Enough to Wear Pink campaign, helped raise almost $2 million for cancer research and awareness from 2007-11.

SISBARRO FAMILY

SISBARRO'S DEAL WITH THE COMMUNITY

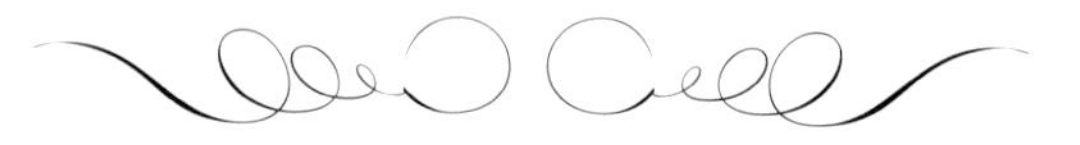

"The Michigan car business was shaky and the winters were getting colder and colder," said a smiling Lou Sisbarro, recalling his 1981 move to Las Cruces to open a car dealership. "That was 30 years ago. I think we made the right move."

With more than 85,000 new and used car sales under his belt, Lou Sisbarro continues to smile.

Employing 200 people, Sisbarro's 10 automotive sales, service, parts and accessory operations stretch along Interstate 10 in New Mexico from Deming across Las Cruces and into Sunland Park. Sisbarro's new car and truck lines include Buick, GMC, Cadillac, Chevrolet, Volkswagen, Mitsubishi, Chrysler, Dodge and Jeep. Sisbarro has been ranked as southern New Mexico's top volume used car dealer since 1991, according to Polk Cross-Sell data.

However, what makes Lou Sisbarro smile more than anything else is his advertising slogan – "Nobody Beats a Sisbarro Deal" – has come to mean much more than the price of a vehicle. The slogan also represents a commitment to his customers and community.

Lou Sisbarro has been a longtime supporter of the Las Cruces community, from the arts to youth activities to New Mexico State University athletics. His family's involvement in local causes mirro his own. His wife, Pat Sisbarro, was a founding co-chair of the "NMSU Aggies Are Tough Enough to Wear Pink" campaign, which, between 2007-11, generated almost $2 million for breast cancer research in southern New Mexico. Son Dan and daughter Nicole Ikard, in addition to holding down key management positions in the Sisbarro organization, are active on local boards and volunteer committees. Another son, Chip, is a teacher in Phoenix.

"There was a time when a car dealership was a central, driving force in a local economy, and dealers put a lot of money back into the community," Sisbarro said. "That's what my wife, Pat, and I have done since we got here. It is so important to be involved and to give back to the people who have supported our business for so long."

What does the future hold for the Sisbarro family and the Sisbarro dealerships?

"I see our business growing and changing with Las Cruces and southern New Mexico," Sisbarro said. "You can't convince me there is a better, more prosperous place to live.

"As we finish our 30th year in business, I hope my children continue the Sisbarro name. But they may have to wait because I have another 30 years left in me."

ALWAYS A GOOD DAY FOR GOLF

Since its inception in 1979 and the subsequent boom of the surrounding housing development, Picacho Hills Country Club has provided a focal point for social activity and great golf. Left and below, golfers in 1982 sport the latest in course fashion.

PICACHO HILLS COUNTRY CLUB

AGAINST THE ROPES

Right, Louie Burke takes a few final seconds to gather his thoughts, moments before his 10-round fight with Charlie Brown on July 24, 1984. Although the majority of spectators felt that he won the fight, Burke was on the short end of the judges' split decision. Both men were previously undefeated.

LOUIE BURKE

MS. PHYSIQUE SOUTHWEST

Left, Las Cruces residents Mary Boris (left) and Kim Clark were the winners of a regional women's body building championship in 1985.

LAS CRUCES BULLETIN

J. PAUL TAYLOR

Born in 1926, J. Paul Taylor has lived a full life in southern New Mexico, and has become one of the most beloved and respected figures in the state.

There are many ways to describe him: a gentleman, an educator, a scholar and a statesman – as he was more than just a legislator. In his 18 years in the New Mexico House of Representatives, he tirelessly campaigned for health care and other services to the poor. He was also a devoted husband to his late wife, Mary, and is an adoring father to his children.

Talk to Taylor and he'll credit his parents for instilling in him the values that have driven him to give back to the people, region and state.

During the Depression, he recalled destitute people camping in his parents' yard. His mother and father would generously feed those in need and offer them a safe place to rest. Taylor describes his mother, Margarita Romero de Taylor, as a "social worker" for the Chamberino community.

It was his mother's side of the family that links Taylor to the area's early development. Just as deep an influence on Taylor as his family was Mary Louise Cable, his fifth-grade teacher. Taylor will tell you it was she who inspired him to learn about history and become an educator.

A STRONG SOUTHERN NEW MEXICAN

J. Paul Taylor flashes a friendly smile in the Mesilla Plaza as he was featured in the Las Cruces Bulletin community guide in 2010.

LAS CRUCES BULLETIN

Taylor's heart was in teaching, and after graduating with a degree from New Mexico State University, he taught sixth grade at Mesilla Park Elementary. He would go on to work as a teacher and principal in the village of Doña Ana and at Alameda Elementary. Taylor went on to central office administration, handling a number of roles, but resisted efforts to have him become the district's superintendent.

After Taylor retired in 1985, Mary Helen Garcia – who now serves as state representative for District 34 – approached Taylor about running for governor.

"I said, 'Forget it,'" recalled Taylor, who is a Democrat. "I had not even intended to get into politics."

When Garcia approached him about running for state representative for District 33, Taylor agreed, and was elected in 1986.

In the House, he would chair the Health and Human Services Committee, where he pushed to improve the state's services for children, youth and families. He also advocated for education – he served as president of the state National Education Association before his retirement – and for cultural affairs.

Taylor carried major bills that improved the infrastructure and wastewater systems in his district, including getting water works for Mesilla.

His legislative accomplishments include adding full-day kindergarten to the system and the creation of an office for early childhood education.

"I thought if kids could have this wonderful background of developmental programs as they grew up ... they would grow up not having to repeat grades or enter programs that require rehabilitation," Taylor said.

Health concerns eventually forced Taylor to retire from the Legislature in 2004. Soon after, Taylor offered one final contribution to the state – the historic home off the Mesilla Plaza where he and his wife, Mary, raised their seven children.

The home, which was first constructed in 1850, will be known as the Taylor-Barela-Reynolds-Mesilla State Monument. Some guided tours are now offered, but it will be opened fully to the public after Taylor no longer lives there.

The home is filled with art and furnishings the Taylors collected over the years, which Taylor said he believes will give people insight into the region's history and culture.

SCHOOL LIFE

Above, Tammy Schutz and Yvette Armendariz, Las Cruces High School band members are all smiles during a football game in 1988. Left, Michael Calderazzo accepts his high school diploma from LCHS in 1989.

NATISHA HALES/COURTNEY FAMILY

GREEN AND GOLD MOMENTS

Below, a senior class at Mayfield High School poses for a picture and enjoy the beautiful Las Cruces weather in 1988.

NMSU LASC

MAKING MEMORIES

Right, Camille Lemons and Ira Cline prepare for the 1989 prom at Mayfield High School. Below, the 1989 graduating class from MHS takes over the Pan American Center.

CAMILLE LIMAS

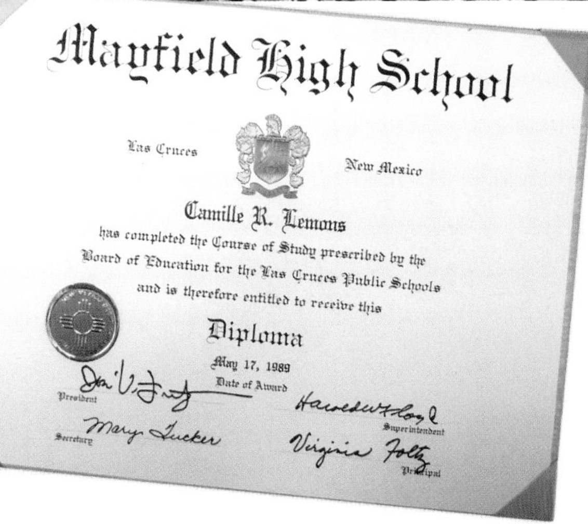

Mayfield High School

Las Cruces New Mexico

Camille R. Lemons

has completed the Course of Study prescribed by the Board of Education for the Las Cruces Public Schools and is therefore entitled to receive this

Diploma

May 17, 1989
Date of Award

President Superintendent

Secretary Principal

THE ARTIST FORMERLY KNOWN AS ...

In March of 1985, Las Cruces residents lined up early in the day to catch Prince perform his Purple Rain tour. The tour was following up on the success of his 1984 movie, "Purple Rain."

NMSU LASC

A THEATER LEGEND

Las Crucen Mark Medoff, center, celebrates the success of his play "Children of a Lesser God" with actors Phyllis Frelich and John Rubenstein at the 1980 Tony Awards. Of four nominations, the work earned three awards – Best Play, Best Performance by a Leading Actress in a Play and Best Performance by a Leading Actor in a Play.

MARK MEDOFF

A STREET CAR NAMED DESIRE

This flyer could be seen around town, advertising the popular play coming to the Las Cruces Community Theatre in 1986 and 1987.

NMSU LASC

GIRLS JUST WANNA HAVE FUN

Cyndi Lauper performs her top hits for Las Cruces at the Pan American Center. She was the first female artist to have her first three charted singles reach the Top 3 Billboard list.

NMSU LASC

ALL THE HYPE

Pop culture played a major role in fashion trends of the 1980s. Metal and punk music as well as movies such as "Flashdance" influenced heavy makeup, baggy pants and outrageous color patterns.

NMSU LASC

WALKING THE RUNWAY AT MESILLA VALLEY MALL

The tailored suit look of the 1980s, with broad shoulder pads being a prominent look for women, was popularized due to several pop culture TV dramas such as "Dynasty" and "Dallas." In Las Cruces, those styles were put on display during a fashion show at the Mesilla Valley Mall in 1984.

NMSU LASC

AN IMPROVED LANDSCAPE

Engineering Complex III at New Mexico State University was built in the 1990s. The complex was one of many new structures that were created on the campus and in Las Cruces during the decade. The '90s was a time of planning for the future of the institution and the city.

NEW MEXICO STATE UNIVERSITY LIBRARY ARCHIVES AND SPECIAL COLLECTIONS

1990-1999

PREPARING FOR GROWTH

A MUSICAL SENSATION

Following suit with other groups hot in the 1990s, P.I.A.D.O.R. (Peace is a Dream of Reality) was a hit, performing its own R&B, gospel and Spanish songs. Formed in 1992, the group of local boys – Eddie Chavez, Victor Lucero, Ronn Reyes, Joaquin "Keen" Hernandez and Jerry Lujan Jr. – started performing around town before traveling across the state and eventually the nation. Before separating in 1996, the group presented an award and performed during the Hispanic Music Awards in Albuquerque, sang the national anthem to a packed Aggie Memorial Stadium on the Fourth of July and played at the Century Club in Beverly Hills.

P.I.A.D.O.R.

THE EXCITING 1990S

The first formal flight test of the Delta Clipper Experimental (DC-X) was completed at White Sands Missile Range in 1996. The single-stage rocket hovered vertically at 300 feet before moving laterally in a straight 350-foot line and descending vertically onto the landing pad. The flight lasted 66 seconds and was considered a success by McDonnell Douglas officials, who built the rocket for the U.S. Ballistic Missile Defense Organization.

U.S. ARMY WHITE SANDS MISSILE RANGE

1990
Thanks to a desirable landscape, temperate weather and major employers, including White Sands Missile Range, NASA and New Mexico State University, the population of Las Cruces reached 62,126.

1990
On Feb. 10, 1990, at Las Cruces Bowl bowling center, four people were murdered and three were severely wounded. Sketches were released, but the suspects were never found.

1990
The first Gulf War begins in August when Iraqi troops invade Kuwait, an act condemned internationally, and one that spurred President George H.W. Bush to deploy American forces into Saudi Arabia.

1991
Rubén Smith is elected mayor of Las Cruces during the city's first official mayoral election at large.

1992
A new phenomenon that would change life around the world: the Internet reaches 1 million websites.

1993
Oñate High School moves from Spruce Avenue to its new location on Mesa Grande Drive off U.S. Highway 70.

NATISHA HALES/LAS CRUCES POLICE DEPARTMENT/LAS CRUCES BULLETIN/CITY OF LAS CRUCES/NMSU LASC/OÑATE HIGH SCHOOL/DOÑA ANA COUNTY/MILLER FAMILY

1990s

Who's Who

Las Cruces Mayors

- 1989-91 ... Tommy Tomlin
- 1991-2003 ... Ruben A. Smith

Postmasters

- 1993 ... William O'Neal
- 1996 ... Bobby H. Alvarez
- 1997 ... Allen Lee Brock
- 1997 ... Samuel Avalos
- 1997 ... Kerby Peterson
- 1998 ... John H. Roark
- 1998 ... Robert M. Dinkel

NMSU Presidents

- 1984-94 ... James E. Halligan
- 1995-97 ... J. Michael Orenduff
- 1994-95, 1997-2000 ... William B. Conroy

Mesilla Mayors

- 1986-90 ... Rosalie Rader
- 1994-95 ... Edward Southworth
- 1995-98 ... Roman Aranda III
- 1998-2010 ... Michael Cadena

Doña Ana County Sheriffs

- 1987-90 ... Cooney Sarracino
- 1991-94 ... Ray Storment
- 1995-98 ... Jan Cary
- 1998 ... Jamas Robles
- 1999-2002 ... Juan Hernandez

New Mexico Governors

- 1987-91 ... Garrey Carruthers
- 1991-95 ... Bruce King
- 1995-2003 ... Gary Johnson

U.S. Senators

- 1983-2011 ... Jeff Bingaman
- 1972-2009 ... Pete Domenici

U.S. Representatives

- 1981-2003 ... Joe R. Skeen
- 1983-97 ... Bill Richardson
- 1989-97 ... Steven Schiff
- 1997-2009 ... Heather Wilson
- 1997-99 ... William T. Redmond

Las Cruces Public Schools Superintendent

- 1989-2001 ... Jesse L. Gonzales

By the Numbers

- 62,126 ... Las Cruces population (1990)
- 135,510 ... Doña Ana County population (1990)
- 46 percent ... Hispanic
- $19,836 ... Average annual income
- $5.15 ... Minimum wage (1997)
- $1.16 ... Gallon of gas (1990)
- 29 cents ... First-class stamp (1991)
- 32 cents ... First-class stamp (1995)
- 33 cents ... First-class stamp (1999)
- 2.59 ... Average number of people per house
- $68,300 ... Home value
- 9,333.54 acres ... City limits
- 1,500 acres ... Acquired by NMSU
- 95,000 sq. ft. ... NMSU Engineering Complex
- $3.830 trillion ... National debt
- 73.1 years ... Life expectancy, men
- 79.1 years ... Life expectancy, women

In the News

March 18, 1990: The largest art theft in U.S. history occurs in Boston, Mass., when two thieves posing as policemen nab 12 paintings worth an estimated $100 to $200 million from the Isabella Stewart Gardner Museum.

April 24, 1990: The Hubble Telescope is placed into orbit by the U.S. Space Shuttle Discovery.

Jan. 26, 1992: The renewed nation of Russia and its leader Boris Yeltsin announce it will stop targeting the United States with nuclear weapons.

April 19, 1993: The 51-day Waco standoff ends when a fire, started by Branch Davidians, kills 75 members of the cult, including leader David Koresh.

June 12, 1994: Former football star O.J. Simpson is arrested and later acquitted for the murder of his ex-wife Nicole Brown Simpson and her lover Ronald Goldman. The Simpson case was one of the highest profile murder cases in the nation's history.

April 19, 1995: Timothy McVeigh and Terry Nichols explode a bomb outside the Alfred P. Murrah Federal Building in Oklahoma City, killing 168 people in the domestic terrorism attack.

Aug. 31, 1997: Princess Diana of Wales was killed in a fatal car crash in Paris after trying to escape the paparazzi. Also killed were boyfriend Dodi Fayed and driver Henri Paul.

Jan. 26, 1998: The Monica Lewinsky scandal begins when President Bill Clinton denies a sexual relationship with the White House intern. He is eventually impeached on the matter.

Jan. 1, 1999: The Euro currency is introduced.

April 20, 1999: Students Eric Harris and Dylan Klebold kill 12 students and one teacher, and injure 21 students before committing suicide during the Columbine High School massacre. This was the fourth deadliest school shooting in U.S. history.

1994
City Council gets the go-ahead from community members to pursue legal action against El Paso Electric Co. that would include nine different lawsuits, including a condemnation lawsuit to take over the utility's distribution.

1996
President Bill Clinton visits the New Mexico State University Horseshoe.

1997
Fernando Macias was a state senator from 1985-2000 and Doña Ana County manager from 1997-2000. Gov. Bill Richardson appointed Macias as judge of Family District Court.

1999
Las Cruces celebrates its sesquicentennial, 150 years after the city was laid out by Delos Bennutt Sackett under the direction of Pablo Melendres in 1849.

1999
After decades of rivalry, Las Cruces and Mayfield high schools football teams meet in the New Mexico High School State Football Championship. LCHS won 24-12.

1999
People internationally prepare for Y2K – a potential crisis that would cause computers around the world to fail once the clock hit midnight on Jan. 1, 2000.

the Bulletin
VOL. 31, NO. 52 • 50¢ "WHERE LOCAL NEWS COMES FIRST" LAS CRUCES, NEW MEXICO

Y2K can't stop the Wilted Chile Awards!

BUILDING FOR THE NEXT GENERATION

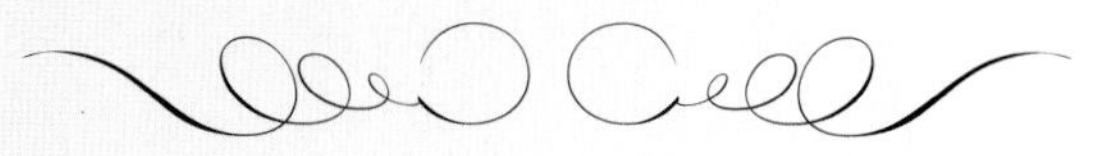

After seeing a tremendous amount of growth in the 1980s, Las Cruces played catch-up in the 1990s and transformed its landscape in regard to new building projects and road construction that served the expanding population.

"The 1990s was when (the city) did a lot of thinking and planning and looked at zoning codes," said Robert Garza, who held several engineering positions with the city in the '90s before his appointment to Las Cruces city manager in 2011. "We set up a long-term master plan that covered drainage, roads and parks."

The '90s saw steady growth, thanks to success at New Mexico State University and White Sands Missile Range, as well as an influx of retirees.

"As the age of the senior population began to increase and people became more affluent and able to relocate, the Southwest became a desirable place," said Eddie Binns, a developer-builder who has been in the Mesilla Valley since the 1950s. "Las Cruces got a percentage of those people looking to relocate."

BUILDINGS OF THE 1990S

The 1990s saw the addition of several buildings, such as the Health and Public Service Building, above, built in 1996 and the Foothills Business Center, below, built in '94.

GENCON CONSTRUCTION

To cater to the new demographic, Binns said in addition to health care, the residential sector saw growth with established neighborhoods, such as High Range, expanding and new subdivisions being built.

"Growth has historically taken place on the eastern side of town," said Binns, who constructed several apartment complexes along Roadrunner Parkway.

To help accommodate growing populations in that area and on the East Mesa, much of which was annexed to the city in the 1990s, the city undertook a project to add frontage roads to U.S. Highway 70.

"The highway department made it a four-lane divided highway," Garza said. "It was one of the largest highway projects since the highway went in."

Brian Denmark, who was the planning director during the decade, said extensive growth on the East Mesa – including the construction of Oñate High School, which relocated from Spruce Avenue – prompted the city to look at ways to relieve the flow of traffic.

"The philosophy was to begin to 'master plan' our community with utilities and build ahead of time," he said. "We were planning for future growth."

One subdivision that was developed in the 1990s was Sonoma Ranch, located off Roadrunner Parkway. Created in 1996, Sonoma Ranch was the brainchild of developers George Rawson, David Steinborn and Dale Schueller.

"In the 1990s, we saw more stuff on Las Cruces being a great place to retire and do business," Rawson said.

A master-planned community that included recreation and various types of housing set against a scenic backdrop, construction on the first houses in Sonoma Ranch began in 1999. Originally on 600 acres, Rawson said as of 2011 it includes 1,200 acres and is an ongoing project.

In addition to growth in the housing sector, commercial industries also began to flourish, with new shopping complexes coming to town or relocating.

"All of the goods and services (retirees) required spurred additional growth," Binns said. "It caused a rollover effect."

Binns said he sold land on opposite sides of Interstate 25 along Lohman Avenue that would become the Walmart Supercenter, previously housed across the street, and the Target-Albertsons complex, a project put together by a developer from Dallas.

To more easily connect community members to business, Garza said the city began various road projects, such as paving

AN IMPROVED LANDSCAPE

New buildings, such as the New Mexico State University Zuhl Library, above, and Memorial Medical Center's Family Practice Centers, below, came to life in the 1990s. The library was named for Herb and Joan Zuhl who made a generous donation to the university, including their world-class petrified wood collection.

NMSU LASC/GENCON CONSTRUCTION

Telshor Boulevard north of Lohman, which helped bring in new developments, such as the Allen Theatres Telshor 12, built in 1998.

Other undertakings included realigning various roads – such as Missouri Avenue to Boutz Road and Picacho Avenue to Spruce – to make commuting more direct. Garza said these tasks uprooted more than a dozen homes in both neighborhoods.

"We had to completely redo the neighborhoods," he said.

Lohman was also extended in the 1990s to meet the needs of residents moving east. The multimillion-dollar extension took five years of planning and one year of construction.

"With density resting east of the flood dam, we needed an arterial to go out there," Garza said. "We started planning in 1993 and finished in 1999.

"In the 1990s, we helped establish the backbone of our transportation system."

"When we grew in demand, we created more services," Rawson said. "Growth at NMSU and in enrollment was key during the '90s."

In the 1990s, NMSU, which employed more than 6,000 during this period, also contributed to Las Cruces' building boom, said Ben Woods, NMSU senior vice president for external relations.

"There were a number of expansions and renovations during the 1990s," he said.

From remodeling Corbett Center Student Union to building new campus housing – Vista del Monte and Cervantes Village – Woods said one major project at the university was the construction of Zuhl Library.

"A lot of projects went through," Woods said. "There was a mix of investments. We were looking at the future and were taking care of what people gave us in the past."

The 1990s also saw Doña Ana Community College – then Doña Ana Branch Community College – expand to Sunland Park and improve its Gadsden center.

"It was the emergence of DACC as a tremendously important asset," said Woods, adding that the institution grew enrollment from 3,700 students in 1995 to 4,700 students in 2000. "(The 1990s) foreshadowed what we've done since then."

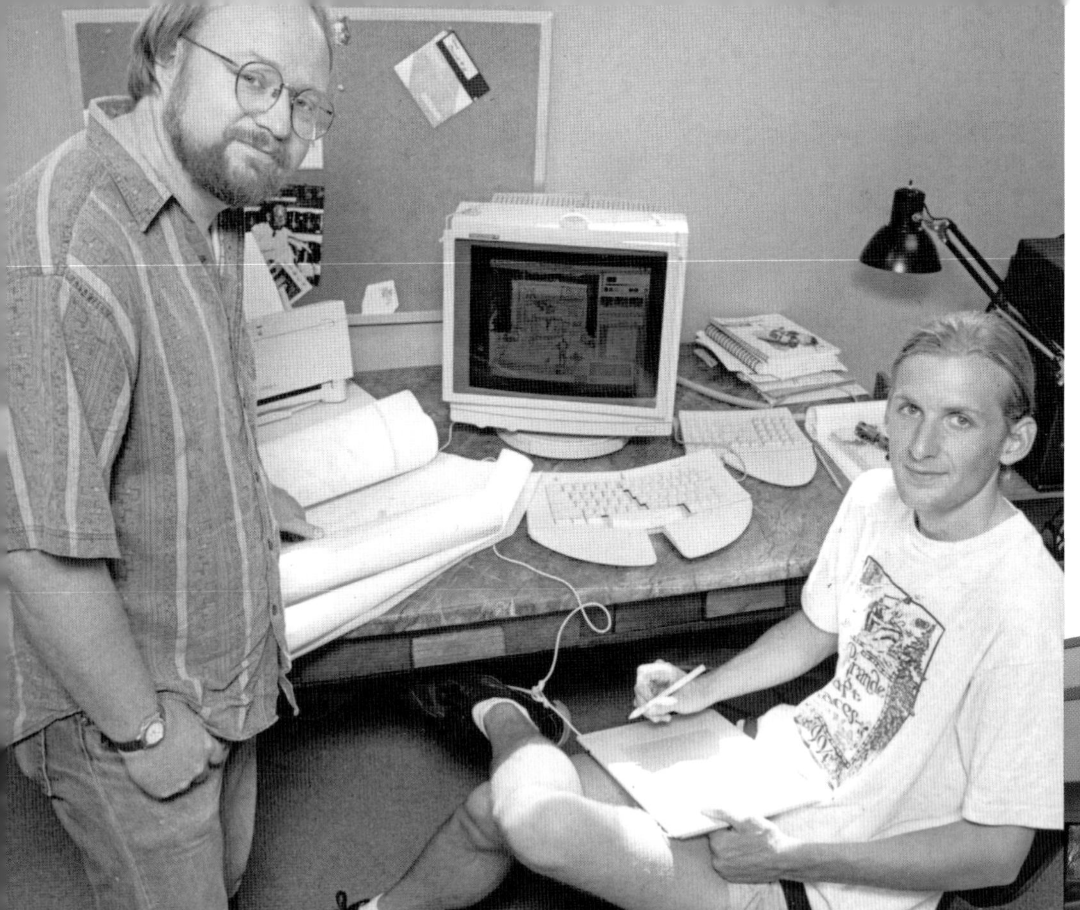

COMPUTERS AND INTERNET

Known as the electronic age, great advances in technology graced the Mesilla Valley in the 1990s. Left, NMSU theater arts professor Jim Billings and student Keith McQueen use the latest computer software to design sets at the American Southwest Theatre Company. While ZiaNet, below, began in Las Cruces as a hobby in 1995, it quickly grew to the largest independently owned Internet service provider (ISP) in the state. Serving more than 2,000 in its first year, it eventually had 30,000 customers in New Mexico.

LAS CRUCES BULLETIN/ZIANET

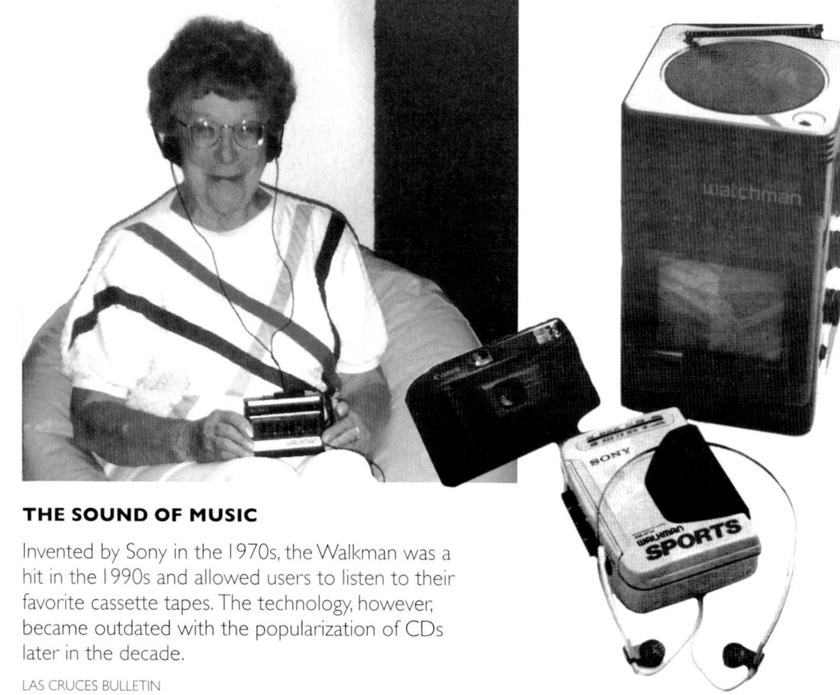

THE SOUND OF MUSIC

Invented by Sony in the 1970s, the Walkman was a hit in the 1990s and allowed users to listen to their favorite cassette tapes. The technology, however, became outdated with the popularization of CDs later in the decade.

LAS CRUCES BULLETIN

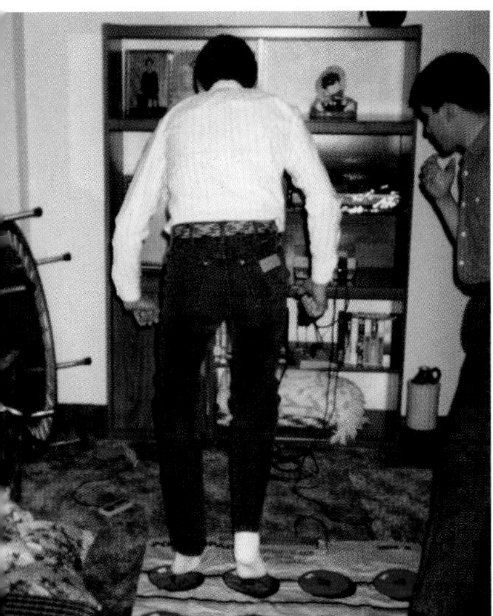

SIGNS OF THE TIME

The 1990s also saw improvements to other forms of technology, such as point-and-shoot cameras, above, and video games. The Nintendo Entertainment System, left, was popular and gave users the chance to interact with their television sets.

LAS CRUCES BULLETIN/NATISHA HALES

SWING STATE

When it comes to election years, New Mexico has witnessed several presidential candidates throwing their weight around to "swing" the state one way or the other.

On Nov. 1, 1996, four days before the election, then President Bill Clinton paid a visit to Las Cruces and touted his current presidency and future plans to a crowd of more than 35,000 people packed on the Horseshoe of New Mexico State University.

"I have worked hard for four years to create America's best future for all of you in the 21st century, to create a country in which everybody – Latino, African-American, Irish-American, Polish-American, Asian-American, you name it – all Americans who are willing to work for it can live out their dreams, an America still standing fast for freedom and peace and security and prosperity all over the world, an America in which we are building an American community of all our people together," Clinton said to the crowd.

"We passed the Family and Medical Leave law over their opposition. And three-and-a-half years later, over 12 million Americans have used it when a baby was born or a family member was sick. We've had record numbers of new small businesses, record numbers of new businesses owned by women and minorities and 10.7 million new jobs, a faster job growth rate than under any administration of the other party since the 1920s."

Clinton won over New Mexico in '96 with 49 percent of the popular vote, compared with 42 percent for his opponent, Republican nominee Bob Dole.

New Mexico has long been considered a "swing state" due to close political races, partisan upheavals, divided political loyalties and tight polling.

People in New Mexico come from many diverse cultural backgrounds, and historically, polling statistics show that candidates who address specific issues important to residents may have a bigger impact than party affiliation.

Put simply, states that have potentially undecided voters are considered very important to presidential candidates.

Since joining the union in 1912, New Mexico has participated in 25 presidential elections, with the results nearly split down the middle – 13 wins for Democrats, 12 for Republicans.

Democratic strongholds in the state include the Santa Fe area, the western and southern portions of the Albuquerque metro area, northern and central regions of the state and most of the Apache, Navajo and Pueblo Indian reservations.

Republican strongholds are considered the eastern and southern parts of the state, also known as "Little Texas" to some, as well as the Albuquerque Northeast Heights area.

Historically, New Mexicans have had a knack for choosing the winning candidate with the popular vote in general elections, with the exception of the elections of 1976 and 2000. While the state voted Democratic in the 2000 election, Republican candidate George Bush, who visited the Mesilla Valley with running mate Dick Cheney that year, was elected to office.

The election that put Democrats ahead was in 2008, with current President Barack Obama winning a popular vote of 57 percent over his opponent John McCain.

Interestingly enough, McCain is from neighboring state Arizona, which makes some political analysts indicate New Mexico may be leaning more Democratically.

However, New Mexico voters in 2011 put a Republican, Susana Martinez, in its governor's seat.

As with the presidential elections, New Mexico's gubernatorial races have similarly flip-flopped between Democrats and Republicans since the election year of 1983.

FOOTBALL GREATS

Tony Samuel, above left, made history as the first African-American head coach of the New Mexico State University football team. Holding the position from 1997-2004, he had a 34-57 record at the university, making him the third winningest coach in program history. As a senior at NMSU in 1998, Denvis Manns, above right, was the Big West Conference co-offensive MVP after rushing for a school record of 1,469 yards. On Oct. 31, 1998, Manns ran for 131 yards against Utah State to become the third player in NCAA Division I-A history to surpass 1,000 yards in four consecutive years. In 2005, at age 28, Manns was inducted into the Aggie Hall of Fame, and as of 2011 still holds the university's career rushing record with 4,962 yards.

NMSU ATHLETICS

A TRADITION BEGINS

It's Burger Time owner Kevin McGrath began the It's Burger Time Football Golf Tournament in 1993 with the hopes of raising funds for local high school football teams. After the death of his wife, Sandra, left, the name was changed to the It's Burger Time Sandra B. McGrath Football Golf Tournament. Generating thousands of dollars, in 2007 the golf tournament changed once again, this time providing funds to all high school activities.

LAS CRUCES BULLETIN/IT'S BURGER TIME

AGGIE STARS

The NMSU men's basketball team saw several greats in the 1990s, such as basketball player and three-time Academic All-American Eric Channing, far left, who is ranked as one of the best all-around shooters in the university's history and was inducted into the NMSU Hall of Fame in 2008. Keith Hill, left, hit the game-winning shot against the UNLV Rebels in 1990, beating the No. 1 ranked team 83-82. Although Lou Henson, below, had already made a name for himself coaching men's basketball at NMSU from 1966-75, he returned as head coach from 1997-2004.

NMSU ATHLETICS

NMSU MEN'S BASKETBALL IN THE 1990S

1989-90: NCAA Tournament First Round

1990-91: NCAA Tournament First Round

1991-92: NCAA Sweet Sixteen

1992-93: NCAA Tournament Second Round

1993-94: NCAA Tournament First Round

1994-95: NIT Quarterfinals

1997-98: Basketball coaching legend Lou Henson returned to coach at the Pan Am Center

1998-99: NCAA Tournament First Round

1999-2000: NIT First Round

TAKING HOME THE CHAMPIONSHIP

In 1999, Las Cruces High School Bulldawgs faced the Mayfield Trojans at Aggie Memorial Stadium in the New Mexico High School Football State Championship. The 'Dawgs won the match 24-12.

MILLER FAMILY

A MUSIC MAN

Former Las Cruces Citizen of the Year William Clark accepted the position of academic department head for the NMSU Music Department in 1990. An educator and musician, Clark greatly impacted the university during his nine years, increasing the faculty and music majors.

LAS CRUCES BULLETIN

ARTS AT NMSU

Students at NMSU occupied their time in creative ways. The Music Department saw many stars, including talented choral performers.

NMSU LASC

LEARNING FROM A LEGEND

Tony Award-winning playwright and NMSU professor Mark Medoff instructs a group of students during a Theatre Arts Department/American Southwest Theatre Company summer camp in 1993.

NMSU LASC

AWARDED, FINALLY

In 1998, 105 years after his death, Sam Steel, pictured top right, was awarded a bachelor's degree by New Mexico State University. At age 17, Steel was supposed to be NMSU's first graduate, but was fatally shot two months before graduation.

STEEL FAMILY

LIVING A STUDENT'S LIFE

Student life in the `90s at New Mexico State University had much to offer, including new student housing, right, recreational activities such as Ultimate Frisbee, above right – a popular pastime at campuses around the country in the 1990s – and opportunities to show off school spirit, above.

NMSU LASC

HOMECOMING COURT

The Homecoming court of 1994 rides through the streets of Las Cruces during the New Mexico State University Homecoming parade. Members of the court were nominated by different university departments and organizations and voted into the position by students.

NMSU LASC

GRANDSON TAKES OVER PECAN LEGACY

Wayne Stahmann, left, took over the second-largest pecan orchard in the country at the time in 1990. His great-grandfather, William J. Stahmann, and grandfather, Deane Stahmann, below, planted the 4,000 acres of Stahmann Farms in 1925 because the Mesilla Valley's climate was ideal for growing the nut.

LAS CRUCES BULLETIN/NMSU LASC

BIG AWARDS FOR RODEO ASSOCIATION

Above top, Aggie Rodeo Association members won several awards at the Grand Canyon Region Rodeo during the decade. The Las Cruces High School FFA Team, above, also won several awards at the AJQHA World Championship Show in 1994.

LAS CRUCES BULLETIN

CHILE EMPIRE FLOURISHES

After several successful decades, Cervantes Enterprises moved its operation to Mesquite in 1998. Since moving to the larger facility, the chile company, led by matriarch Emma Jean Cervantes, has provided its products around the world and can be found in 85 percent of commercial salsas available in most grocery stores.

CERVANTES FAMILY

A LIVING HISTORY BOOK

Since 1998, the New Mexico Farm & Ranch Heritage Museum has told the story of the vital roles farming and ranching have played in New Mexico history.

NEW MEXICO FARM & RANCH HERITAGE MUSEUM

New Mexico Farm & Ranch Heritage Museum

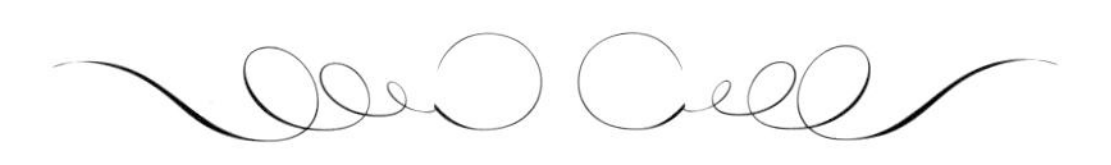

The New Mexico Farm & Ranch Heritage Museum is a history book in the form of interactive exhibits, live plants, animals and hundreds of artifacts. Every page is a new experience. It's a demonstration, an exhibit or an oral history interview that tells the fascinating story of New Mexico's 3,000 years of agricultural history.

The museum also is a family scrapbook of sorts. The stories told on this sprawling 47-acre campus are real stories about real people – our grandparents or great-grandparents. The museum connects generations of New Mexicans and reminds us the production of food and fiber is a common thread that weaves us all together.

The idea of preserving this history and telling New Mexico's agricultural story in the form of a museum came from William P. Stephens, the state's former Secretary of Agriculture. In the 1970s, Stephens, along with former New Mexico State University President Gerald Thomas, began laying the groundwork for the museum.

In 1991, the movement picked up steam. The previous year, the New Mexico Office of Cultural Affairs received a $50,000 appropriation to provide for a study and plan for a comprehensive Farm and Ranch Heritage complex.

During the 1991 Legislative session, Sen. Ben Altamirano of Silver City introduced Senate Bill 250. "An act relating to agriculture; enacting the Farm and Ranch Heritage Museum Act; creating a board, providing for powers and duties." With that piece of legislation, the Farm and Ranch Heritage program became a part of the state Office of Cultural Affairs.

In May 1991, Gov. Bruce King attended a New Mexico Farm and Ranch Heritage Institute Foundation meeting and pledged his support for a three-year, $8 million project. In November of that year, King appointed the Farm and Ranch Heritage Museum Board, created by Altamirano's Senate Bill 250.

After the New Mexico Legislature passed a $7 million appropriation for Phase One of the museum in 1994, the NMSU Board of Regents approved the lease of 47 acres on Dripping Springs Road for the museum site.

The museum board approved the final design of the building at its meeting on Aug. 11, 1995, and a ground-breaking ceremony took place the next day. The event was not a typical groundbreaking get-together. After the Heritage Riders rode down the hill on horseback and delivered shovels and a post-hole digger to the dignitaries, museum volunteer Alvin Davidson plowed across the property with a 1937 John Deere tractor.

Construction on the main building (since renamed the Bruce King Building) began in late December 1995 and about the same time, the museum received its first animals when 19 longhorn cattle were sent south from Chicosa Lake State Park in northern New Mexico. The museum opened to the public in 1998 and has welcomed visitors from all over the world.

Other structures have been added to the museum over the years, including the adobe Blacksmith Shop, Skaggs Dairy Barn, the Horse and Cattle Barn, the Sheep and Goat Barn and the Greenhouse. In 2007, the Historic Green Bridge from Lincoln County was brought to the museum and reassembled over the Tortugas Arroyo.

BOWLING ALLEY MASSACRE

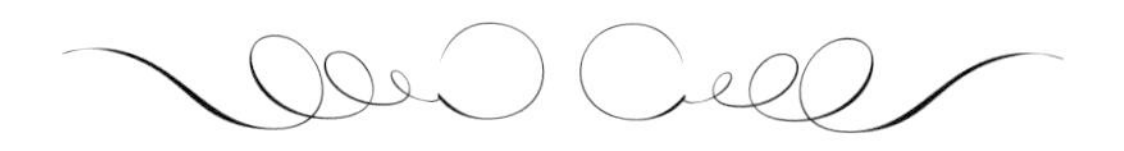

Early in the morning on Feb. 10, 1990, the Las Cruces Police Department received a phone call from a 12-year-old girl who had been shot in the head after two armed men entered the Las Cruces Bowl on Amador Avenue. The men shot seven people at close range, killing four.

Twenty-five bullets struck the victims – manager Stephanie Senac; her daughter Melissia Repass, 12, who made the 911 call; cook Ida Holguin; 13-year-old Amy Houser, who died; and Steven Teran and his two daughters, Paula Holguin, 6, and Valerie Teran, 2, all of whom died.

THE VICTIMS

Victims murdered in the Bowling Alley Massacre included Paula Holguin, 6, Valerie Teran, 2, Amy Houser, 13, and Steven Teran.

LAS CRUCES POLICE DEPARTMENT

After the shooting, the assailants took between $4,000 and $5,000 from the safe – leaving some money behind – and set the office on fire.

More than 100 tips an hour flooded into the Las Cruces Police Department, still, officials were unable to find a motive or suspects. Several theories about the motivation behind the horrific crime came out, including revenge against then owner Ronald Senac, who was out of town during the event; revenge against one of the adults, possibly related to debt or out-of-state organized crime; or a simple robbery.

The suspects were described as Hispanic, with one possibly ranging from 28 to 34 years old at the time and the other age 48 to 54. Baffling many involved, the shooting was featured on "Unsolved Mysteries" and "America's Most Wanted."

In 2010, a documentary on the case was created, titled "A Nightmare in Las Cruces." Still, despite its publicity, no arrests have been made, and the Bowling Alley Massacre, the worst mass murder in Las Cruces history, remains unsolved as of 2011.

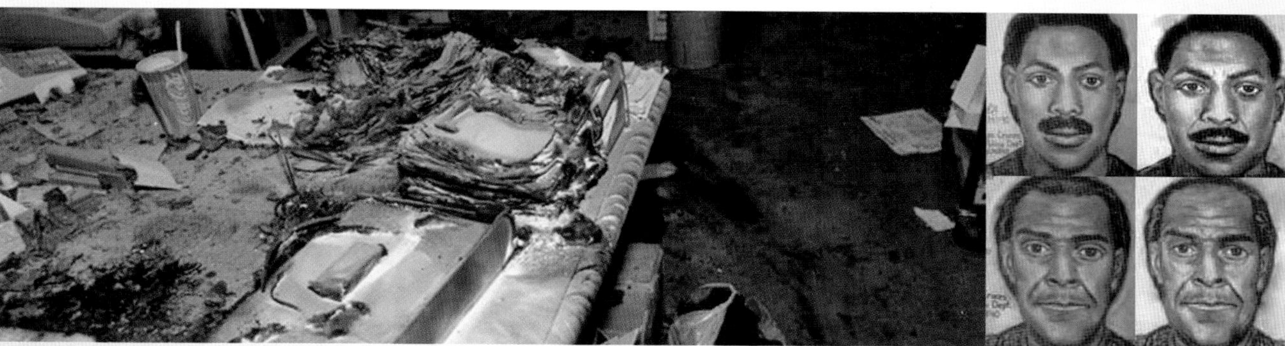

TRAGEDY STRIKES

The office of Las Cruces Bowl, above left, was set on fire by the assailants after they shot seven people, killing four in 1990. Sketches of the suspects, above right, were widely distributed at the time and later updated to show them as they may have aged. The suspects were never found.

LAS CRUCES POLICE DEPARTMENT

BUILDING A SUBSTATION

In the 1990s, the City of Las Cruces built the West Mesa Substation. Offering residents in the area 20 percent lower rates than El Paso Electric Co., the city eventually embarked on a legal battle with the utility company to take over electrical service in the area. The battle included nine different lawsuits. One of the suits, filed in 1999, was for eminent domain.

NMSU LASC

FIGHTING FOR LOWER RATES

Las Cruces attorney Robert Kelley, left, leans on his stack of documents relating to the El Paso Electric Co. rate-moderation case. The legal battle, above, came to an end in 2000. It resulted in the city receiving a settlement of $21 million, which covered the cost of building the substation and litigation.

LAS CRUCES BULLETIN

A VISION OF DOWNTOWN

This wood diorama, above left, built in 1996, shows how officials envisioned the revitalization of Downtown Main Street, which had been turned into a pedestrian mall in the 1970s. The process of reinventing Downtown Las Cruces began in 1992, thanks to the work of several concerned citizens. Officials wanted to create an area that brought in business, while providing quality-of-life elements in the "heart" of the city and preserving its rich history, as seen by the addition of the St. Genevieve's Memorial, above right. The iron monument was completed in 1998 by welder Sam Torres. The re-visioning of Downtown finally came to fruition in 2010.

NMSU LASC/LAS CRUCES BULLETIN

AREAS OF GROWTH

This postcard, above left, shows the growth that occurred on Lohman Avenue during the decade. In addition to creating frontage-road access to businesses, the street was extended beyond Telshor Boulevard to Roadrunner Parkway. Above center, another area of growth occurred at Doña Ana Branch Community College and its educational centers, such as the one in Gadsden. The 1990s also saw the addition of fire stations No. 5, above right, to serve the East Mesa, and No. 6, to serve Sonoma Ranch, High Range and Las Colinas.

JEFF BARNET/NMSU LASC

IMPROVING QUALITY OF LIFE

With the city's population steadily increasing and hitting more than 60,000 at the beginning of the decade, Las Cruces added more quality-of-life elements, including a new park in honor of the area's veterans off Roadrunner Parkway, below. Veteran's Memorial Park is home to the Bataan Death March Monument as well as a Veteran's Wall of names of soldiers from Doña Ana County who served in the military.

NMSU LASC

STEVE NEWBY ARCHITECTS

Steve Newby arrived in Las Cruces with his beautiful bride Pamela in 1974, as the architectural firm he was working for was putting the final touches on the Downtown pedestrian mall, with its bricked Main Street and metal awnings.

As New Mexico entered its second century of statehood, Newby was one of the key figures in Las Cruces' Downtown revitalization, which saw the removal of the awnings and traffic flowing through Main Street once again.

In fact, Newby has worked toward the revitalization for more than 25 years. He designed one of Downtown's key renovations: La Iguana restaurant in the old Popular Dry Goods building.

The re-envisioned Downtown will not look like it did in the 1960s, Newby said. Nor will it look like Santa Fe. Newby hopes a number of different architectural styles will give Downtown a classic but fresh look, and will allow the past and present to meet in the living room of the city.

CHANGE BY DESIGN

Architect Steve Newby arrived in Las Cruces in the 1970s. He's worked for years to help the city re-envision itself.

STEVE NEWBY ARCHITECTS/LAS CRUCES BULLETIN

Newby established his own firm in 1988, and by 2011 had nine colleagues. The architects and staff work in a collaborative atmosphere that the firm fosters. Although there is a lot of responsibility in running one's own firm, Newby said he and his co-workers enjoy the freedom as well.

"We'll throw a design on the wall, challenge each other and make changes," he said. "The discovery process of questioning, reasoning and creation are essential parts to the design process."

From the very beginning, Steve Newby Architects designed energy-efficient, sustainable buildings. By 2011, the firm had achieved six LEED Silver and Gold designations on their building designs.

Newby and his team have made their mark on the city of Las Cruces with a variety of striking buildings in a range of styles. The Las Cruces Aquatic Center, which opened in 2010, with its bright colors and big windows, is set at a 45-degree angle on the lot.

"We wanted a building that was visually exciting," he said.

Newby loves to design historically based projects and to renovate historic buildings, believing that culture and history can illuminate good design. The Villa Esperanza condominiums on Avenida de Mesilla are designed in an elegant, historic Santa Barbara style, while the 77,000-square-foot Roadrunner Plaza was designed to emulate different urban designs in a combined setting.

Another one of the firm's designs opened in 2011: the Las Cruces Convention Center, done in collaboration with HNTB Architects. The building has a sleek, minimalist design with strong lines and has achieved LEED Gold status, a first in Las Cruces.

In New Mexico's second century, Newby believes the opening of Downtown Las Cruces and continued growth of Las Cruces will provide architects an opportunity to create unique buildings and community-oriented neighborhood spaces.

All over the country, Newby believes, people are rediscovering the value of pedestrian-friendly downtowns and close-knit neighborhoods.

He also believes there is more to running a firm than just designing buildings. It is important to give back to the community, Newby said, in such ways as doing pro bono designs for nonprofit organizations.

He also believes that a building design should not be the autobiography of the architect.

The entire firm has been involved in numerous boards and community events and has taken leadership positions with the Vision 2040 plan, Downtown revitalization and the Greater Las Cruces Chamber of Commerce. The firm's architects have also served in local, state and national architectural organizations. Newby was chosen as the Greater Las Cruces Chamber of Commerce Citizen of the Year in 2004.

The firm also believes in working for social change, and became involved in helping establish the Amador Avenue home for the Gospel Rescue Mission and provided the design of the building.

"We hope to be part of creating a vibrant city," he said. "I think people still want the front-porch experience, with community, neighborhood, timeless design and a sense of belonging. To deliver this, you need to listen closely, restrain the ego and pay attention to the memories that define a place and make it unique."

GIVING ART A HOME

Las Crucens celebrate the re-opening of the Court Youth Center in September 1996. Originally built in 1941 as Court Junior High, the school was closed in 1984. After almost a decade, enough money was raised to renovate the historic structure as a youth center for the arts. In 2004, the building became home to the city's first charter high school, Alma d'arte.

NMSU LASC

PROVIDING SHELTER

In 1997, ground broke on the Mesilla Valley Community of Hope, a facility dedicated to providing services to the homeless. With Phase I completed in 1999, the final project was finished in 2001 and includes a day shelter, child care, health care, a soup kitchen and food bank.

NMSU LASC

MAKING AN EASIER CONNECTION

In '96, work on connecting Missouri Avenue and Boutz Road was in full swing as officials toured the area, above left. After several months of work and relocating a dozen families in order to bulldoze their homes, a ribbon cutting was held for the newly opened road, above right.

NMSU LASC

IF YOU BUILD IT, THEY WILL COME

In 1993, the need for a regional sports complex in Las Cruces was established and the wheels to create the Field of Dreams were set in motion. Championed by 50 community volunteers, the complex was designed to be a multi-purpose football stadium along with seven soccer fields, a softball complex and a three-field baseball complex on Tashiro Road. Construction broke ground in 1998 and was completed in 2003.

WOOTEN CONSTRUCTION

A NEW HOME FOR OÑATE

Originally located on Spruce Avenue, where Sierra Middle School is housed as of 2011, Oñate High School, the third high school in the city, quickly outgrew its location. After conducting a land exchange with the Bureau of Land Management, Las Cruces Public Schools relocated the high school to a state-of-the-art structure on Mesa Grande Drive. With construction completed in 1993, the school hosted its first graduation in 1994.

OÑATE HIGH SCHOOL

LIVIN' THE STUDENT LIFE

Student life at the new Oñate High School was bustling. From learning about sewing and fashion, above top, to hanging out on campus, above, students such as Laura Montoya, below, had plenty to keep them busy.

LAS CRUCES BULLETIN/RACHEL COURTNEY/LAURA DELGADO

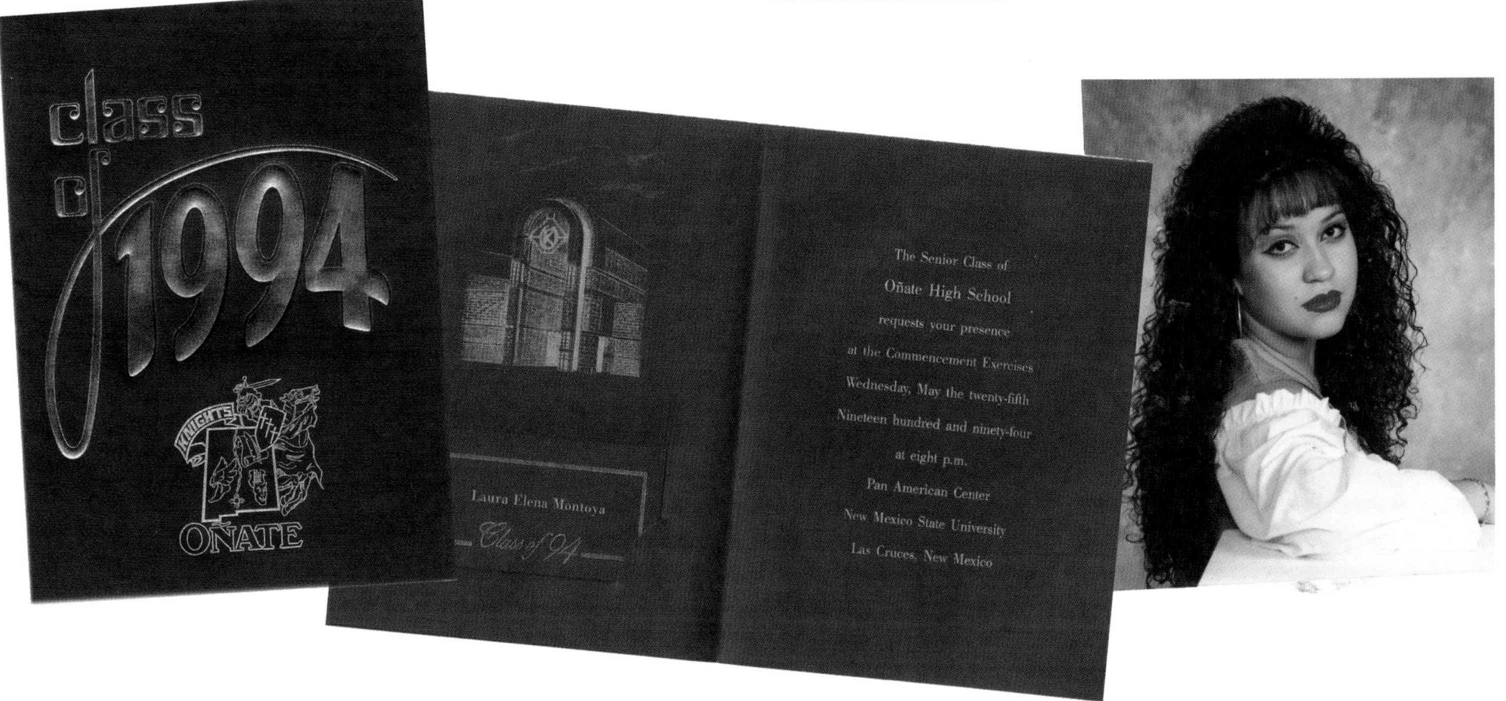

LAS CRUCES CHAMBER BALLET

Founded in 1983 by Michele and Kevin Self, the Las Cruces Chamber Ballet offered dancers in the Mesilla Valley the opportunity to develop their talents with a professional performance experience. Possibly the most well-known chamber ballet performance is "The Nutcracker," presented every December to get Las Crucens into the holiday spirit.

LAS CRUCES BULLETIN

A CREATIVE OUTLET

Las Cruces High School students painted murals throughout the school to add beauty to their environment.

LAS CRUCES BULLETIN

PERFORMING ARTS IN LAS CRUCES

The Las Cruces arts scene was hot with various acts drawing in the public's attention, such as the sharply dressed Sweet Carolines, above left. Singer/songwriter Bob Diven, above center, performed his original songs about life, love and roadkill in the 1990s. Richard Rundell as King Sextimus, Jennifer Damon as Queen Agravain and Lennie Rainwater as Princess Winnifred starred in "Once Upon a Mattress" at the Las Cruces Community Theatre in 1993, above right.

LAS CRUCES BULLETIN

STYLISH MEN

Locals kicking back at El Patio Bar, left, show off popular men's style trends of the 1990s, such as baggy jeans. The members of the musical group P.I.A.D.O.R., below, also model the styles of the time, which included long-sleeve polo shirts and acid-washed jeans.

FOUNTAIN FAMILY/P.I.A.D.O.R.

FASHION, BIG HAIR AND TIARAS

The styles of the 1990s were very distinct: big hair, floral patterns and flashy accessories, left. Another fashion must have – Glamour Shots. A phenomenon made popular in the 1980s and '90s, glamour shots allowed everyday women to show off their fashionable, stylish sides in malls and shopping centers throughout the United States. Puffy sleeves and lace adorned wedding gowns, while quinceañera dresses, such as the one Esmerelda Bustamante wore in 1995, right, second from the bottom, were accented with pearls. Prom dresses also shimmered during the decade.

NATISHA HALES/THERESA MONTOYA BALSALDUA/PAUL BOWMAN/ISELA ALVAREZ/RACHEL COURTNEY

2000-2009

LIVING THE DREAM

RIO GRANDE VINEYARDS & WINERY

Nestled in the Mesilla Valley and across from the Organ Mountains, the Rio Grande Vineyards & Winery opened in 2004 on 10 acres, growing eight European grape varieties.

EFRAIN M. PADRO

DREAMS COME TRUE

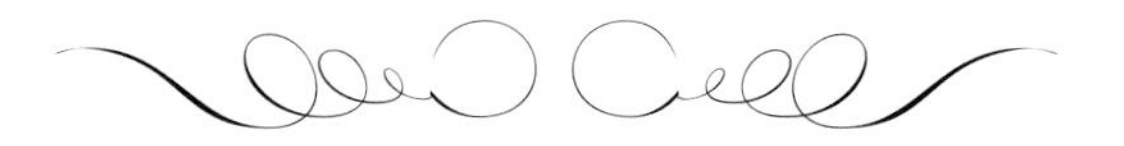

As Las Cruces roared into the new millennium, the city's growth seemed unstoppable.

The Sonoma Ranch development, spearheaded by George and Yvonne Rawson, David Steinborn and Dale Schueller, was continuing the transformation of the East Mesa, driving the edge of the city further east.

In 2009, the estimated population was 93,570, a 26 percent increase from the 2000 official count of 74,267.

New arrivals to Las Cruces were mostly baby boomers, many of whom had been able to retire in their 50s, and sought out Las Cruces because of its mild climate, open spaces and urban amenities. Even though Las Cruces remained the second largest city in New Mexico, it maintained a small-town feel.

Leading the charge was a rapid succession of national rankings, starting with Where to Retire magazine listing Las Cruces as one of the top 100 retirement towns in the U.S. The city continued its accolades with one of the best places to live or retire by Family Digest and Money Magazine in 2002 and 2005; a best ranking for business by the Forbes/Milken Institute in 2002, 2003, 2004 and 2005; a top city for Hispanics to live in 2002 and 2003; and AARP declaring it a "dream town to retire" in 2006.

IMPROVED FACILITIES

With these retirees came a desire for better access to high-quality medical care, which resulted in the city's second – and first privately created – hospital, MountainView Regional Medical Center, opening in 2002. MountainView provided comprehensive intensive care services with a medical plaza and an outpatient surgery center.

Other medical facilities, such as the Rehabilitation Hospital of Southern New Mexico and a southern outreach cancer clinic from the University of New Mexico Cancer Center, would soon follow and vastly improve the quality of medical care to residents.

Also in 2002, Bill Richardson was elected governor of New Mexico, and while rising oil prices hurt consumers at the gas pumps, revenues from the oil and gas extraction industries filled the state with money that mostly went to "one-time" capital outlay expenditures.

This abundance of state money helped local officials to finally succeed in acquiring funding for long sought-after projects.

In January 2004, the Las Cruces City Council approved the Las Cruces Downtown Revitalization Plan, developed by design consultants Sites Southwest and modeled after Albuquerque's successful Downtown revitalization.

2000
Created by artist Olin Calk, using refuse from a local dump, the Recycled Roadrunner is 20 feet tall and 42 feet long. Built at the city dump, the large bird – touted as the world's largest roadrunner – was moved to the West Mesa in 2000 and can be found on the south side of Interstate 10, east of Picacho Avenue and overlooking Las Cruces.

2001
The first Walmart Supercenter in Las Cruces boasts the most sales of any Walmart in the nation.

2002
MountainView Regional Medical Center opens, providing a second hospital option for Las Crucens that included comprehensive intensive care services. The hospital included a medical plaza and an outpatient surgery center.

2003
David and Jaki McCollum form FIG Publications LLC and purchase the Las Cruces Bulletin.

2004
Burt Rutan wins the X PRIZE to prove that a privately developed spacecraft could make repeated flights into suborbital space, which gave support to passage of legislation to create a spaceport between Las Cruces and Truth or Consequences, N.M.

JESSICA GRADY-MAULDIN/LAS CRUCES BULLETIN/X PRIZE FOUNDATION/NMSU UNIVERSITY COMMUNICATIONS/DOÑA ANA COUNTY

2000s

Who's Who

Las Cruces Mayors

1991-2003 .... Rubén Smith
2003-07 .... William Mattiace
2007-11 .... Ken Miyagishima

Postmasters

1998-2007 .... Robert Dinkel
2007-10 .... Le Gretta Ross-Rawlins

NMSU Presidents

1997-2000 .... William Conroy
2000-03 .... G. Jay Gogue
2004-08 .... Michael V. Martin

Mesilla Mayor

1998-2010 .... Michael Cadena

Las Cruces Police Chief

2004-09 .... Harry Romero

Las Cruces Fire Chief

1998-2001 .... Adolf Zubia

New Mexico Governors

1995-2003 .... Gary Johnson
2003-11 .... Bill Richardson

U.S. Senators

1973-2009 .... Pete Domenici
1983-2011 .... Jeff Bingaman
2009-11 .... Tom Udall

U.S. Representatives

1981-2003 .... Joe R. Skeen
1997-2009 .... Heather Wilson
1999-2009 .... Tom Udall
2003-09, 2011 .... Steve Pearce
2009-11 .... Harry Teague
2009-11 .... Martin Heinrich
2009-11 .... Ben R. Luján

Las Cruces Public Schools Superintendents

1989-2001 .... Jesse L. Gonzales
2001-03 .... Virginia Foltz
2003-05 .... Louis D. Martinez
2005-06 .... Joann Patton
2006 .... Sonia Diaz
2006-11 .... Stan Rounds

WSMR Commanders

1999-2001 .... Brig. Gen. Steven Flohr
2001-03 .... Brig. Gen. William Engel
2003 .... Col. Lawrence Sowa
2003-05 .... Brig. Gen. Robert Reese
2005-07 .... Thomas R. Bernard
2007-08 .... Brig. Gen. Richard L. McCabe
2008-09 .... Brig. Gen. David L. Mann
2009-11 .... Brig. Gen. John S. Regan

By the Numbers

74,267 .... Las Cruces population (2000)
174,682 .... Doña Ana County population (2000)
52 percent .... Hispanic population
$37,670 .... Median household income (2000)
$52,053 .... Median household income (2009)
$5.85 .... Minimum wage (2007)
$6.55 .... Minimum wage (2008)
$7.25 .... Minimum wage (2009)
$153,713 .... Median home price (2009)
31.5 .... Median age
$1.95 .... Gallon of gas (2000)
$3.34 .... Gallon of gas (2008)
34 cents .... First-class stamp (2001)
37 cents .... First-class stamp (2002)
39 cents .... First-class stamp (2006)
41 cents .... First-class stamp (2007)
42 cents .... First-class stamp (2008)
44 cents .... First-class stamp (2009)
36 .... Las Cruces Public Schools

In the News

April 8, 2001: Tiger Woods becomes the first golfer to hold all four major titles simultaneously.

Sept. 11, 2001: Islamic terrorists hijack four U.S. airliners and crash two into the World Trade Center and one into the Pentagon, while the fourth crashes in Pennsylvania after passengers attempt to retake the airliner.

Feb. 1, 2003: A tragedy at NASA occurs when the Space Shuttle Columbia explodes upon re-entry. All seven astronauts aboard are killed.

Oct. 27, 2004: The Boston Red Sox win the World Series, its first since 1918.

July 24, 2005: American cyclist Lance Armstrong wins his record seventh straight Tour de France.

Aug. 29, 2005: Hurricane Katrina devastates the city of New Orleans.

Oct. 26, 2005: The Chicago White Sox win the World Series, its first since 1917.

Jan. 4, 2007: The first female speaker of the U.S. House of Representatives, Nancy Pelosi, is sworn into office.

Oct. 3, 2008: Congress passes the Emergency Economic Stabilization Act legislation, giving a $700 billion bailout to distressed Wall Street and banking businesses.

Nov. 4, 2008: Barack Obama becomes the first African-American president.

June 1, 2009: The H1N1 virus – swine flu – is deemed a global pandemic.

2004
Michael Martin begins term as president of New Mexico State University. Though he only stayed at NMSU four years, he significantly reorganized the university and raised his profile.

2005
Las Cruces City Council adopts a plan to revitalize Downtown through a series of actions and strategies, including re-opening Main Street.

2006
Extreme monsoon rain causes widespread flooding, especially in Hatch where an arroyo is breeched and the center of town is flooded in four feet of water.

2007
First NMSU Aggies are Tough Enough to Wear Pink event is held in conjunction with a football game.

2009
October: Filming of scenes for "Due Date" with Robert Downey Jr. close parts of U.S. Highway 70, causing traffic headaches.

MAIN STREET REVITALIZATION

In 2008, the awnings that shaded the Downtown pedestrian mall were removed in preparation for the re-opening of Main Street.

LAS CRUCES BULLETIN

The main feature of the Las Cruces Downtown revitalization plan was to tear down the metal awning that covered the "yellow brick road" walking mall and to re-open Main Street as a car-friendly road. Plans also included new retail stores, restaurants, entertainment businesses, a plaza and "loft" housing in a mixed-use approach to make Downtown a place where people worked, played and lived.

In addition to re-opening the middle section of Main Street, one of the revitalization effort's first accomplishments was the restoration of the Rio Grande Theatre, one of the few surviving adobe theaters in the Southwest.

Spaceport America and Sapphire Energy

As the Downtown revitalization efforts gained momentum, so did long-dormant plans to create a spaceport in southern New Mexico. With Virgin Galactic planning a spaceliner service to take tourists to suborbital space, the effort was revived and the Legislature approved the more than $200 million project. Voters in Doña Ana and Sierra counties also approved an increase in gross receipts taxes to help fund construction.

With concerns about greenhouse gases and the volatility of the Middle East driving the energy industry to look at new ways to produce energy, Las Cruces again attracted attention. Sapphire Energy, one of the major efforts to create fuels from algae oils, built its research and development facility on the West Mesa Industrial Park.

The region's great climate also caught the eye of companies considering solar generation projects. The spaceport and such "green" industries gave promise that there would be new economic opportunities on the horizon.

Development Controversy

An unexpected dynamic occurred, however, at the height of the city's growth. Many of the new retirees began to question whether the city was growing too fast for city services to keep pace. There were problems and complaints about the roads and emergency services on the East Mesa.

In 2007, Vistas at Presidio's development proposal to guide the city's growth on the East Mesa for the next 20 to 30 years was introduced. Brokered by State Land Commissioner Pat Lyons with a master planning and business development contract to Las Cruces developer Philip Philippou, the more than 4,000-acre plan and annexation was approved by the City Council amid controversy about the single-source contract award and political donations made by Philippou.

Coupled with an earlier approved phase of Vistas at Presidio of more than 1,700 acres, it was too much growth too fast for some. Opponents organized politically and systematically removed all but one of the council members in the following election. Ken Miyagishima, who had cast the single lone vote on the City Council against the annexation, was elected mayor in 2007.

In 2008, the housing bubble imploded and new housing construction slowed dramatically. Some have estimated that 7,000 construction jobs were lost.

However, the city did complete projects started during the more flush economic times, including the new federal courthouse, a regional aquatic center, the new City Hall and a convention center.

With Downtown taking on a new face, Las Cruces wasn't as hard hit by the recession because of support from institutions such as White Sands Missile Range (WSMR) and New Mexico State University.

After the 9/11 attacks, WSMR became home to much of the modern warfare training because of its arid terrain and similarities to Iraq and Afghanistan. With military reorganization, WSMR also became home to the 2nd Engineer Battalion whose members were deployed to both wars. Also, Las Cruces hosts a New Mexico National Guard unit that had been deployed to the Middle East.

In the summer of 2009, longtime Doña Ana County District Attorney Susana Martinez announced her run for governor in which the Republican candidate said she was the race's "underdog." Martinez won in 2010 and became the first woman to be elected governor in New Mexico and the first Hispanic female governor in the United States.

BANKING BOOM

First American Bank opened its Las Cruces headquarters.

LAS CRUCES BULLETIN

THE NEW O'DONNELL HALL

Originally built in 1968, O'Donnell Hall, named after former professor and dean William B. O'Donnell, underwent renovations for two years, reopening in 2008. As part of the face lift, windows were placed in faculty offices and classroom technologies were updated.

LAS CRUCES BULLETIN

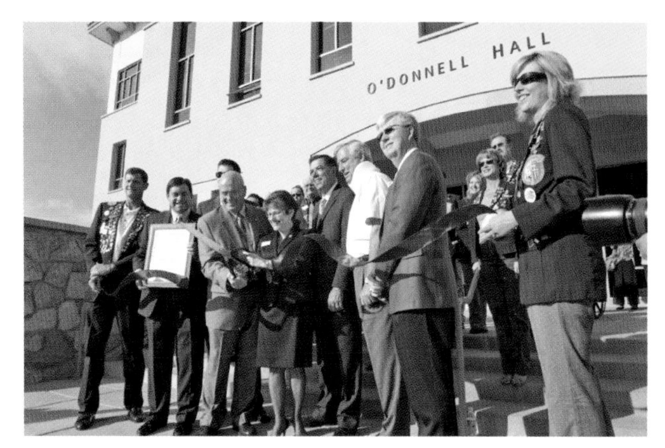

CINEPORT 10

Construction of Cineport 10 in the Mesilla Valley Mall was completed in 2009. The theater included 10 screens with stadium seating, digital projection and a full-service restaurant – The Launch Pad Café.

LAS CRUCES BULLETIN

SOLDIERS

The New Mexico Army National Guard 642nd Maintenance Company stand outside of the Field of Dreams before their welcome home ceremony January 2006 following a deployment. The Guard and members of the Second Engineer Battalion stationed at White Sands Missile Range have had to endure long and repeated tours of duty in the Iraq and Afghanistan wars.

LAS CRUCES BULLETIN

HONOR FLIGHT AND HONOR MARCH

Through the Honor Flight of Southern New Mexico program, 77 WWII veterans, above, traveled Oct. 7, 2008, to the National World War II Memorial in Washington, D.C. In honor of all soldiers, each March thousands gather at White Sands Missile Range to complete long desert treks for the Bataan Memorial Death March.

LAS CRUCES BULLETIN

MISSILES IN SOUTHERN NEW MEXICO

A PAC-3 Patriot interceptor is fired at White Sands Missile Range during the week of Sept. 15, 2008. High-elevation missile tests conducted at the range have sometimes left remarkable and otherworldly patterns in the sky.

WSMR

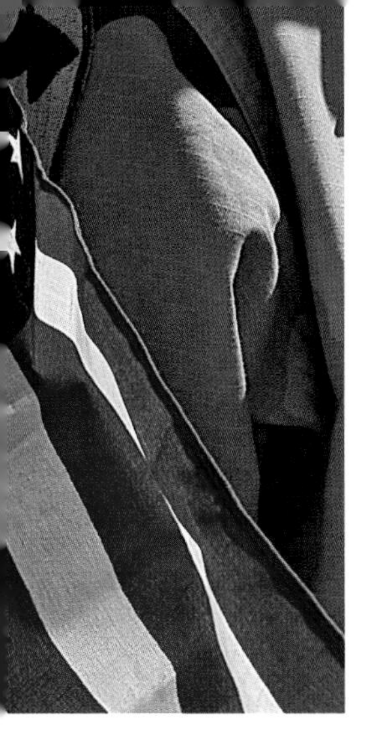

HIZZONER BILL MATTIACE

William "Bill" Mattiace, originally from New York, ran twice for mayor in 2003, in a special election in March and then the general election in November. He won both times. Four years later, in November 2007, Mattiace narrowly lost re-election to Ken Miyagishima.

LAS CRUCES BULLETIN

WATCHDOG

Las Cruces Mayor Ken Miyagishima answers questions from resident Tamie Smith after his first State of the City address, Feb. 13, 2007. Miyagishima would win a second mayoral term with a decisive victory in November 2011.

LAS CRUCES BULLETIN

SÍ SE PUEDE

Below left and center, as part of his presidential campaign, Barack Obama visited Las Cruces May 26, 2008. His campaign message advocating change in America was well received and he became the first African American president in 2009. Below right, his acceptance speech after winning the election evoked emotion from many of his supporters.

LAS CRUCES BULLETIN

FRESH PRODUCE

The Mesilla Valley in the 2000s gave Las Crucens plentiful access to locally grown produce. The Downtown Farmers & Crafts Market was a popular place to shop for fruits and vegetables. Top right, people would line up to have their chile roasted during the late summer, such as the scene from Lowe's Fiesta Foods with employee Craig Pyle.

LAS CRUCES BULLETIN

TECHNOLOGY CHANGING FARMING

A mechanical harvester strips chile pods from the plants, saving farmers from having to hire laborers to pick the chile by hand.

LAS CRUCES BULLETIN

WATER WOES

The lack of water in Elephant Butte Lake, above, forced Mesilla Valley farmers to pump well water. Though the area saw some agriculture hardship, onions remained one of the valley's cash crops.

LAS CRUCES BULLETIN

PRESERVING THE GREEN BELT

As farms began to give way to housing developments, local officials looked for ways to preserve the "green belt" surrounding the towns and cities.

TANA HEMINGWAY

GROWING THE FORCE

The Doña Ana County Commission Chambers frequently was the location for graduation ceremonies for academies to increase the number of officers serving the Sheriff's Department and Detention Center.

LAS CRUCES BULLETIN

KATIE'S LAW

The Katie Sepich Enhanced DNA Collection Act of 2010, also known as Katie's Law, is a proposed federal law to provide funding to states to implement minimum and enhanced DNA collection processes for felony arrests. The bill is named after Katie Sepich, above, who was brutally attacked and murdered in August 2003.

THE ROUND UP

TRAFFIC CAMERAS

A worker for RedFlex installs one of four traffic light enforcement cameras placed at the busiest intersections of Las Cruces. The cameras became operational in late February 2009 with citations issued the following month. The state forced the shutdown of two of the cameras, which have been controversial. Some believe the cameras have made the intersections safer, while others contend the photo enforcement violated their consitutional rights.

LAS CRUCES BULLETIN

FIRE ON THE MOUNTAIN

Dry conditions in southern New Mexico contributed to this fire in the Organ Mountains in June 2008 that was started by military activities on the east side of the range. Fire crews set up burn lines that prevented the blaze from reaching homes in the Soledad Canyon area.

LAS CRUCES BULLETIN

Basilica of San Albino

No matter where you live in the town of Mesilla, you can hear the melodic bells of the Basilica of San Albino ringing out, calling parishioners to Mass.

Two copper bells – Sagrado Corazón and María Albina – were cast in 1876. The large bell, Campana Grande, was cast in Milwaukee, Wisconsin in 1884. In keeping with Catholic tradition, the bells were christened and given padrinos (godparents) to care for them.

The history of San Albino parish spans more than a century and a half, two countries, five dioceses, and four church buildings.

The first church, finished in 1852 when Mesilla was part of Mexico, was a sapling-chinked mud structure at the south end of Mesilla's plaza. In 1857, parishioners completed an adobe fortress-style church – to provide protection from raids – on the north end of the plaza. A single-spire, French-European style church replaced the adobe in 1885. Finally, construction began on the present-day Romanesque church in 1906 and was completed in 1908.

When the parish was founded, it was part of the Diocese of Durango, Mexico. Throughout the years, it would also be part of the Diocese of Santa Fe, the Diocese of Arizona and the Diocese of El Paso before becoming part of the Diocese of Las Cruces created by Pope John Paul II in 1982.

For its historic and spiritual importance to the people of Mesilla and southern New Mexico, in 2008 Pope Benedict XVI raised the church of San Albino to minor basilica status.

The parish is named for a French saint of the sixth century, St. Aubin, Bishop of Angers. He was generous in helping the poor, and tradition states he often used his funds to free hostages who had been captured by pirates on the Loire River. Most important, many sick people would find healing after venerating his tomb.

As the building of the Basilica of San Albino enters its second 100 years, it faces an ongoing conservation project. Past renovations have trapped moisture within the bricks, causing cracks to form up the church walls.

Parishioners themselves did a heroic and large-scale renovation of the church in 1966, redoing the roof, adding support to the walls and restoring sacred images.

For more than a century, one family has had the honor and duty of ringing the bells of the Basilica of San Albino. Manuel Valles started ringing the bells in 1908 and today his great-great-great grandson Eric Gallegos continues the tradition.

The bells are rung by Gallegos and others 30 and 15 minutes prior to Mass so as to call the faithful. The bells also ring to notify the community when a parishioner has died and at the funeral Mass.

So deeply ingrained in the heart of Mesilla, the bells of San Albino are a reminder the church has been the center of the community from the days the town was founded.

A CHURCH OF HISTORICAL AND SPIRITUAL IMPORTANCE

The cornerstone of San Albino Catholic Church was laid in 1906. A 2009 retablo of San Albino made by Virginia Romero. Parishioners leaving San Albino after Mass, circa 1908. The large bell, Campana Grande, was cast in Milwaukee, Wisc., in 1884. The Coat of Arms for the Basilica of San Albino was created in 2009.

JESSICA GRADY-MAULDIN/BASILICA OF SAN ALBINO

RELIGION IN THE MESILLA VALLEY

Built in 1908, San Albino, above left, received minor basilica status from the Vatican in 2008 on the Feast of All Saints. Temple Beth-El came into formation in 1953, with its new building, above right, constructed in 2004-5. St. Genevieve's Catholic Church, below, celebrated its 150th anniversary in 2009. In 1969, the church moved to its new home on Espina Street.

LAS CRUCES BULLETIN

ENJOYING THE OUTDOORS

Residents and visitors alike take advantage of the Mesilla Valley's temperate weather and scenic landscape by participating in outdoor activities, such as ballooning, above left. Another popular event is the annual Raft the Rio, left, which the Southwest Environmental Center began in 1997.

LAS CRUCES BULLETIN

MORE SERVICES

Above left, the Hispano Chamber of Commerce de Las Cruces' board in 2001, which was formed to provide a voice for minority owned and small businesses in southern New Mexico. To better serve the community, The Bridge of Southern New Mexico, above center, was created in 2007. The Bridge is a unique partnership between community members and businesses and the educational system. The group works to ensure there is a "bridge" enabling students to cross into the post-graduation world with the skills and knowledge valued by employers. Also in 2007, La Casa Inc., the area's domestic violence shelter, held a ribbon cutting for its additional and renovated space.

HISPANO CHAMBER OF COMMERCE DE LAS CRUCES/LAS CRUCES BULLETIN

SPACEPORT TAKES OFF

The idea of constructing a spaceport in the New Mexico desert had been kicked around since the 1990s. In the 2000s, it finally took flight with the help of billionaire and Virgin Galactic CEO Sir Richard Branson. Ground broke on the facility in 2009 on 27 square miles of state-owned land 45 miles north of Las Cruces.

VIRGIN GALACTIC

SOLAR POTENTIAL

Gov. Bill Richardson praised efforts such as the Southwest Environmental Center's installation of solar panels to contribute to the commercial building's power needs.

LAS CRUCES BULLETIN

APPLE CRAZE

With Steve Jobs taking over again as CEO of Macintosh in 2000, Apple computers began to regain market value with the introduction of innovative computer products, including the iPod, iBook and iMac.

LAS CRUCES BULLETIN

NEVER SAY NEVER

Len Sugerman was a testament to the idea that if you believed in something strongly enough and didn't give up, dreams could come true.

Spaceport America is a monument to Sugerman's belief.

He was among a group at New Mexico State University's Physical Science Laboratory (PSL) who in the early 1990s began pushing for the creation of a spaceport in southern New Mexico.

At the time, McDonnell-Douglas was testing a single-stage-to-orbit rocket called the Delta Clipper and its commercial potential gave the idea of building a spaceport more credibility.

Unfortunately, the Delta Clipper wasn't fully developed by NASA following the demise of the Star Wars missile defense program that started it, which put the spaceport project on hold.

But as NASA began looking to develop a replacement vehicle for the space shuttle, the spaceport efforts gained momentum again in the late 1990s as a test site for the VentureStar X-33 technology demonstration vehicle. However, that effort was also unable to be developed after some initial design problems.

LEN SUGERMAN

Keeping his faith in a spaceport, Len Sugerman was instrumental in making commercial space travel dreams a reality in southern New Mexico. Sugerman was also known for his work with the Greater Las Cruces Chamber of Commerce Conquistadores.

LAS CRUCES BULLETIN

While others lost hope for the spaceport during these stops and starts, Surgerman never lost faith in the idea. One of the first people to make it a point to talk to Bill Richardson after taking office in 2003 was Sugerman. Understanding the power of perception, he got Richardson to have the state Highway Department put up a sign by the Upham exit on Interstate 25 that pointed to the future spaceport.

Somehow, having that sign on the road made what was to come as inevitable as Sugerman's belief in the project. By 2005, Virgin Galactic agreed to fly out of that future spaceport. A year later, just a few weeks shy of the first UP Aerospace sounding rocket launch from Spaceport America, Sugerman died at the age of 86.

Those who knew Sugerman understood that once he believed in an idea, a person, a place or an institution, his faith was unshakeable and his support unfailing.

Besides the spaceport, Sugerman believed in New Mexico State University and its Physical Science Laboratory, where he had worked since 1977. Not a rich man, he supported scholarships for students and the New Mexico Space Grant Consortium named its building after Sugerman, an honor usually bestowed to large donors.

He was also very involved in the Las Cruces community and was a long-serving member of the Conquistadores, the goodwill ambassadors for the Greater Las Cruces Chamber of Commerce.

Sugerman, a native of New York City, joined the Air Force in 1942 and retired 33 years later as a colonel.

During World War II, he helped build runways for B-52 bombers on Pacific islands. In the 1950s and '60s, he served in the Pentagon and at Andrews Air Force Base, while earning a bachelor's degree in engineering from Massachusetts Institute of Technology and a MBA from the University of Chicago.

Sugerman was first stationed in New Mexico in 1964 at the Air Force Missile Development Center at Holloman Air Force Base, where he served as the director of the Central Inertial Guidance Test Facility. He then became the Air Force deputy to the commanding general at White Sands Missile Range. Sugerman ended his Air Force career in 1975 at the Air Force Special Weapons Center at Kirtland Air Force Base in Albuquerque.

Sugerman then became assistant to the PSL director and participated in the launching of sounding rockets, missiles and high-altitude balloons on every continent. Sugerman received a master's degree in public administration from NMSU in 1984.

He remained active until his death. "Len died as he would have wished, with his boots on," said Patricia Hynes, director of the New Mexico Space Grant Consortium. "He was at home, in the community he loved, and he was busy until the end."

REGGIE NATION

Reggie Theus, right, was coach of the New Mexico State Aggie basketball team in 2005-07 and led the team to an appearance in the NCAA Tournament in 2007. Elijah Ingram, below right, was a key player during his years at NMSU.

NMSU ATHLETICS

A MAKEOVER FOR PISTOL PETE

In 2005, the beloved NMSU mascot, Pistol Pete, returned with a fresh look after a community uproar demanded the removal of his replacement, "Lasso Larry." His first replacement had his guns carelessly pointed into the air. The next version featured a safer Pete.

NMSU

DACC ANNIVERSARY

Led by President Margie Huerta, Doña Ana Community College celebrated its 35th anniversary in 2008 with a ribbon cutting.

LAS CRUCES BULLETIN

NMSU VOLLEYBALL AND COACH JORDAN

Throughout the 2000s, New Mexico State University volleyball coach Mike Jordan transformed his team and has been the winningest coach at NMSU as of 2011. He was named coach of the year five times in his career, three times with the WAC (2005, 2006, 2008) and twice with the Sun Belt Conference (2003, 2004). Jordan has led the Aggies to the NCAA Tournament five times – 2003, 2004, 2006, 2007, 2008.

LAS CRUCES BULLETIN

A LIVELY BUNCH

Las Cruces was not short on entertainment in the 2000s, including the annual Renaissance ArtsFaire held in Young Park, above, the Mayor's Ball, above right, and SalsaFest!, right.

LAS CRUCES BULLETIN

VANS WARPED TOUR

The Vans Warped Tour started in Las Cruces in 2003 and features crowds of 8,000 to 12,000. The NMSU intramural fields are typically filled with people aged 16-30 and includes multiple stages featuring various acts, multiple booths and vendors.

STEVEN PARRA

BORDER BOOK FESTIVAL

The Border Book Festival was established in the mid-'90s with the hope to bridge the arts and the community. The festival had great success throughout the 2000s, and continues to grow, incorporating education and entertainment. "We have worked to bring literature, literacy and storytelling to our borderland region. The deeper and closer we work in our home place and in our vecinidad, the more we realize how that impacts the greater world and becomes global in scope," said Denise Chavez, organizer of the festival.

LAS CRUCES BULLETIN

CENTER OF OPPORTUNITY

Former New Mexico Gov. Garrey Carruthers is quick to point out that Las Cruces has a stellar record when it comes to placing a local in the governor's residence in Santa Fe.

Edwin Mechem, governor from the 1950s and 1960s, was raised and educated in Las Cruces. Jerry Apodaca in the late 1970s, was a Las Crucen, and Gov. Susana Martinez was a long-time district attorney for Doña Ana County.

"Since the '50s we've had as many governors as anybody," Carruthers said.

Carruthers, who was New Mexico governor from 1987-91, was born in Alamosa, Colo., on Aug. 29, 1939, the son of a gold miner. Due to a heart condition, his father had to leave the high altitudes of southern Colorado and began farming and raising dairy cows in the Animas Valley near Aztec, N.M.

GARREY CARRUTHERS

Garrey Carruthers, a former governor, is no less active as New Mexico State University's Business College dean. With Arrowhead Research Park, Carruthers still plays a role in creating more economic opportunities for New Mexicans.

GARREY CARRUTHERS

After graduating high school in Aztec, Carruthers came to Las Cruces to study at New Mexico A&M in 1957, where he earned a bachelor's degree in agriculture and a master's degree in agricultural economics. He attended Iowa State University to earn his doctorate in economics.

Returning to New Mexico, he joined the faculty at NMSU. He said his aspiration was to be "a really great college professor."

His academic career took a detour, however, when his dean asked him to apply as a White House Fellow.

"I didn't know what I was getting into," he said. "I went through a couple of interviews and ended up as a special assistant to the Secretary of Agriculture Earl Butz – Earl was kind of a famous guy in his days.

"I was selected when Richard Nixon was president, but I went to my fellowship when Gerald Ford had taken over."

Those were dark days for the Republican Party.

"(Vice President) Spiro Agnew had apparently been corrupt when he was in Baltimore, so he left office and Nixon had resigned," Carruthers said.

"Butz told me – he knew I was a Republican – 'The Republican Party is in real trouble, we need some new leadership.'"

Carruthers came back to New Mexico and did some volunteering for the party on the local level. When Ronald Reagan defeated Carter for president, the New Mexico Farm & Livestock Bureau pushed hard to have somebody from New Mexico as an assistant secretary of the Interior.

"I had given them a speech right after the election – I used to give a really stem-winding speech about free enterprise – they liked it a lot and they asked me to send my credentials to the White House to be assistant secretary," he said

At the Interior Department, Carruthers set up a series of meetings for a group of New Mexicans called the Amigos, a group of businessmen and professionals who were visiting Washington to advocate for business related issues. Members of that group asked Carruthers to return to New Mexico and run for governor. "So I just decided 'What the heck' after this term with Reagan I'll come home and take a look at it," he said.

As governor, Carruthers said he spent most of his time working on education.

"I actually asked for – and some Republicans have never forgiven me for it – I asked for a quarter (of a) cent gross receipts tax to pay teachers a higher salary. It passed the Legislature and I signed it," he said.

"It was kind of my death as a Republican because Republicans are not supposed to do that, but I thought our teachers were so poorly paid that we had to do something about it."

After leaving the governorship, Carruthers was president and CEO of Cimmarron Health, basically an HMO.

But Carruthers couldn't stay away from education. In 2003, he became the dean of the NMSU College of Business and vice president for economic development. Still in that position in 2011, he is closely involved in NMSU's Arrowhead Park and Arrowhead Park Early College High School, a partnership with Las Cruces Public Schools and Doña Ana Community College.

OÑATE HIGH SCHOOL

Oñate High School students celebrate graduation, above, and its marching band performs, below, at the annual Tournament of Bands. Oñate High School opened on the East Mesa in 1993 and is known for its unique architecture.

LAS CRUCES BULLETIN

MAYFIELD HIGH SCHOOL FOOTBALL

The Mayfield High School Trojan football team has been the most successful school athletic program in New Mexico with 15 appearances in the state title game, winning the state championship eight times, including 2005, 2006, 2007 and 2010. The team has finished as runner-up seven times, including 2001, 2002, 2003 and 2009.

LAS CRUCES BULLETIN

ALMA D'ARTE

The 2009 class of Alma d'arte Charter High School, an art-based public high school in Doña Ana County, poses for a photo during graduation.

LAS CRUCES BULLETIN

HIGH SCHOOL BASKETBALL

The Mayfield High School girls basketball teams were state champion in 2004 and 2007 and runners-up in 2005 and 2006. In 2002, Mayfield and Oñate boys finished as runners-up in the state championship in their respective districts.

LAS CRUCES BULLETIN

MountainView Regional Medical Center

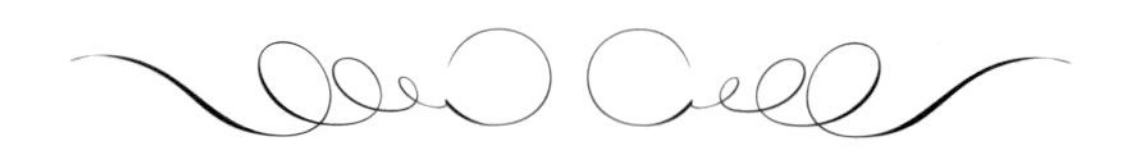

When Denny Shelton, chairman and CEO of Triad Hospitals, Inc., announced in March 2000 that the company intended to build a state-of-the-art hospital in Las Cruces, the idea was met with skepticism from some community leaders. Prior to 2000, several companies had promised to build a hospital, but did not follow through on their plans.

Shelton committed to buy land and to hire and relocate a CEO to Las Cruces by July 2000. Two years later, in August 2002, MountainView Regional Medical Center – Las Cruces' second hospital – opened on schedule due in large part to the coordinating efforts of the first CEO, John Hummer.

Hummer helped develop community support and participation. Community steering committees helped define what was needed to meet local health care needs. The community also voted for the name MountainView via newspaper ballots and voting booths set up around the city. MountainView received 68 percent of the votes, topping the other two proposals, Mission Regional and Alta Vista.

Gallup polls commissioned by Triad showed 80 percent of Las Crucens wanted a second hospital, and their primary reason was to have a greater choice of doctors and services. In keeping with these results, MountainView selected the slogan: "A New Choice for Healthcare."

By the time MountainView Regional Medical Center opened, the population of Las Cruces had reached 75,000 and would grow by more than 31 percent in the decade between 2000 and 2010.

MountainView not only made a tremendous impact on available healthcare services in the area, but also made a substantial economic impact as well. According to John Hummer, by August 2002, the new hospital was expending $1 million per month in salaries. In addition, he said, $68 million had been spent on the two-year construction of the hospital.

Later in 2002, another $14 million was spent on the construction of the adjacent, four-story Medical Office Plaza.

Even before the hospital was completed, MountainView Regional Medical Center made a commitment to becoming an anchor in the community. That commitment was reflected in many ways — by paying much-higher-than-average salaries to its workers, providing scholarships for New Mexico State University and Doña Ana Community College health care students and partnering with several nonprofit agencies in the area.

A decade later, MountainView Regional Medical Center is now an important member of the larger community. MountainView has achieved chest pain certification and certifications from the Joint Commission in Hip and Knee Replacement. In 2011, MountainView became the first hospital in New Mexico to unveil a Wall of Heroes, which honors MountainView patients who have given the gift of life through organ and tissue donations.

As envisioned, MountainView Regional Medical Center has become a vital health care resource committed to attracting top physicians and improving the quality of life in southern New Mexico.

JEFFREY ARTERBURN

Research projects in Jeffrey Arterburn's lab, right, at New Mexico State University are partially funded through the NMSU Aggies are Tough Enough to Wear Pink campaign, below, in hopes of helping cure cancer. The annual campaign started in 2007 and became the most successful Tough Enough to Wear Pink fundraiser in the nation.

LAS CRUCES BULLETIN

NEW MEXICO SENIOR OLYMPICS

The New Mexico Senior Olympics State Games have taken place in Las Cruces from 2007-11, bringing active seniors to compete in dozens of events, ranging from line dancing to swimming.

LAS CRUCES BULLETIN

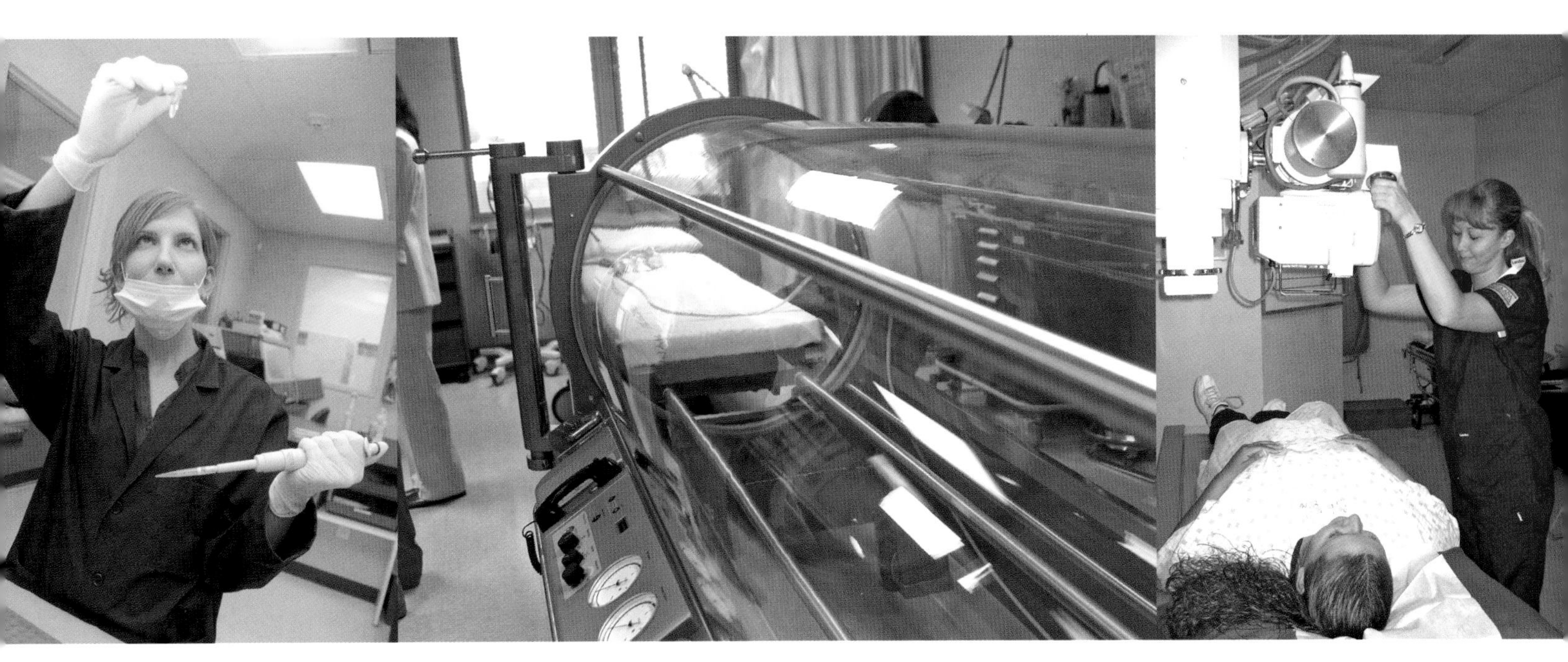

ADVANCED TECHNOLOGY

Medical technology in Las Cruces moved just as fast as other parts of the country in the 2000s, including advanced forms of treatment and improved health care training programs offered at New Mexico State University and Doña Ana Community College.

LAS CRUCES BULLETIN

LAS CRUCES' GROWTH

Throughout the 2000s, Las Cruces saw a tremendous amount of growth, including apartments on Roadrunner Parkway, left.

LAS CRUCES BULLETIN

PHILIP PHILIPPOU

In 2007, the Vistas at Presidio proposal to guide the city's growth on the East Mesa was approved. The 4,000-acre plan was brokered by State Land Commissioner Pat Lyons; the master planning and business development contract went to developer Philip Philippou, pictured below with his wife, Bibi.

LAS CRUCES BULLETIN/PHILIP PHILIPPOU

NEW DEVELOPMENTS

The Sonoma Ranch development, spearheaded by George and Yvonne Rawson, David Steinborn and Dale Schueller, was at the height of Las Cruces' growth in the 2000s. Other developments during the decade included El Dorado, Ridge and High Range.

LAS CRUCES BULLETIN

MESILLA VALLEY HOSPICE

More than 30 years ago, a small group of people in Las Cruces had a dream. They wanted to create an organization to allow people to spend their last days at home surrounded by loved ones, rather than in a sterile hospital setting.

That dream became Mesilla Valley Hospice.

In 1982, Mesilla Valley Hospice opened its doors in a small office on Idaho Avenue with one volunteer nurse, five volunteer board members, a part-time chaplain and a full-time executive director/social worker.

In 1998, Mesilla Valley Hospice moved into its permanent home at 299 E. Montana Avenue. As of 2011, La Posada (The Inn) was the first and only free-standing hospice care facility in New Mexico and one of less than 100 in the United States.

The staff and volunteers believe every life is precious, every person has value, and each person's day should have meaning and be free from pain, fear and uncertainty.

Mesilla Valley Hospice provides compassionate care using a team approach. The team develops a unique plan of care to meet the physical, emotional and spiritual needs of each individual patient coping with a life-limiting illness – and his or her entire family.

In hospice philosophy, the patient and family are considered a unit of care. Family is not just the traditional family, but the patient's family of choice.

Volunteers are at the heart of hospice. Mesilla Valley Hospice volunteers provide a special kind of caring. The volunteers, who come from all walks of life, are caring, dependable people committed to helping individuals and their families deal with end-of-life issues.

Mesilla Valley Hospice services can be provided in a family home, assisted living facility, hospital, nursing home or residence of choice.

Hospice care enables patients to remain near their loved ones, support systems and churches in their own community. Mesilla Valley Hospice serves families in homes from Sunland Park and Santa Teresa to Hatch and Garfield – and all points in between.

Nurses, social workers, certified nursing assistants, chaplains and volunteers are available to serve patients and their families 24 hours a day, seven days a week.

La Posada is available to patients of all ages and diagnoses in the Doña Ana County area. In contrast to the typical hospital setting, there are no limited visiting hours or restrictions at La Posada. Family and friends, including pets and children, are encouraged to come and go as they please.

La Posada becomes the patient's home away from home – a place of comfort, a place of care, a place of compassion.

As New Mexico turns 100 in 2012, the Mesilla Valley Hospice dream will celebrate its 30th year of keeping life precious for the region's citizens and their families.

A PLACE OF COMFORT, CARE AND COMPASSION

Mesilla Valley Hospice enables families to focus on their loved ones. Staff and volunteers at the original Idaho Avenue location. La Posada's courtyard provides a verdant, serene setting. Patients are encouraged to celebrate important moments of life.

MESILLA VALLEY HOSPICE

SUSANA MARTINEZ
SUSANA MARTINEZ
GOVERNOR

2010-2011

MOVING AHEAD

A NEW GOVERNOR

Confetti flies through the air at the Hotel Encanto de Las Cruces after Susana Martinez gives her acceptance speech upon winning the New Mexico gubernatorial election on Nov. 2, 2010. Martinez, a former district attorney of Doña Ana County, is the first female to be elected governor of New Mexico and the first Hispanic woman to be elected governor in the country.

LAS CRUCES BULLETIN

City Projects Bring New Beginnings

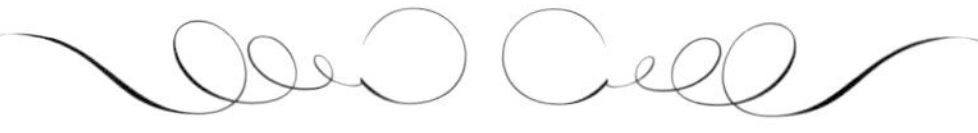

From the start to the finish of 2010, it was a year of new beginnings and grand openings of government facilities that would change the face of Las Cruces forever.

Nowhere was that change more pronounced than Downtown with the opening of a new City Hall and federal courthouse and the first phase of re-opening Main Street.

Borrowing on the city's early territorial architecture, the $37.7 million, three-story City Hall south of Branigan Memorial Library was designed to accommodate future growth.

On April 5, 2010, the City Council held its first meeting in the complex's round, kiva-inspired council chambers. The 117,000-square-foot building was not only Leadership in Energy and Environmental Design (LEED) certified for its construction, but also its operations with a variety of energy-saving systems and the requirement that all powered equipment have an Energy Star rating.

Meanwhile, a few blocks south, next to the former city hall, the new federal district courthouse was built with twice the height of the new City Hall and a more modern take on pueblo and Southwestern elements, using copper and stone details.

Made possible by unrelenting former U.S. Sen. Pete Domenici, the $91.2 million federal courthouse project is a six-story, 96,000-square-foot building with eight courtrooms, basement and a penthouse with a unique blast-proof design. Judges' chambers utilize bulletproof glass and the prisoners' holding cell features special security measures to prevent escape.

Along with these additions, the Downtown landscape changed in 2011 with the removal of the pedestrian mall. With the north end complete, including a roundabout, the south end was expected to be opened in the fall of 2012.

By October 2010, the new $14 million Las Cruces Regional Aquatic Center opened on the corner of Solano Drive and Hadley Avenue. The indoor aquatic facility has 5,000 square feet of water surface area, including a recreational pool with water slide and play features, a 25-meter lap pool, a lazy river and therapeutic pool. Using the latest technology for water purification, it is LEED certified.

The center was the brainchild of state Rep. Joseph Cervantes, who persuaded Gov. Bill Richardson to match funds with southern New Mexico lawmakers who put up their capital outlay funds for the project.

In December 2010, the new $26 million Las Cruces Convention Center opened on the corner of University and Union avenues. A project that was under debate by officials for more than 25 years, it marks a partnership between the city and New Mexico State University, with funding made possible through an additional lodger's tax.

The convention center includes a 14,500-square-foot exhibition hall as well as a 8,950-square-foot ballroom. There are six breakout rooms totaling nearly 3,000 square feet, more than 5,000 square feet of outdoor space and 8,500 square feet of indoor pre-function space. It is LEED gold certified.

The first major function held at the convention center was the send-off to Santa Fe of newly elected Gov. Susana Martinez, a longtime Doña Ana County district attorney and prosecutor. Martinez is not only the first woman to be elected governor of New Mexico, she is the first Hispanic woman to be a governor in the United States.

Another local milestone for women was the selection of Barbara Couture as NMSU's new president. Hired in December 2010, she had barely unpacked before being thrown into a 30-day legislative session with state government facing a $500 million shortfall.

Besides the local educational systems having to tighten their belts, Doña Ana County and Las Cruces also have been making budget cuts as the recession saw mild recovery through 2011.

Leading the city into the more austere times was Las Cruces City Manager Robert Garza, a structural engineer by training who worked his way up through city government for 25 years before being named city manager in 2011.

"I'm a trained problem-solver," Garza said about his approach to the challenges ahead.

2 0 1 0 - 1 1

Who's Who

Las Cruces Mayor

2007-2011	Ken Miyagishima

Postmaster

2010	LeGretta Ross-Rawlins

NMSU President

2010-2011	Barbara Couture

Mesilla Mayor

2010	Nora Barraza

Doña Ana County Sheriff

2006-2011	Todd Garrison

Las Cruces Police Chief

2010-2011	Richard S. Williams

Las Cruces Fire Chief

2010-2011	Travis Brown

New Mexico Governors

2003-2010	Bill Richardson
2011	Susana Martinez

U.S. Senators

1983-2011	Jeff Bingaman
2009-2011	Tom Udall

U.S. Representatives

2009-2011	Harry Teague
2009-2011	Martin Heinrich
2009-2011	Ben R. Luján
2011	Steve Pearce

Las Cruces Public Schools Superintendent

2007-2011	Stan Rounds

White Sands Missile Range Commanders

2009-11	Brig. Gen. John S. Regan
2011	Robert S. Carter
2011	Col. John G. Ferrari

Las Cruces City Managers

2005-10	Terrence Moore
2011	Robert Garza

By the Numbers

97,618	Las Cruces population (2010)
51.3	Percentage of women
56.8	Percentage Hispanic
209,233	Doña Ana County population (2010)
$37,441	Average household income
$7.25	Minimum wage (2009)
$2.86	Gallon of gas (2010)
44 cents	First-class stamp (2010)
45 cents	First-class stamp (2012)
24,400	Enrollment at NMSU
38	Schools in Las Cruces
117,000	Square feet in the new City Hall
96,000	Square feet in the new federal district courthouse
4 inches	Rio Grande water allotted per acre
95	Average temperatures (June/July 2010)
29	Average low temperature (December/January)

In the News

Jan. 12, 2010: A 7.0-magnitude earthquake hits Haiti, killing more than 230,000.

Feb. 27, 2010: An 8.8-magnitude earthquake rocks Chile, triggering a tsunami in the Pacific.

April 14, 2010: Volcanic ash from Iceland disrupts air traffic across Europe.

April 20, 2010: BP's Deepwater Horizon oil platform explodes in the Gulf of Mexico, killing eleven workers. The resulting Horizon oil spill, one of the largest in history, spreads for several months, damaging the waters and the United States coastline.

March 11, 2011: A 9.0-magnitude earthquake off the coast of Japan devastates the country from heavy tremors and a resulting massive tsunami, including the meltdowns of three reactors in the Fukushima I Nuclear Power Plant complex.

May 2, 2011: An elite team of Navy SEALS kills Osama bin Laden in Pakistan.

Aug. 2, 2011: President Barack Obama signs debt ceiling deal.

Oct. 21, 2011: Obama announces U.S. troops to leave Iraq by year's end.

2010
Barbara Couture starts her tenure as New Mexico State University president. She came to NMSU from the University of Nebraska-Lincoln.

2011
Gov. Susana Martinez begins her term as governor. Following a regular 60-day session in which a balanced budget was passed, she called for a special session in October to draw new political boundaries and pass other legislation, but lawmakers failed to complete redistricting and passed only a few other bills.

2011
SalsaFest is the official opening event for state Centennial events and the northern end of Downtown's Main Street is re-opened.

2011
Virgin Galactic begins work on the interior of the Spaceport America terminal hangar, a year after the spaceport's runway was dedicated.

LAS CRUCES BULLETIN

GOVERNOR MARTINEZ

On Jan. 1, 2011, New Mexico made history when Gov. Susana Martinez was sworn into office, making her the first Hispanic female governor in the United States.

Born and raised in El Paso, Martinez made a name for herself as the district attorney for Doña Ana County. After being re-elected three times and serving 15 years as the county's lead prosecutor, she took her mission to the state level when she ran for governor as a Republican.

"The first eight months have been nonstop," she said. "Nonstop because it truly is, about 99 percent of time, it is seven days a week and about 12- to 15-hour days, but it's very challenging and exciting at the same time."

Since taking office, Martinez said she has been able to accomplish several of the goals she set for herself during her campaign.

"One of the highlights has been, No. 1, we balanced the budget knowing we had a deficit," she said. "That was very challenging (to do) without raising taxes on small businesses."

Martinez, a proponent of small government, said supporting small businesses and creating a supportive environment for incoming businesses is essential to New Mexico's growth.

"I can see (growth) happening in the southern part of the state here in Doña Ana County, a place where we did not have a lot of opportunity for growth, but with Union Pacific it has been phenomenal," she said, adding that she sees similar companies coming to the state. "(Companies) are looking at our state more and more because they're looking at the predictability that we bring as an administration – that we're looking at regulations that exist and saying 'Does this make sense, what are we getting in exchange for this regulation? Is there something environmentally positive we're getting or is it a regulation in place that makes it harder for businesses to come here?'"

There are several factors, she said, that will help New Mexico grow and bring in business, especially education and providing a top workforce.

"Education is one issue that, if done right, will outlive us all and the benefits are everlasting," she said.

Along with helping New Mexico prosper, Martinez is also shouldering the responsibility of making not only the state, but the nation proud.

"I know I'm the first Hispanic female governor in the country, and it's very humbling, but I also understand the enormous responsibility I have to do this job as governor of New Mexico and do it right because there are little girls who come to me, and now in our discussions, they realize they can become more than they ever thought they could," she said.

Becoming a sort of celebrity nationwide, rumors had swirled around Martinez possibly on the short list for the GOP vice presidential nomination.

"As far as vice president, I would not consider that because it would require me to do that now and not what I was elected to do," she said.

"I have four years as governor, and I'm committed to those four years. ... They will get the absolute most from me to make sure we do this right. I cannot abandon this job for another."

REMEMBRANCE AT CITY HALL

Las Cruces Mayor Ken Miyagishima, right, welcomes the public into the new City Hall in 2010, which was also the setting for the 10th anniversary of 9/11, co-hosted by Police Chief Richard Williams, below.

LAS CRUCES BULLETIN

NEW TO THE LANDSCAPE

In addition to a new City Hall, above left, 2010 also saw the opening of the Las Cruces Convention Center and Las Cruces Regional Aquatic Center. The Convention Center, above center, was made possible by a local lodger's tax. The aquatic center, above right, was built with state funds from local lawmakers pooling their capital outlay funds, which was matched by Gov. Bill Richardson's building fund.

LAS CRUCES BULLETIN

CENSUS COUNT PUSH

Herb Torres of Las Cruces Public Schools urges people to participate in the 2010 census, which counted 97,618 residents in city limits. Many local officials hoped the city population would exceed 100,000 in the official count.

LAS CRUCES BULLETIN

SPACEPORT AMERICA LANDS SAFELY

Virgin Galactic's Richard Branson and his new spaceliner have made two landings at Spaceport America – in October 2010 to dedicate the two-mile-long runway and October 2011 to ceremoniously get the "Keys to a New Dawn" for the terminal hangar. The $209 million project was started during Gov. Bill Richardson's administration and Gov. Susana Martinez is seeing the project through.

VIRGIN GALACTIC/LAS CRUCES BULLETIN

PREPARING TO DEPLOY AGAIN

Prior to their departure to Afghanistan, members of the 2nd Engineer Battalion roll up the group's flag for the Casing of the Colors during the Deployment Ceremony held at White Sands Missile Range in April 2010.

LAS CRUCES BULLETIN

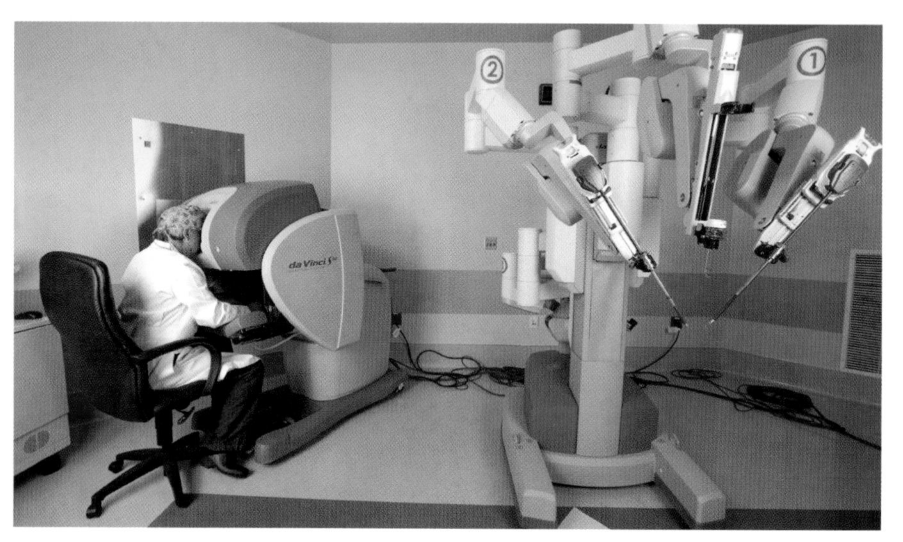

FUTURE MEDICINE ARRIVES

In June 2010, MountainView Regional Medical Center welcomed its newest surgeon – the da Vinci robotic surgical system, the first of its kind in southern New Mexico. Da Vinci's guided arms are compared to "operating with chopsticks" to replicate the surgeon's movements. Though the technology is costly, use of robotics in surgery is expected to improve patient recovery time.

LAS CRUCES BULLETIN

NEW SCHOOL ON CAMPUS

Arrowhead Park Early College High School opened in 2011. A first for New Mexico, APECHS allows high schoolers to take classes at New Mexico State University and Doña Ana Community College.

LAS CRUCES BULLETIN

LA FIESTA DE LA FRONTERA

In July 1940, at La Fiesta de la Frontera, Father Henry Buchanan presided over a "Blessing of the Crosses." A 1950s New Mexico roadside historical marker.

NMSU LASC

LAS CRUCES:
THE HISTORY BEHIND THE NAME

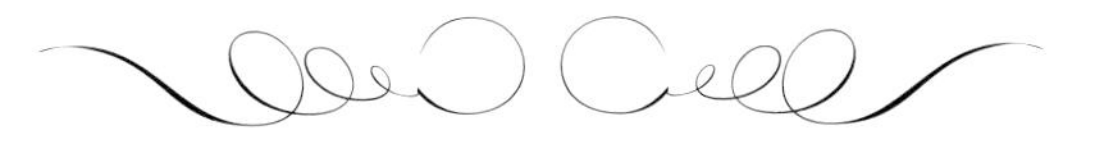

In 2006, the City of Las Cruces successfully defended itself in federal court against a lawsuit that targeted the use of crosses in its official logo: a sunburst with three crosses in the center. The lawsuit sought to force the city to remove the crosses from its logo, claiming it was a Christian symbol and therefore in violation of the First Amendment tenet: "Congress shall make no law respecting an establishment of religion, or prohibiting the free exercise thereof."

In its defense, the City of Las Cruces provided the following information as evidence in the federal trial.

Las Cruces is Spanish for "the crosses." According to widely held belief, the name Las Cruces described groups of crosses placed on graves and the sites of Indian massacres that occurred in the area between 1712 and 1840. In historical accounts, several massacres occurred along the Camino Real de la Tierra Adentro near present day Las Cruces. In 1712, a group of colonists traveling north to Santa Fe were attacked by Apaches at the campsite about 30 to 45 miles north of Paso del Norte (present day El Paso, Texas and Ciudad Juárez, Mexico). Soldiers from Paso del Norte buried the victims and erected crosses over the graves.

In 1787, a group with a bishop, a priest, two Mexican military officers, four trappers and four choirboys was attacked in the Las Cruces area near the Rio Grande. Only one boy survived.

In yet another account, this one dated 1830, a caravan of 40 people traveling south from Taos were all killed in the area, resulting in "a forest of crosses."

Another theory holds that the brush along the river provided such fine cover for the Apaches that there were several small clusters of crosses, each marking a massacre, scattered around the river bank.

On Feb. 12, 1847, an eyewitness recorded the following observation in her diary: "Yesterday, we passed over the spot where a few years since, a party of Apaches attacked Gen. Armijo as he returned from the Pass with a party of troops, and killed some 14 of his men, the graves of whom, marked by a rude cross, are now seen."

This firsthand report is the most compelling evidence of crosses standing in the area that would eventually become known as Las Cruces, "The City of the Crosses."

YESTERDAY AND TODAY

From its earliest days, Las Cruces has stood at the crossroads of east-west and north-south highways, which are most recently known as U.S. Highway 70 that provides the east-west traffic, and Interstate 25 that is the primary north-south route.

NMSU LASC

ENTREPRENEURIAL SPIRIT

Fate Dickerson and Jason Ivy in front of the Fairacres Post Office in the early 1900s. Sybil Lee Clagett Dickerson and Juanita Denton were the first two female letter winners at New Mexico A&M College, and were pioneers in the Aggie women's athletic program in 1938. Charles F. Dickerson as a kid in the early 1950s.

MARCI DICKERSON

THE DICKERSON FAMILY

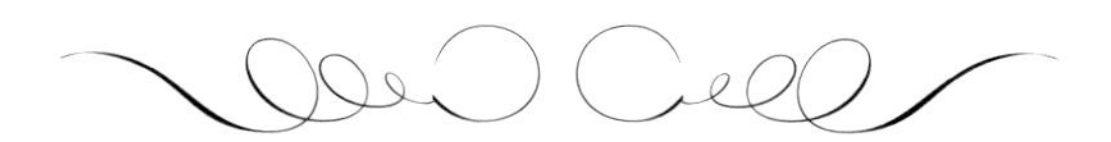

In the early 1900s, Fate and Etta Dickerson ran a general store just west of Las Cruces in Fairacres, where the locals, who got there by horseback and later by Model T, would gather around the heater and visit during wintertime.

The Dickersons provided mail service and, later, a post office was established there with Fate Dickerson as postmaster.

For more than a century, the Dickerson family has continued to establish and grow entrepreneurial enterprises as they have seen opportunities to bring new businesses and services to the people of the Mesilla Valley. In addition, three generations of the family have graduated from New Mexico State University.

Fate's son Morris Dickerson grew up in the family business and succeeded him as the postmaster of Fairacres. His wife, Sybel Lee Clagett Dickerson, was one of the first two Aggie women to ever receive letters in athletics, and helped establish the women's athletic program at NMSU. Morris and Sybel were active members in the Masons and the Rebekas, major civic organizations at the time.

Their son, banker Charles F. Dickerson, started an auction business in an old cotton gin on land adjacent to the family store on Picacho Avenue. Soon, he became a full-time auctioneer and by the mid-1970s was renting "the barn" for parties and events, which led him and his wife, Jeanette Hitson Dickerson, to cater these events.

"Food and people, that's always been the main thing," Jeanette Dickerson said.

In 1981 they opened the Smokehouse Barbecue inside Dickerson's Barn because Charles could not find "good BBQ in this town." Through a series of large building projects, the family created Dickerson's Event Center. Here, several Las Cruces traditions were established: the annual Toys for Tots motorcycle run, the La Casa Christmas Bazaar, and the Cowboys for Cancer Research Dinner Dance.

Charles devoted years to the community. He was involved in regional events such as the Hatch Chile Festival, the Renaissance ArtsFaire and the Southern New Mexico State Fair & Rodeo, for which he served as volunteer general manager for more than 20 years. Jeanette served on the Board of the Las Cruces Public Schools for 16 years.

Charles and Jeanette's three daughters – Marci, Kari and Kristin – all grew up in the restaurant business.

Marci Dickerson built on the success of Dickerson's Event Center success, launching other businesses, including Dickerson's Catering, The Game Sports Bar & Grill and Hurricane Alley. The Event Center was scheduled to become the Rio Grande Rifle Company, Gun Store and Indoor Shooting Range. Plans for the range include a storefront with couches where people will visit and talk just as Fate and Etta's customers did in the early 1900s.

By recognizing needs in the community and responding creatively, the Dickerson family has for more than a century demonstrated entrepreneurial genius in service to people.

"We make it personal, we make it local," Jeanette said.

NMSU MAKES ADVANCES ON MANY FRONTS

Above, New Mexico State University opened its new Barnes & Noble University Bookstore on the corner of University Avenue and Jordan Road. People swarmed to see the new store, which has the first escalator in Las Cruces. Below left, Barbara Couture is lavished with NMSU clothing upon her arrival in January 2010 as the first woman to be selected as NMSU's permanent president. Bottom right, Aggie forward Wendell McKines cuts the net after the Aggies won the Western Athletic Conference Tournament March 13, 2010, in Reno, Nev. The Aggies defeated Utah State 69-63 to earn an automatic bid to the NCAA Tournament. In the first round, the Aggies lost a heartbreaker to Michigan State University, 69-67. The Spartans advanced to the Final Four.

LAS CRUCES BULLETIN/NMSU COMMUNICATIONS

LEADER OF THE FLOCK

Las Cruces Diocese Bishop Ricardo Ramírez, pictured at the Basilica of San Albino in Mesilla, was the first bishop of the Roman Catholic Diocese of Las Cruces, which was created in 1982 by Pope John Paul II. When he turned 75 in 2011, he offered his resignation in accordance with church law. He served the diocese and its people for nearly three decades and emphasized social justice issues, such as the plight of the poor and migrant workers.

LAS CRUCES BULLETN

SAVING A HISTORICAL AND SPIRITUAL TREASURE

The oldest African-American church in Las Cruces, Phillips Chapel CME Church – built in 1911 by the grandfather of Clarence Fielder, left, an NMSU history professor – was the center of a restoration project held by building students at Doña Ana Community College and concerned community members beginning in 2010. The goal of those involved is to save the one-room adobe building, which used to be a social center and school in addition to serving the spiritual needs of those in the Mesquite neighborhood.

LAS CRUCES BULLETIN

A TAPESTRY OF FAITH

One Mesilla Valley family's roots: Felicitas G. Montes, Ernest and Consuelo Ríos Lerma, Ronald and Olivia Lerma McDonald, María Montes Ríos, Consuelo Lerma.

MCDONALD FAMILY

HUMBLE BEGINNINGS, LASTING CONTRIBUTIONS

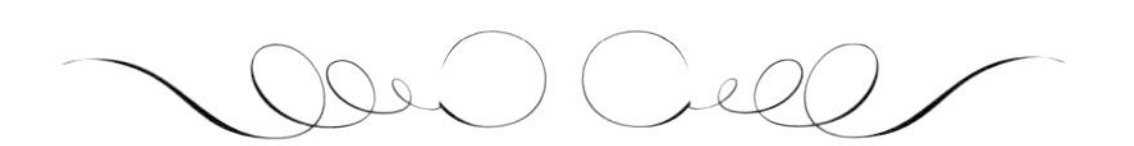

The greatness of New Mexico is not measured only by its resources, its size, or its beauty; nor solely from politicians, large landowners, or influential investors. A generous portion of its greatness was built on the backs of humble citizens who made lasting contributions in their way. Many New Mexicans can trace their ancestry to this unnoticed population of remarkable, unsung Hispanic pioneers whose lives strengthened the fiber of the state.

The Montes and Ríos families were typical of settlers whose heritages stem from those who came when it was New Spain, Mexico, and New Mexico territory. They were here when it became a state. They were never mentioned in newspapers' society pages or pictured on walls of museums. Only their descendants remain to testify proudly to their contributions.

When red-headed Albino Montes was gone, his wife Felicitas Garcia Montes supported her family as a midwife delivering hundreds of babies throughout the Mesilla Valley. How many New Mexican families can be tied to the expertise and caring of this lady who hitched her horse to a buggy and carried her small black bag to help so many mothers?

Sepia toned photos in the family album speak silently of Hispanic heritage, revealing features and a mixture of fair-skinned Spanish influence. Her own widowed father entrusted Felicitas' and her sister's education to nuns at a convent boarding school, arming her to contend with being sole supporter of her children, difficult in any era.

Doroteo Ríos, with slightly darker skin tones, hinting at Native American lineage, or firm evidence of toiling in the sun, helped build the railroad which lined the way for 19th century progress and helped New Mexico prosper. His blue-eyed Elena bore sons Jesús and José and saw to their education in reading, writing and catechism. They farmed and older residents tell of the orchard Doroteo tended. Elena died quite young and rests beside her husband in San Albino's Cemetery in what was then called La Mesilla.

Jesús Ríos married María Montes, Felicitas and Albino's daughter, in San Albino Catholic Church. They settled to farm on the west side of Las Cruces. Of nine children, they lost one to smallpox, one to tetanus, and one to influenza. When arroyos were uncontrolled, one stormy night brought unrestrained water, destroying their farmland, barn, home, and all their belongings. They moved to the edge of the original town site of Las Cruces, a block from the route of the 16th century El Camino Real, where Jesús and his sons made adobe bricks and built a new home that stands to this day. Its image is featured on street signs designating the Mesquite Historic District.

The Great Depression brought the Civilian Conservation Corps, and among the workers was Ernest Lerma, a heavy equipment operator who built levees along the Rio Grande. In Las Cruces he found Consuelo Ríos, who taught sewing and sold sewing machines to hundreds of women during her 40-year career. As a widow, she dedicated her time and influence to found an organization honoring and preserving the history and culture of her beloved neighborhood.

Continuing the family pattern of history and faith in God, daughter Olivia, with husband Ronald McDonald, returned to the land of her birth and settled in the area. Their blend of Anglo and Hispanic cultures reflects New Mexico's heritage, especially in the last century. At the request of their parish priest, Msgr. Robert , and approval by the bishop, they were privileged to complete a successful, detailed petition to the Vatican to elevate tiny San Albino church to the status of minor basilica, where generations have worshipped.

Presenting the Montes, Ríos, Lerma, and McDonald family line shows but a small branch of New Mexico's family tree. They represent a standard of many generations of other families who also lived simply, but contributed greatly to New Mexico's growth, prosperity, and greatness during these last 100 years.

FUTURE TRAVEL

With construction under way on Spaceport America near Truth or Consequences, N.M., in 2008, the state-of-the-art facility for space travel is coming into existence. Possibly opening as early as 2013, the spaceport is the world's first commercial spaceport designed with the needs of the commercial space business in mind. In addition to bringing travelers looking to visit space, the spaceport will also spur the economy by bringing in tourism-related industries and those in aerospace and accompanying fields.

NEW MEXICO SPACEPORT AUTHORITY

2012 AND BEYOND

LOOKING FORWARD

CENTENNIAL HIGH SCHOOL

The fourth public high school in Las Cruces, Centennial High School, will open its doors in August 2012. It was designed using the school-within-a-school approach, which breaks the main academic portion of the school into separate structures, providing each grade with its own facility. Featuring 344,000 square feet sitting on a 110-acre campus, Centennial High School will include 82 classrooms.

ARCHITECT: ASA ARCHITECTS; LAS CRUCES; ASSOC. ARCHITECT: DEKKER/PERICH/SABATINI; ALBUQUERQUE; CONTRACTOR: GERALD A. MARTIN; LTD.; ALBUQUERQUE

Ready for the Next 100 Years

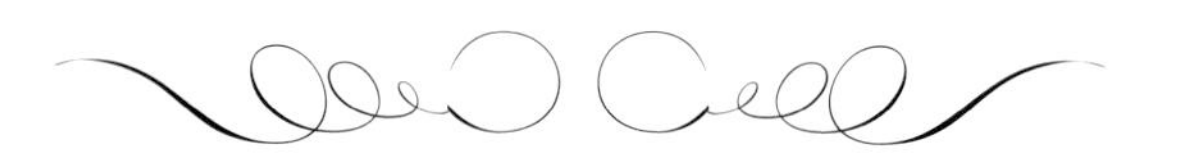

While the entire nation has struggled to get out of the economic downturn, Las Cruces and Doña Ana County are still in positions to grow, thanks to the scenic landscape, temperate weather and open spaces.

"If you look at how the city has changed by decade, it indicates that there has been a lot of growth in the last 60 years. I don't see that (trend) changing," said Las Cruces City Manager Robert Garza in 2011. "Because of our quality of life here, people want to move here and people want to stay here."

Continuing to prosper, the future is bright for the area, according to industry experts.

Growth in Las Cruces

With the U.S. leaving an economic recession, the 15th the nation has experienced since the Great Depression, in 2011, Lowell Catlett, dean and chief administrative officer for the New Mexico State University College of Agricultural, Consumer and Environmental Sciences, said the future of business in Las Cruces is already looking up.

"(The recession) was nothing but a pause for people to take a breath, and industry to restructure itself," he said. "Recessions are a natural part of the landscape."

Featuring a diverse economy that includes industries such as higher education, agriculture and the military, Catlett said the area has services that can't be reproduced anywhere else, such as test facilities at White Sands Missile Range.

"We have a fairly stable base," he said. "Basically, that's why Las Cruces has been able to grow and prosper."

The unique landscape of the Mesilla Valley is also a driving force behind bringing new industries and people. In addition to potentially providing a hub for various alternative-energy industries, Catlett said Las Cruces will also make strides in health care.

With health care already a pillar of the local economy, Catlett said more people will venture to the area for two new services – end-of-life assisted care and low-maintenance lifestyles.

"People want places that are physically beautiful," he said. "There is a revolution in health care and we are suited for it."

With these new lifestyle facilities possibly coming to town, end-of-life assisted care would allow people to spend their final years or months in a relaxing, soothing environment.

"Humans are naturally attracted to plants, animals and people," he said. "Our area is situated to attract this new type of health care. We have great potential here."

Another lifestyle change the Mesilla Valley will see is more people purchasing farmland for pleasure rather than for making a living, Catlett said.

"We see people who want 5 acres," he said. "They want that lifestyle."

In addition to changes in lifestyle and health care, the future of

Las Cruces is in the stars – or more specifically, in Spaceport America, located in Upham, N.M., near Truth or Consequences.

"The spaceport will be a destination resort, as we call it," Catlett said. "People will come to the area for that one thing."

While visitors will come for the spaceport, they will need other amenities, such as recreation and dining, which will create jobs throughout the area, Garza said.

He added that, along with these services, the spaceport will bring aerospace and support-industry experts who will want to live in an area that fulfills their basic needs and then some.

"Those people will likely want to live in Las Cruces versus other areas," Garza said.

"It's about critical mass," Catlett said. "Basically, can people get their basic needs filled and feel that they have more than one choice?"

With such growth potential, Brian Denmark, assistant city manager, said once the economy has realigned itself, the city will once again see 3 percent growth in population each year.

"Once we get out of this lag period, we will see another period of growth," he said.

To accommodate future growth, Garza said the city is working on several construction projects. This includes several major endeavors with the New Mexico Department of Transportation in the coming years, such as a new interchange at interstates 10 and 25.

Preserving Public Land

With about 1 million acres of the more than 2 million acres of Doña Ana County owned by the Bureau of Land Management, the federal department has several plans on how to best use it to serve the environment and the community.

Dwayne Sykes, planning and environmental coordinator and TriCounty Resource Management Plan team leader, said they are addressing many prescriptions for the remaining BLM land in Doña Ana, Sierra and Otero counties.

"There is a lot of (BLM) land around Las Cruces," he said. "We're looking at how we're going to provide for future community development. We're identifying land that is suitable for disposal."

Conducting land exchanges for acreage needed for community development, Sykes said BLM recently conducted such a transaction with a small parcel of land for a new state police station near Sonoma Ranch Boulevard.

"Land disposal is a big part of the plan we're working on," he said. "We work closely with the city and county to make sure what we plan matches up with them."

The plan also looks at conserving open spaces, such as a buffer zone around the Organ Mountains, and creating designated areas identified for special management, such as wilderness and national conservation areas.

"The key is trying to create an appropriate use of land available for disposal, but also land we're maintaining," said Bill Childress,

LIVING GREEN

When developers began Picacho Mountain, below, a master-planned community, they didn't just envision luxurious and green homes, but also a retail village, creating a mini community in the area. Still in the works, it will include various businesses, from a general store to a boutique hotel operated by La Tour Signature Hotels.

PICACHO MOUNTAIN

DRIVING GREEN

Above, El Paso Electric Co. is currently conducting research with the City of El Paso on adopting electric car-charging stations. Based on the response, Las Cruces also showed an interest in such stations.

EL PASO ELECTRIC CO.

PRESERVING THE TRACKWAYS

Established in 2009, the Prehistoric Trackways National Monument, the 100th national monument in the United States, covers approximately 5,280 acres in the Robledo Mountains near Las Cruces.

ROBERT WICK

district manager for BLM.

Other areas that are being considered for special designation, whether for scenic value or because they're a habitat for rare plants and animals, are Broad Canyon, Tortugas Mountain, Picacho Peak and Butterfield Trail.

Once Congress determines the appropriate designation, Childress said it is the responsibility of BLM to carry it out. He said designations cover a wide range of uses, including areas for all-terrain vehicles – known as off-highway vehicle (OHV) areas – and other recreational activities.

"There are areas for protecting and areas designated for ultimate use," he said.

"One thing we're wrestling with is OHV in the (Prehistoric Trackways National Monument)," said Sykes, explaining that the annual Chile Challenge for rock crawlers takes place on existing trails in the area.

Childress said BLM is currently developing a plan for future use of the Prehistoric Trackways National Monument in Doña Ana County, ensuring there are areas for recreation, such as hiking, as well as scientific research.

The bureau is also partnering with the Las Cruces Museum of Natural History to display trackway specimens at the future museum, which will be located in Downtown Las Cruces.

"We're very excited about that," he said.

Another possible use of BLM land in Doña Ana County includes bringing more renewable-energy development, especially solar panels and possibly wind-generated energy.

An area of about 70,000 acres near Interstate 10, south of the Industrial Park, known as the Afton Solar Study Area, could be transformed into a solar field. Another site, the Mason Solar Study Area, consists of more than 23,000 acres that could be devoted to the renewable energy.

"We're looking at reducing those sizes," Sykes said. "We're looking at the need."

"We're trying to provide a balance of use and conservation," Childress said. "We're trying to position ourselves to accommodate renewable energy sources."

Along with the possibility of solar energy comes the potential of transmission lines set in place to get the energy generated to where it is needed. Childress said they have received applications from SunZia Transmission LLC and Southline Transmission LLC for such lines.

"The future holds a lot of additional proposals for infrastructure and all different types of use," said Jim McCormick, assistant district manager for BLM. "The land-use plan covers most of those uses, but not all."

McCormick said BLM is also developing new ways to monitor the health of the land to ensure it will be available for future

LOOKING TO THE SUN

Near Interstate 10, south of the West Mesa Industrial Park, 70,000 acres are being considered to be transformed into the Afton Solar Study Area for solar energy. If the solar field takes shape, transmission lines will also need to be installed to transfer the energy created to where it is needed, most likely in other states.

BUREAU OF LAND MANAGEMENT

CULTURE OF CARING

In the late 1800s and the early 1900s, New Mexico was a destination for those with tuberculosis. The climate and the care frequently brought recovery.

AMBERCARE

AMBERCARE

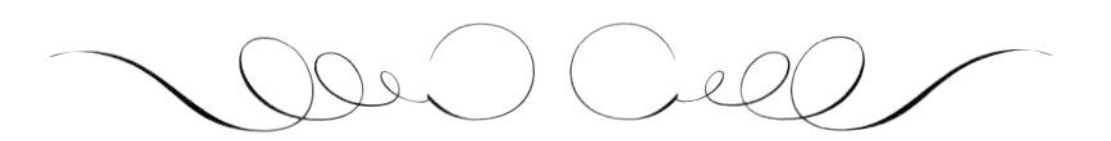

A century ago, people suffering from tuberculosis came to New Mexico in search of a cure for this dreaded disease. The Las Cruces area, with multiple care centers, was a key destination for those seeking comfort. There was a facility near Dripping Springs, as well as the Alameda Ranch Resort, situated near the intersection of Alameda Boulevard and Hoagland Road.

The care patients received was exceptional, and many not only recovered, but became prominent citizens and community leaders. The "lungers," as they were known, may have planted the seed for a culture of caring that inspired the creation of Ambercare.

Ambercare began in 1994, founded by New Mexicans Michael and Mary Merrell in Valencia County, N.M.

The organization provides New Mexicans with home health care, hospice, medical equipment and personal care services. The Merrells started with just a few employees, embracing a holistic method of care delivery, using a "bridge" model to provide flexibility to accommodate the shifting needs of patients.

The services have proven valuable, as evidenced by Ambercare's swift and steady growth. By 2011, Ambercare was serving many communities in New Mexico, from Las Cruces to Las Vegas.

Ambercare became employee-owned, so every patient is cared for by an owner. The Merrells and Ambercare employees attend to the needs of tens of thousands of homebound patients each year.

Poised to enter New Mexico's second century, Ambercare works to follow the tradition of caring established in the Land of Enchantment even before statehood.

CARING THEN AND NOW

The Alameda Ranch Resort, shown here circa 1905, attracted patients from around the country who sought the benefits of the dry Las Cruces climate.

NMSU LASC

Greater Las Cruces Chamber of Commerce

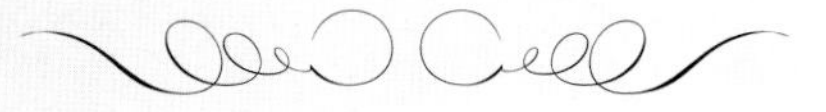

In 1963, the president of the Greater Las Cruces Chamber of Commerce was Sonny Klein. He ran the chamber out of a 500-square-foot, donated space in the old Branigan Library. The "one-man chamber," as he described it, was supported only by Main Street retail merchants.

In an effort to grow the chamber, Klein advocated hiring a chamber manager. With a manager and a host of volunteers, Klein started a fundraising and membership drive entitled "Keep Pace with Tomorrow." The goal was to recruit members beyond retail merchants – lawyers, doctors, farmers and ranchers – and bring all the factions together to promote and support the local business community.

"We wanted a real community chamber of commerce that served and represented everyone," Klein said. The effort was successful, and diversity of the chamber continues to be an important goal of the organization.

Kent Evans, president of the chamber from 1988-89, said his best memories include The Whole Enchilada Fiesta, originally organized by the chamber, and Business Executives of Tomorrow. The Fiesta became a destination event, drawing 50,000 visitors during the three-day September event. Business Executives evolved into Leadership Las Cruces, a program that educates professionals on community diversity and provides training for tomorrow's leaders. Through 2011, more than 500 professionals had participated in the program.

The chamber also was the genesis for The Bridge, a regional educational initiative that "bridges the gap" between students and the needs of the workforce, through public-private collaboration.

In late 2010, the chamber had grown to more than 1,000 members, and hired Bill Allen as president/CEO. Allen quickly became involved with a key project: The chamber was outgrowing its 760 W. Picacho Ave. location. In late 2011, the chamber announced plans to move to the historic Armijo House at 150 E. Lohman Ave. in the Loretto Towne Center. The chamber initiated a capital campaign, "Our Future is Our History," to raise $2.3 million for the renovation of the Armijo House.

"Our architects, Steve Newby Architects & Associates, have developed a Southwestern-style compound that will include two buildings (the Armijo House being one) and a courtyard surrounded by a low wall," Allen said. "We see multiple uses for the facility, both inside and out, that both the chamber and its members will be able to take advantage of."

Moving into New Mexico's second century, the chamber is poised to help the business community prosper in the future. With a 2013 move into the Armijo House, the chamber is honoring Las Cruces history, and living the slogan, "Our Future is Our History."

500 SQUARE FEET

In 1963, the Greater Las Cruces Chamber of Commerce operated from a 500-square-foot, donated space in the old Branigan Library in Downtown Las Cruces.

GREATER LAS CRUCES CHAMBER OF COMMERCE

PICACHO PRESENCE

By 2010, the Greater Las Cruces Chamber of Commerce was outgrowing the office on 760 W. Picacho Ave., its home since 1968.

LAS CRUCES BULLETIN

HISTORY IN THE FUTURE

In 2013, the chamber is scheduled to move into the historic Armijo House. The "Our Future is Our History" campaign was launched in 2011 to raise funds for renovation.

GREATER LAS CRUCES CHAMBER OF COMMERCE

THE FUTURE OF DOÑA ANA COMMUNITY COLLEGE

With phases six and seven already in full swing by 2011, the Doña Ana Community College East Mesa branch is slated to be the institution's main campus.

DOÑA ANA COMMUNITY COLLEGE

CHILE DESTEMMER

Among the areas of research New Mexico State University is making strides in is the chile destemmer. In the works since the early 2000s, the chile destemmer is a project of the NMSU Manufacturing Technology and Engineering Center, and will allow growers of green chile, cayenne pepper and jalapeños to mechanically harvest the pepper.

NEW MEXICO STATE UNIVERSITY

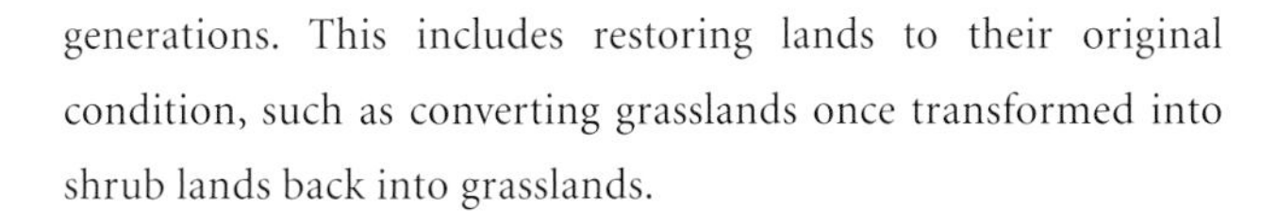

generations. This includes restoring lands to their original condition, such as converting grasslands once transformed into shrub lands back into grasslands.

NMSU PLANS AHEAD

Also looking to the future is New Mexico State University. NMSU Senior Vice President for External Relations Ben Woods said that in the 1990s, university officials purchased 1,500 acres east of the campus. This landholding was set aside for future growth at the institution.

"We're not going to build on it just because it's there," he said. "We're going to use it efficiently and wisely, so in 50, 60 years from now, it's there."

While that land won't be used for several decades, there are other construction projects changing the face of the university campus as Las Cruces knows it.

"We have a number of major projects currently in construction," Woods said.

From new student housing and the Center for the Arts to improvements to the chilled water systems around campus, the university is changing – as is Doña Ana Community College, which will open satellite locations in Hatch and Chaparral as well as move its main operations to the East Mesa branch.

"The East Mesa branch is currently in phases six and seven (and) are under construction," Woods said.

In addition to construction, NMSU is making great strides in the field of research, Woods said. Teaming up with emerging industries, the students at the university have a role in the development of algae biofuel and unmanned aerial systems (UAS), to name a few.

UNMANNED AERIAL VEHICLES

The Physical Science Laboratory at New Mexico State University is partnering with the U.S. Defense Advanced Research Projects Agency in developing and testing the agency's Vulture unmanned aerial vehicle program. The Vulture Program II, a joint venture with Boeing, is centered around a new UAV with a 400-foot wingspan and a weight of 5,000 pounds. The objective is to develop and demonstrate the technology to enable an airborne payload to remain on-station, uninterrupted for more than five years, performing intelligence, surveillance, reconnaissance and communication missions. The NMSU/PSL portion of the project will continue through the conclusion of flight testing, which is expected to last into the third quarter of fiscal year 2014.

PHYSICAL SCIENCE LABORATORY; NEW MEXICO STATE UNIVERSITY

NMSU CENTER FOR THE ARTS

The New Mexico State University Center for the Arts, which broke ground on the corner of Espina Street and University Avenue in July 2010, will be constructed in three phases and will include a 400-seat dance and theater art performance hall, a visual arts center and a grand performance hall, which will seat 1,200. The university plans for the center to be open to the public in 2012.

ARCHITECTS: HOLZMAN MOSS BOTTINO ARCHITECTURE/ASA ARCHITECTS; CONTRACTOR: MCCARTHY

"We're receiving national recognition for what the (Physical Science Laboratory) folks are doing," Woods said of the UAV project, adding that NMSU is the only FFA Authorized Unmanned Aircraft System Flight Test Center in the U.S.

With the economic downturn slowly coming to an end, Woods said he thinks the university will see more funding from the federal government that had been cut the last three years.

"I see us continuing to grow," Woods said. "I see the next decade as a good, strong period for the university under President Barbara Couture."

Water worries

Since civilization first moved into New Mexico and the Mesilla Valley, a great concern has focused on the issue of water; will it last and what will happen if it doesn't?

Even in the 21st century, the debate is still raging, with many wondering what the future holds and how it will affect different facets of the community.

"It's an ongoing and continuous battle over water, its use, its re-use and its conservation," Garza said. "Preservation is a growing top priority of the community."

Gary Esslinger, treasurer and manager of Elephant Butte Irrigation District, the largest supplier of surface water in New Mexico, said in 2011 the reservoir held 190,000 acre-feet of water, even though it has the capacity to hold 2.2 million acre-feet.

"It's much lower than normal," he said. "There has been a down trend since 1999, but there have been a few intermittent good years."

A major cause of the reduction of water in the reservoir is climate change due to El Niño and La Niña.

Phil King, associate professor and associate department head at the NMSU College of Engineering, said when the waters near the Pacific equator are warm, El Niño occurs and the Mesilla Valley will get a big monsoon and snow pack runoff from Colorado, which supplies the reservoir.

During La Niña, he said, the waters are colder, causing the Gulf Stream to push storms north and away from the Southwest. This cycle occurs about every four years and can lead to drought.

"Groundwater use is going to be high this year because there is so little surface water," King said. "I expect the same (in 2012) because it's so low."

Esslinger said it isn't new for farmers in the Mesilla Valley to see the reservoir so low, adding that there were significant droughts in the 1950s and '70s.

"What happens in a drought is you shake out a lot of water users," said King, adding that farmers will re-evaluate what they're growing and crop size because of costs.

As with past droughts, Esslinger said farmers in the county will avoid high-water-usage plants, such as alfalfa, and will focus on low-water-usage plants, such as cotton.

"You'll see the area continue to grow vegetables," he said. "Right now, New Mexico has a pretty well-established onion market. Vegetables like onions, lettuce and chile will continue to grow until fuel costs to pump water become a factor."

Unable to predict La Niña-El Niño cycles, King said, in 20 years the climate in Doña Ana County could be wetter or drier than in 2011.

"There are more variables, so there will be more severe dry and wet cycles," he said.

More extreme wet cycles can also have a negative impact on the area's watershed, which is an area of land that drains water to a particular stream, river or lake. McCormick said with more concrete

Hotel Encanto de Las Cruces

A quinceañera. A wedding. A 50th anniversary. A party honoring a son or a daughter's graduation from New Mexico State University. In Las Cruces, these celebrations of life often share a common thread – an uncommon venue.

Perched high on a hill, Hotel Encanto de Las Cruces is perfectly positioned to take in the glorious New Mexico sunset in the west, and the mystical moonrise over the Organ Mountains to the east.

Encanto is Spanish for enchantment, and the hotel's setting helps visitors understand New Mexico's reputation as the Land of Enchantment. Locals often refer to it as "Hotel E."

When built in 1986 off of Telshor Boulevard, the hotel was on the eastern edge of Las Cruces. Nearby was the Mesilla Valley Mall and not much else. By the time of its 25th anniversary in 2011, Las Cruces had grown to the point the hotel almost felt like the physical center of the city.

In 1994, native New Mexican Jim Long and his partners acquired the property. The hotel debuted as Hotel Encanto de Las Cruces as a Heritage Hotels and Resorts property in November 2006.

Designed in grand Mexican colonial style, the hotel reflects the region's rich Spanish and Mexican history. The hotel features one-of-a-kind pieces from villages along the historic Camino Real – the trail that linked Mexico City to Santa Fe. Guestrooms are furnished with unique pieces from the Palace of the Governors Collection.

Hotel Encanto's key people are the employees themselves: They are the heart of the hotel. In 2011, the most tenured employees of Hotel Encanto had totaled more than 260 years of experience in the hotel and hospitality industry. The staff and management at the hotel work to make sure guests experiences are as enchanted as the name implies. The team has grown to more than 100 employees and have helped make the hotel a stellar part of the Heritage Hotels and Resort family, as well as a signature destination in Las Cruces.

Guests have included singing cowboys (George Strait, Randy Travis, Alan Jackson and Garth Brooks) and Dallas Cowboys (Emmitt Smith, Michael Irvin, Danny White and Danny Villanueva). Politicians (George Bush, Bill Richardson, Pete Domenici and Joe Skeen) and musicians (Carlos Santana, Willie Nelson, Los Lobos and War). An astronaut (Buzz Aldrin) and an icon (Johnny Cash). Kings (NBA's Sacramento version) and Mavericks (NBA's Dallas version, not to mention John McCain). Actors (Kate Winslet, Val Kilmer, Kim Basinger and Edward James Olmos) and chanteuses (Sheryl Crow, Whitney Houston, Reba McEntire and Linda Ronstadt).

But while Hotel Encanto attracts its share of stars, the real star is Las Cruces itself. From the ancient White Sands to the futuristic Spaceport America, southern New Mexico's many attractions draw people from all over the world. And when they come, many seek a place such as Hotel Encanto de Las Cruces.

HERITAGE HOTELS

HIGH FLIGHT

Little Joe II launch at White Sands Missile Range, 1963. Shuttle Forward Reaction Control System firing. STS-3 Shuttle Columbia landing at White Sands Space Harbor, 1982. Through these efforts and more, NASA White Sands Test Facility has been and will continue to be vital to the nation's space flight program.

WHITE SANDS TEST FACILITY

WHITE SANDS TEST FACILITY

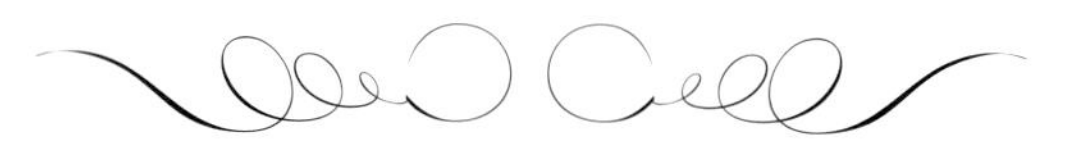

Established in 1963 to test propulsion systems for the Apollo spacecraft, the NASA White Sands Test Facility (WSTF) became a center of technical excellence in the fields of rocket propulsion testing and high-pressure oxygen systems safety. That tradition has continued for nearly 50 years. Considered a national asset, WSTF has supported every U.S. human space flight from Apollo to the Shuttle Program and the International Space Station (ISS). Chosen for its isolated location and topography, WSTF is nestled in the foothills of the San Andres Mountains, just east of Las Cruces, with a moderate desert climate ideal for year-round testing.

WSTF has tested more than 550 rocket engines in more than 3.5 million firings for NASA, the Department of Defense, the Department of Energy and private industry. About 90 percent of all nonmetallic materials flown on Apollo and the space shuttle were tested at WSTF.

With demonstration of the Apollo launch escape system at White Sands Missile Range (WSMR) in 1963, Little Joe II provided the capability for our astronauts to safely escape in the event of an anomaly and began a long history of WSTF support to NASA programs and missions. WSTF began developing expertise in improving oxygen safety in response to the tragic 1967 Apollo 1 fire at Cape Canaveral, Fla., that took the lives of three astronauts. Today, WSTF continues to be a leader in pressurized oxygen systems.

In 1973, WSTF demonstrated dominance in the area of rocket propulsion testing through its work on the space shuttle orbital maneuvering system engine as well as the work performed on the forward and aft reaction control system engines. Tests of these engines continued throughout the entire Shuttle Program.

In 1982, the Shuttle Columbia (STS-3) landed at what was then known as Northrup Strip, 30 miles west of Alamogordo. The strip was then renamed White Sands Space Harbor (WSSH). WSSH runways, navigational aids, and control facilities continuously stood ready as contingency landing support for every shuttle mission.

By performing low-velocity, ice-impact testing on shuttle thermal tiles, WSTF played a role in the Shuttle Program return to flight efforts following the 2003 Columbia disaster.

Since 2006, Jacobs, a private company, has provided technical, engineering and construction services to support NASA projects and testing at WSTF.

With experienced and talented personnel and unique testing capabilities and resources, WSTF will continue to support ISS human spaceflight activities, and will be involved in the design and development of the new NASA Multi-Purpose Crew Vehicle, which will enable human deep space exploration. WSTF also continues to provide testing and research services for other government agencies and is partnering with commercial space companies to continue successful exploration of space.

As NASA defines future missions, WSTF is poised to support these programs in exploration, technology development, and scientific research.

and pavement being spread throughout the Mesilla Valley, water will run off faster, increasing the risk of flooding.

"Everything – roads, agriculture – depends on the watershed," McCormick said.

To help improve the watershed, McCormick said BLM has a program that will strengthen the landscape, such as maintaining easements around arroyos instead of developing them with concrete.

Catlett said many people are attracted to the area because of the plants and wildlife, all of which are dependent on water.

"You'll see some shift," he said of water usage in the area. "But agricultural people will have to move to more efficient uses of their water."

Catlett said one such option is drip irrigation, although Esslinger said the cost to install may deter some farmers.

"The problem with drip irrigation is that the well water pumped out of the ground is high in saline," he said, adding that over long periods of time, this can hurt crops. "You have to make sure to rotate the crops out and rotate drip farms around."

To help farmers, Esslinger said EBID is trying to convert more lateral canals to pipes, which have less seepage and loss, moving water from Caballo reservoir more efficiently. Currently, he said EBID has piped 23 out of 90 miles and has saved 10,000 to 13,000 acre feet of water every year.

With southern New Mexico constantly seeing growth, Esslinger said there will be more demand on the groundwater supply, which in return will affect agriculture, the river, habitats, wildlife and communities.

"You're going to see city restrictions on when people can use water," he said. "You're going to see restriction on agriculture. You're going to see all different situations and conflicts."

Garza said the city has a 40-year water plan that looks ahead and monitors wells to ensure the area has an ample supply. One such possibility for the future is for the city to use brac, or recycled, water.

"It's not out of the question for the city to put in a desalination plant," he said.

While some ponder the possibility of running pipes from areas high in water to areas suffering from drought, Esslinger said the environmental impact of such a feat could stop it in its tracks.

"It would take a lot of Congressional effort and a lot of environmental effort," he said. "It's feasible, but it wouldn't be easy."

With plans set in motion on the city and county levels as well as at NMSU to accommodate growth, experts believe there is plenty of opportunity for the future of the Mesilla Valley.

SAPPHIRE ENERGY

Sapphire Energy, an algae biofuel research company, is currently building a site in Columbus, N.M. The Columbus site is expected to be open by the spring or summer of 2012 with 100 acres and will spread over 300 acres upon final completion in 2015. It is expected to produce 100 million gallons of diesel fuel per year.

LAS CRUCES BULLETIN

WATER WORK

To help preserve the watershed, crews build up arroyos using dirt instead of concrete. The use of concrete promotes water runoff and can lead to flooding.

BUREAU OF LAND MANAGEMENT

WETLANDS PROJECT

Southwest Environmental Center (SWEC) has begun a project to restore La Mancha Wetland, an aquatic and wetland habitat along the Rio Grande in southern New Mexico. Wetlands have diminished over the past century, which has contributed to the disappearance of about two-thirds of the original native fish species. La Mancha Project will be on 3 acres of private land owned by SWEC and adjacent federal land on the west side of the Rio Grande between Interstate 10 and the Calle del Norte Bridge. The goal is for La Mancha to be a place the public can go to learn about and enjoy nature. Guided tours and field trips will take place at the site when it is completed.

SOUTHWEST ENVIRONMENTAL CENTER

INDEX

OLIVIA MCDONALD

ACKNOWLEDGEMENTS

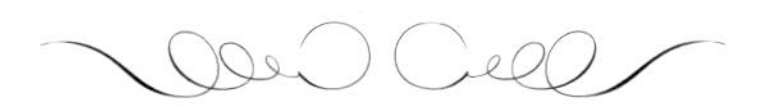

FIG Publications, LLC and owner/publishers Jaki and David McCollum offer a heartfelt thanks to the following individuals and organizations who have contributed to the development and production of "Las Cruces: A Photographic Journey." Without their assistance with writing, photography, researching, storytelling, editing and design, this special Centennial book might never have been completed.

Las Cruces Bulletin team members: Section editors – Natisha Hales, Samantha Roberts, Beth Sitzler, Rachel Christiansen, Jim Hilley, Todd Dickson; special feature/profiles – Richard Coltharp, Jeff Barnet and Terry Bierwirth; design – Theresa Montoya Basaldua, Jessica Grady-Mauldin, Rafael Torres; support staff – Cyndi Armijo, Marissa Barrio, Rachel Courtney, Claire Frohs, Ray Gonzalez, Sid Graft, Amanda Green, Stephanie Griffin, Jorge Lopez, Shellie McNabb, Joey Morales, Steven Parra, Pam Rossi, Tim Smith, Marvin Tessneer

Special thanks to our friends and partners in this project at New Mexico State University and the NMSU Library Archives & Special Collections: Barbara Couture, Elizabeth A. Titus, Kristina Martinez, Laurence S. Creider, Dean Wilkey, Charles Stanford, Elizabeth Flores, Leonard Silverman, Cecelia Carrasco, Kris Laumbach

Las Cruces organizations who donated photographs, shared their stories, verified information and provided advice and insight into Las Cruces over the past 100 years include: Albuquerque Journal: Greg Sorber and Karen Moses; **Allen Theatres:** Asa Allen, Heather Gandy, Larry Allen and Russell G. Allen; **Amador Hotel Foundation:** Dawn Starostka; **Ambercare:** Michael and Mary Merrell, Michelle Merrell and Dianne DeLeon; **ASA Architects:** Gary Yabumoto; **Ashley Furniture HomeStore:** Paul and Wanda Bowman, Lou Hendren; **Basilica of San Albino:** Father Richard Catanach; **Binns Construction:** Eddie Binns; **Black Box Theatre:** Ceil and Peter Herman; **Bureau of Land Management:** Bill Childress, Dwayne Sykes and Jim McCormick; **Cervantes Enterprises:** Emma Jean Cervantes and family; **Citizens Bank of Las Cruces:** Irene Juarez, Justin Harper and Ruth Christopher; **City of Las Cruces:** Brian Denmark, Esther Martinez, Letty Garcia, Mike Johnson, Paul Michaud, Pete Conley, Robert Garza and Udell Vigil; **COAS Bookstore:** Brandon Beckett, Brett Beckett, Mike Beckett, Pat Beckett and Veronica Beckett; **Doña Ana Community College:** Andrew Burke, Dr. Margie Huerta, Fred Lillibridge, John Paulman, Kathy Reddington and Mary Beth Worley; **Doña Ana County Sheriff's Office Museum; El Paso Electric Co.:** Armando Reyes, Billy Massie and Chris Montoya; **El Patio Bar:** Altie Fountain; **Elephant Butte Irrigation District:** Gary Esslinger; **First Baptist Church:** Rev. Maurice Hollingsworth; **First Presbyterian Church:** Larry Felhauer; **Greater Las Cruces Chamber of Commerce:** Bill Allen, Joel Courtney, Kent Evans and Sonny Klein; **Heritage Hotels & Resorts:** Jim Long and Kristelle Siarza; **Herzstein Memorial Museum; Hispano Chamber of Commerce de Las Cruces:** John Muñoz; **Institute of Historical Survey Foundation:** Evan Davies; **Honor Flight of Southern New Mexico:** David Melcher; **Human Systems Research Inc.:** Deborah Dennis; **IMA Inc.:** Edgar Lopez; **It's Burger Time:** Kathy Gonzales; **Jacobs Technology:** Jamie G. Puentes, Keith Beck and Sandy Hodgin; **La Posta de Mesilla:** Jerean and Tom Hutchinson; **Las Cruces Blog:** David Thomas; **Las Cruces Community Theatre:** P.J. Waggaman; **Las Cruces Farmers & Crafts Market:** Eric Montgomery, Dodds Cupit, Dorothy Andress, Jenny Yorston and Craig Dougherty; **Las Cruces Police Department:** Danny Trujillo; **Las Cruces Railroad Museum; Memorial Medical Center:** Dr. Bill Einig, Mandy Leatherwood and Paul Herzog; **Mesilla Valley Christian Schools:** Lori Conn; **Mesilla Valley Hospice:** Terra Van Winter; **Mountain View Market:** Andrew Rader, Heather Rische, Mike Perriguey, Mo Valko and Shahid Mustafa; **MountainView Regional Medical Center:** Denten Park, Audrey Hardman-Hartley, Don Harlow and Kelly Duke; **Moy Surveying:** Jorge Moy; **New Mexico Centennial:** Sarah Ives; **New Mexico Department of Transportation:** Bridget Spedalieri; **New Mexico Farm & Heritage Museum:** Craig Massey, Dave Lundy and Mark Santiago; **New Mexico Museum of Space History:** Michael Shinabery, George House and Wayne Mattson; **New Mexico Palace of the Governors Museum Archives:** Dan Kosharek; **New Mexico State University President's Office:** Ben Woods; **NMSU Athletics:** Jeremy Strachan, Tiffany Franklin and Tyler Dunkel; **NMSU College of Agriculture, Consumer and Environmental Sciences:** Lowell Catlett; **NMSU College of Business:** Garrey Carruthers; **NMSU College of Engineering:** Phil King and Ricardo Jacquez; **NMSU Communications:** Darren Phillips, Ellen Costello and Minerva Baumann; **NMSU Pan American Center:** Shacoy Parra; **NMSU Physical Science Laboratory:** David May; **NMSU Water Resources Research Institute:** Cathy Klett; **Oñate High School; P.I.A.D.O.R.; Palace of the Governors Photo Archives:** Daniel Kosharek; **Picacho Hills Country Club; Picacho Mountain:** Tiffany Etterling; **Rawson Family:** George Rawson, Joan Rawson and Lee Rawson; **Roman Catholic Diocese of Las Cruces:** Bishop Ricardo Ramírez and J. David McNamara; **Sisbarro Dealerships:** Lou Sisbarro and Rick Nezzer; **Solar Electric:** Devlyn R. McNabb and Mary A. Garza; **Sonoma Ranch:** George Rawson; **Southwest Environmental Center:** Kevin Bixby; **St. Andrew's Episcopal Church:** Father Scott Ruthven and Trish Higdon; **St. Paul's United Methodist Church:** Alice Ward and Pastor James Large; **Stahmann Farms:** Eva Valerio and Sally Stahmann-Solis; **Steinborn & Associates Real Estate:** Morgan Switzer; **Steve Newby Architects:** Steve Newby and Tammy Gates; **Thomas Branigan Memorial Library; Tom Udall's Office:** Xochitl Torres; **Town of Mesilla:** Nick Eckert; **Tularosa Basin Historical Society; U.S. Library of Congress; White Sands Federal Credit Union:** Sharon Sumner; **White Sands Missile Range:** Darren Court, Monte Marlin and Lisa Blevins; **Williams Design Group:** Alex Salcido; **Wooten Construction:** Ken Wooten and Ray Wooten; **Ziatel Inc.:** Anthony Smith.

Las Cruces community members who donated photographs, shared their stories, verified information and provided advice and insight into Las Cruces over the past 100 years include: Amador family; Diane Allen; Isela and Philip Alvarez; Gilbert Apodaca; Rudy Apodaca; Dolores Archuleta; Jeff Barnet; Marissa Barrio; Theresa Montoya Basaldua; Tresa Berleman; Jim Bradley; Evelyn Bruder; Elba Garcia-Burke; Louie Burke; Bob Burns; Bruce Cabot; Martin Campbell Jr.; Father Daniel Cave; Laura Conniff; Dolores Connor; David Corn; Rachel Courtney; Rebecca Courtney; Laura Delgado; Jeanette and Marci Dickerson; Todd Dickson; Bob and Ona Fern; James Flanagan Jr.; Jeanette Foreman; Fountain family; Sen. Mary Jane Garcia; Vicky Gibson; Sid Graft; Norma Jean Gryder; John Hadsell; Natisha Hales; Linda Harris; Jerry Harrell; Duncan Hayse; Fred Heinrich; Tanah Hemingway; Lou and Mary Henson; Glenda Hilley; Jim Hilley; Barbara Hubbard; David Ikard; Christina Chavez Kelley; Jorge Lopez; Charles and Mary Ann Lucero; Marisa Lucero; Wanda Mattiace; Josh Mauldin; Ronald and Olivia Lerma McDonald; Janet Mechem; Mark Medoff; Stuart Meerscheidt; Leon Metz; Miller family; Bobbie Montana; Paula Moore; Chris Mortenson; Jo Galvan Nash; Erik Ness; Eva A. Northcutt; Steve Parra; Steven Parra; John Papen; Sen. Mary Kay Papen; Richard Petrillo; Jerry Phillips; Heather Pollard; Bob Porter; Lee Rawson; Kathy Salopek; Jerry Smith; Joshua Smith; Nancy Barnes-Smith; Rubén Smith; Gordon Steel; Kathy Stout; J. Paul Taylor; Arvil Thomas; Roland Thomas; Robert Wick; John Yarbrough

Families and businesses that also helped to make this Centennial project a reality through their financial support are: Allen Theatres, Ambercare, Basilica of San Albino, Bowman family/Ashley Furniture, Cervantes family, Citizens Bank of Las Cruces, City of Las Cruces, COAS Bookstore, Dickerson family, Doña Ana Community College, New Mexico Farm & Ranch Heritage Museum, First Baptist Church, First Presbyterian Church, Greater Las Cruces Chamber of Commerce, Heritage Hotels & Resorts, Hotel E, Jacobs Technologies/NASA, La Posta (Tom and Jerean Hutchinson), Lou Henson family, McDonald family, Memorial Medical Center, Mesilla Valley Hospice, Mountain View Market, MountainView Regional Medical Center, Moy Surveying, NMSU, Rawson family, Ritter family (Buddy), Rubén Smith family, Salopek family, Sen. Mary Jane Garcia family, Sisbarro, Solar Electric, St. Andrew's Episcopal Church, St. Paul's United Methodist Church, Stahmanns, Steel family, Steve Newby Architects, The Roman Catholic Diocese of Las Cruces, White Sands Federal Credit Union, Wooten family.